UNTANGLED
THE PSYCHOLOGICAL CHAINS OF HUMAN ABUSE

BRIGHTWELL DUBE

Copyright © Brightwell Dube

All rights reserved. No part of this South African published book may be reproduced in any manner, mechanically or electronically, including tape or other audio recordings and photocopying, without the prior written permission of the publisher, except in the case of brief quotations embodied in critical reviews and certain other non-commercial uses permitted by copyright law. For permission requests, write to the author, addressed "Attention: Permissions" at brightwellsiza@gmail.com

First print edition 2021

Print ISBN: 978-0-620-91009-5

Amazon ISBN:979-871-586819-0

Typesetting by Human 1st Publishers

Cover design by Gregg Davies

Printed by Grant Walton

Published by Human 1st Publishers

Edited by Brightwell Dube, Skhumbuzo Khumalo, Juan de Beer Odendal, David Baloyi, Cecil Robert Jordaan & Sizalobuhle Khumalo

+2768 579 4288

DISCLAIMER

The author of this book does not dispense medical or psychological advice or prescribe the use of any substance or technique as a form of treatment for physical, medical, or psychological problems without the advice of a registered medical practitioner, either directly or indirectly. The intent of the author is only to offer information of a general nature to help you in your quest for general wellbeing. In the event, you utilize neither any of the information provided in this book for yourself, which is your constitutional right, neither the author, the publisher nor any of their associates assume liability for your actions.

'Untangled' 'The Psychological Chains Of Human Abuse' reads like a great self-help guide, but as a golden one, it is a very loud masterpiece, it raises a lot of unresolved issues that people always avoid, and it ventures into the uncharted waters. Most significantly it captures the emotions and mood of both the abused and the perpetrators.

Skhumbuzo Khumalo – (*BA in English and Communication Studies*)

"There is no keener revelation of a society's soul than how it treats its children"

- Nelson Rolihlahla Mandela
(18 July 1918 – 5 December 2013)

Table of Contents

PREFACE	12
ACKNOWLEDGEMENTS	17
PART ONE	**20**
1. INTRODUCTION	21
2. STOP IT!	32
3. THE LONG-TERM SOLUTION	37
4. IGOLIDE	42
5. SEARCH FOR MEANING AND BELONGING	48
6. YOU ARE ENOUGH!	55
7. SYNDROMES OF ENTITLEMENT	59
8. MADNESS	65
9. DARE NOT TOUCH…ITS FIRE	70
10. THE POWER OF INTENTION	74
11. ROLE-PLAYING	78
12. IMPERFECT BEINGS	83
13. BEAUTY STANDARDS	87
14. HOPE FOR THE PERPETRATOR.	92
15. THE VISION	97
16. THE BEST WAY OF WALKING AWAY	101
17. CHECK YOUR POSITION	106
18. THE POWER OF TOLD STORIES	111
19. THE POWER OF A COMPLIMENT	118
20. THE UNIVERSE APPLAUDS	123
21. THE POWER OF REFLECTION	127

22. THE POWER OF POWER   132
23. THE HERO WITHIN   137
24. SELF-ESTEEM AND SELF-WORTH   142
25. H-A-B-IT   148

PART TWO 153

26. SCARS UNTOLD — 154
27. AN IMAGE OF GOD — 158
28. THE COMPARISON DISEASE — 162
29. I-DENTITY — 167
30. THE POWER OF SPOKEN-WORD — 171
31. THE POWER OF BALANCE — 175
32. A TWO-WAY STREET — 179
33. A BALANCED STATE OF CONFIDENCE — 183
34. THE KINGDOM WITHIN — 187
35. CAUTIOUSLY LETTING GO — 191
36. CHEERS TO THE UPLIFTING OVERCOMERS — 195
37. THE FAVORITISM POISON — 199
38. BE AUTHENTICALLY YOU — 203
39. THE POWER OF HUMAN-WILL — 207
40. THE POWER OF PERCEPTION — 211
41. SINGLE PARENTING — 216
42. THE FLAWS OF MEDIA — 221
43. THE SPOTLIGHT — 226
44. THE HUSTLE — 231
45. THE CRYING BABY — 236
46. PASSION — 241
47. LIFE SEASONS — 246
48. THE BLAME GAME — 250
49. THE SEE-SAW — 254
50. REJECTION — 259

PART THREE   **263**

- 51. PATTERNS   264
- 52. BROKEN VESSELS   268
- 53. NOBODY IS DIS-ABLED!   272
- 54. OCEANS   276
- 55. I AM THE LIGHT   280
- 56. THE OVER-SIZE SHOE   284
- 57. JUDGEMENT   288
- 58. THE UNATTAINABLE   293
- 59. THE POWER OF ENTHUSIASM   296
- 60. RUN-AWAY   301
- 61. SORRY   305
- 62. AWARDS   309
- 63. INDEPENDENCE   313
- 64. THE CELL-PHONE BUCKET   317
- 65. MAN-HOOD   320
- 66. THE AGONY OF A BLACK CHILD   324
- 67. THE POWER OF MENTAL STRENGTH   328
- 68. EXPECTATIONS   335
- 69. FORCED-LOVE   337
- 70. TRUST   341
- 71. CALCULATED ACCURACY   345
- 72. OPPORTUNITY COST   349
- 73. A 'COMMON-PRINCIPLED VILLAGE'   352
- 74. THE MIRROR   356
- 75. POINT OF CORRECTION   360

PART FOUR	364
76. INTERPRETATION OF ART	365
77. THE POWER OF SOLITUDE	369
78. THE POWER OF SERVING	374
79. STATUS	379
80. THE CHILD-BIRTH CRISIS	384
81. THE AUDIENCE APPLAUDS	388
82. MY DEFINITION OF WEALTH	392
83. ISOLATION	397
84. THE GOLDEN VOICES	401
85. KINDNESS	406
86. EDUCATION INTO ACTION	409
87. IRREPLACEABLE	413
88. EXTRAVAGANZA	417
89. PUZZLES	421
90. THE POWER OF INFLUENCE	425
91. THE POWER OF MUSIC	428
92. THE TRIP	431
93. HUMAN CHARACTER FOR HUMAN COLOR	434
94. CHEERS TO THE PILLARS	437
95. RESOURCES: HELPLINE FOR LGBTQI+	440
96. HELPLINE FOR MEN	442
97. HELPLINE FOR CHILDREN	443
98. HELPLINE FOR WOMEN	445
99. CONCLUSION	447
100. THE COURAGE TO LOVE	449

ABOUT THE AUTHOR

PREFACE

If you are sick and tired of the dilemma of gender-based violence and want to broaden your knowledge to do something rather than sitting on a fence and lament, this is your perfect guide. Tormented by an abusive environment, and on realizing the depth of the scourge of human abuse, I was reborn and inspired to turn a new leaf ... became an enthusiastic activist of human abuse, to single-handedly from my perspective fight the scourge. The guide aims to empower you. Charity starts from home and so is abuse. Both are in one way or the other nurtured within familial settings. Parents, beware, there is no middle line. You cannot sit on a fence when it comes to parenting. You either instill genuine love or plant seeds of abuse that will consequently torment the future.

There are various ways of sowing human violence. And we point at different sources, from patriarchy, matriarchy, socialization, and the other vices and virtues. The common denominator is what happens after birth. Once a child is born, what you sow in the mind of the child as a parent is what begins the process. Seeing with my naked eyes and listening to human abuse true stories made me conclude that parenting can become an effective way to curb the scourge at its budding place ... birth.

The guide is a whispering sound to all of us ... a clarion call from my inner voice, it urges everyone to be silent so one can hear his /her 'inner voice' and do what is right. Take note, a plethora of books are breaking bookshelves on topics in Domestic violence, Parenting, and Gender-based violence, but there is none-perfect. Take one that works for you and implement it. What makes this guide unique, relevant, and powerful is that it consists of a wide spectrum of sizable topics that can be implemented immediately; it also challenges humanity to begin to put into action mechanisms that will offer long-term solutions in uprooting the taproot of human violence. And the solution is genuine love from birth - A love button to be handed over from generation to generation.

'Untangled' 'The Psychological Chains Of Human Abuse' aims to:

- Encourage parents to groom children in love.
- Empower and heal the abused and the perpetrator through practical philosophical truths.
- Activate a healing mechanism for parents, caregivers, and guardians.

- Make young people realize, it is within them to turn into a new leaf, rather than perpetuate wrong behavior learned during socialization or bad parenting.
- Appeal to everyone to take a bold stand against abuse.

This is my bitter truth, but a truth that most of us have swallowed, and do not know how to vomit it out. Use the guide to cleanse yourself.

Once upon a time, deep within the heart of the African continent, surrounded by roaring oceans of great intensity and the only song that filled the sky was a peaceful melody from birds, and the splashing waves. There was a distinct village founded and anchored in the roots of profound love. The love was so significant, coherent, and powerful to such an extent that humans and carnivores lived in perfect harmony without fear of being abused. It was ... I'm certain ... a glimpse of paradise on earth ... It was called Ikhaya Lothando (*A village of Love*). Upholding of that love was a daily responsibility for all. However, inhabitants failed to transmit the love from one generation to the next with time. As such that love gradually eroded to a state below that of animal species. We must restore that love, but it is not going to be a walk in the park. We need all hands-on deck to revive a world that has been entangled by the psychological chains of human abuse. This Guide aims to rekindle such love into the 21st century. To create societies that are guided by wise words of great leaders like Nelson Mandela who left an eternal mark of their existence: "There is no keener revelation of a society's soul than how it treats its children"

I strongly believe that the genuine and persistent positive affirmation of love will instill in any child deep-rooted love to an extent of not allowing him /her to abuse another human being. Such love will ultimately create enzymes within human beings that will instill in them psychological empowerment to abhor any form of violence against another being. That is my genetic code for cultivating a mind and behaviorally transformed genealogy of love ... a kind of love that untangles the psychological chains of human abuse. '**Untangled**' '**The Psychological Chains Of Human Abuse**' is a wealth of wisdom and philosophical truth that seeks to highlight the root-cause of human abuse and assist in up-rooting it for the greater liberation of humanity. This is a self-help guide that not only shouts justice for the abused but further brings about fully fleshed truths on the noble role that parenting plays in curbing abuse.

Preparing the way forward to pen my work, I did some desktop research and interviewed some victims and perpetrators. My findings firmly concluded that the scarcity of love at a parental level is the main source contributing to the powerful magnitude at which the pandemic of human abuse is felt today.

The World Health organization says: Globally, it is estimated that within a year - up to 1 billion children aged 2 – 17 years, experience physical, sexual, emotional, or mental abuse either from parents, caregivers, or guardians, and such childhood violence colors the rest of their lives to do the same as adults.

As a young adult, who has added to the above statistical figure. I solely took an initiative not to be a bystander, but in trying to heal myself, felt the need to also heal others … YOU. The publication success of this self-help guide is the definite response that seeks to answer the first question asked by my psychologist:

"What will be effective enough to heal you?"

Eleanor Roosevelt confirms:

"When you have decided what you believe, what you feel must be done; you dare to stand alone and be counted"

ACKNOWLEDGEMENTS

I send my deepest gratitude and heartfelt thanks to the following:

- Lethabo Phala, you gave me the best gift a friend would ever give. You believed in my ability, even when I doubted myself.

- Juan de Beer Odendal, my mentor, friend, and inspiration. Your guidance and motivation are a tapestry of wisdom, and power to my soul. You continuously remind me that the world seizes to revolve without our immense contribution to humanity.

- Garen Rangasamy and Cecil Robert Jordaan. I always have had the pleasure of tapping into your divine grace and wisdom. You will remain dearly loved.

- Gregg Davies, amidst all the leaf, branch, and root friends I have – I am so honored to call you my root friend. Amid my challenges, you were a pillar of support, hope, and courage.

- Skhumbuzo Khumalo, the seeds of commitment you planted in me as my High school teacher, has now blossomed into a flower whose scent cannot be ignored – a scent of comfort and healing. Thank you for being proud of me.

- Professor David Baloyi, your contribution to the literary world is much appreciated; you are like gold for a writer. May your legacy live on.

- Nick Williams, thank you for affirming me. You made me realize that my deepest fear is not that I am inadequate, but my deepest fear is that I am powerful beyond measure.

- New Model Private College, you catapulted me into the position of the school's Head Leader, and the President of the Debate Club. These made me realize that there is something in me that can be shared with the world. The outstanding essays and debates prophesized my destiny.

- Urban Life Church, I dearly appreciate you for the guidance, motivation, relentless support, and willingness to make inroads to preach the subject of sexuality with an open heart and mind.

- Big thanks to all my educational background teachers who unknowingly instilled in me the courage to challenge situations.

- My parents, families, and friends, for always cheering me up. Today, I dare to dance in the path of greatness because of your unwavering support.

- The Almighty ... King of Glory for entrusting me with a gift of writing. The tears I brought to you in my earnest and persistent prayers have finally touched the heavens' heart.

- And

- The Universe for conspiring in my favor.

PART ONE

1
INTRODUCTION

Despite unrelenting efforts and cries of concerned citizens to curb the animalistic nature of the human species, the spiraling levels of human abuse in this age and time are uncalled for. A million-dollar question is: "Are we doing enough as a people to deal with the root cause of abuse?" My clarion-call is that we need to reflect and revise what we raised as weapons to fight this pandemic. On conducting research, I reviewed what can be the root-cause, and concluded that the scarcity of love and care within families may be one of the central pillars that contribute to escalating levels of abuse, which ultimately, continues to spill over to all areas of human interaction and relationships. To me, it appears, one of the most effective pills for this psychological illness must be given to homes ... families. And should be in the form of practicing the use of three little but powerful words on nurturing children: "I love you". Interactions with young people and everybody within familial situations and relationships must be colored in true love, care, understanding, sympathy, empathy, and positive affirmations. Take note, every baby is born with primal instincts, such as aggression, violence, and selfishness. It becomes a parental task and responsibility to mitigate, these animalistic instincts with loving experiences, like altruism, compassion, care, empathy, and selflessness. Brad Henry says: "Families are the compass that guides us, the inspiration to reach great heights, and comfort when we occasionally falter." However, love is like self-understanding, it is a lifetime endeavor, not a weekend seminar, and never comes in capsule form, and needs to be practiced from generation to generation.

The psychological impact of embracing young people in love is enormous; fills the void in their souls. A youngster, who has been persistently told 'I love you', is most likely to pass this act of affection to his or her family in the future. From that small act, abuse is gradually untangled in families. However, the effects of arrogance and lack of genuine love have far-reaching negative impacts. A young person, who was never been shown love and affection from birth, tends to have a fickle or a warped view of life. Grows up with a sense of hunger and thirst for love and ends up filling the void with abuse. He or she ends up giving birth to low self-esteem that may be characterized by dysfunctional behaviors such as insecurity, anger, and violence. These turn to be coping mechanisms in their relationships.

To untangle the psychological chains of human abuse, parents, and all people, in general, are to occupy the front seat of love when interacting with young people. Parents must ensure that their offspring know and understand unconditional love to radiate it to others, and to pass such positive behavior to future generations. I believe that it is one of the surest ways of dealing with some of the root causes of the scourge. As in the words of Nelson Mandela: "There is no keener revelation of a society's soul than how it treats its children". Teach young people how to love, so that they can start to love and accept themselves and see that love flowing over to others. Eleanor Roosevelt confirms; "Friendship with one's self is all-important because without it one cannot be friends with anyone else in the world"

I emphasize the term 'human abuse', with no connotations. Amongst all others, one of my purposes is to eradicate the belief that abuse is prevalent in certain racial groups. Whereas reality and progression of time relentlessly teach us that human beings of all portfolios if not raised in a loving environment turn to become abusers and or perpetrators of abuse irrespective of race, gender, or sexuality. Men, women, and young people from heterosexual or same-sex relationships can become victims or perpetrators. Thus, I strongly believe it is in small acts of love taken in faith and hope that a radically-mind-transformed generation can be born to further preach and practice TRUE love ... a seed to make love blossom and ripple out to suppress abuse, and gradually loosen its pangs on people. It does not cost a dime to say the three universal words affirming affection … 'I LOVE YOU.' It only needs a caring and genuine heart from anyone, irrespective of age, race, religion, or status. Affirming the words, I love you to a young person may prove to be rocket science to transform attitudes, behavior, and action, and suppress the perpetration of abuse. However, the approach needs practice, practice, and practice. Positive saturated minds agree:

"The best angle to approach every problem is the try-angle".

Try to embrace and exhume love and notice people's responses around you.

General observation reflects that a young man told that: "You are a tiger and must never cry or show your emotions to anyone." Finds it even difficult to embrace or show love and affection even to his children. What is taught to young boys and girls determines how they will cope as parents in the future. The belief that men are tigers and women are sheep gave birth to abusers and the abused. And for some time, the status quo was left unchallenged. The era of buying blue clothes for boys and pink for girls is long gone; make them wear dresses and trousers indiscriminately, the previous practice created a generation of 'strong' men with a warped and propped-up ideology of manhood. And women who maintain that their roles are in the kitchen and bedroom, with lowered womanhood that accepts any form of abuse as part of being a woman. To me, a warped-up manhood may be an ideology that fosters abuse of the fairer sex, a girl child, and a boy child. At most, individuals with a warped understanding of manhood cannot control their own emotions.

Harboring emotions has a dire effect on the well-being of humanity. Anger that is not expressed builds bitterness, and love that is not expressed seizes to make an impact on anyone. Harbored emotions are at most released in violence and abuse; these become building stones of abusive relationships. Everyone is challenged to open-up, to express emotions; be it anger, love, or dissatisfaction. My advice is not to withhold emotions in any way. Emotions need to be released through love and affection irrespective of their tone, so as not to harm, devaluate or dehumanize other beings. An attitude of openness does not usually start when one is old, but it is a virtue that is nurtured from a young age and grows with time. An open and considerate parent is open enough to share emotions and wise enough to seek professional advice when necessary. I equate openness to a key to being a holistic person – one with a great sense of awareness. Take note, I am not Doctor Love but trust me, it is in openness that we start enjoying the fruits of an honest, authentic, and sustainable relationship. I bring to light some psychological chains that if not considered at an early age come back to haunt and propel human beings to various forms of violence and abuse. The lesson is openness and immediate expression of emotion within the appropriate channel slowly but surely build up a paradigm of an abuse-free society.

Let it be a norm for the child 's ears to hear the words, 'I love you', said in happiness without buying a face. The effects affirm their dignity and worth. It assures that one is loved regardless of flaws and weaknesses. Scarcity of love may result in young people becoming entangled in abusive relationships. Research confirms; "University students subconsciously get involved in abusive relationships in search of meaning or need to belong. Even when abused, they blindly stick to such relationships,

It is indisputable that a parent, who never knew love and care in his /her upbringing, perpetrates the status quo in his /her parenting role - does what he knows best; scolds-slaps and abuses others, unless an intervention is made, and that parent has a greater will to tap into the courage to love. Refer to my poem at the end of the guide that conveys the message that it is terrifying to acknowledge weaknesses and humble ourselves to others. If intervention is freely sorted, then there will be a glimpse of hope. The power to accept weakness activates and speeds up healing, builds love that will overshadow past or future pain. That is what the power of love does to our souls if our will is not compromised. It is not easy but possible...highly possible.

Wisdom says: a seed that has not been nurtured by its gardener fails to produce abundant fruit. The quality of fruits that a tree yields are determined by the extent of nurturing that stems from the gardener. Similarly, young people are like seeds, their growth, attitude, and character are to a large extent dependent on the love and care received from parents ... gardeners. In the same breath, a cracked or bruised mirror reflects a distorted or bruised image. So, parents should give young people a true reflection of love.

The reality is: I don't know your abusive experience – you certainly know your pains more than I do. Considering that truth, I challenge you to positively use your nasty experience to uplift the lives of others. I challenge you to use your mishaps as stepping-stones for others. Some write, some preach, counsel, teach, motivate, and sing. I urge you to also do something. You are unique and so is your story. Find the light in your darkness and shine it for the world the best way you can. Mathew 5: 14 – 16 says: *"You are like light for the whole world. A city built on a hill cannot be hidden. No one lights a lamp and puts it under a bowl; instead puts it on a lampstand, where it gives light for everyone in the house. In the same way, your light must shine before people, so that they will see the good things you do and praise your Father in Heaven."*

I believe counseling is necessary when a perpetrator is ready to commit and change. Remember, you can be taken to the best counselor the world has ever seen, but if you are in denial, or refuse to accept the reality you will never change, and you remain a perpetrator right into an early grave. Remember, you can take a donkey to a drinking place, but you cannot push water up to its throat. Change remains a challenge to most people.

In taking my time to listen to stories of the abused and perpetrators, it was perplexing to discover that both the abused and the perpetrator have got the victim element in their story. Their stories have a common denominator ... the perpetrator grew up in an abusive family and that gave them a satisfying meaning of how a family is raised and believed it is what life is all about. Oftentimes, the perpetrator is channeled to grow up with a warped sense of conviction that there is no love if there is no pain. The perpetrator reflects an understanding of the ghostly side of marriage. In response to probing their turning point, the perpetrator would respond; "I now accept that I have a problem, hence, I feel free to talk to you, and believe I'm on the path of change, not to hurt anyone anymore." It is through similar responses that I decided to pen this guide ... realized abuse can be 'Untangled'. There is hope and untangling the psychological chains of human abuse is one of these greatest hopes.

The pandemic of human abuse has raised and continues to raise alarming concerns to the world at large. So alarming are the effects of human abuse – they have caused governments to invest capital for solutions in the form of, research, counseling centers, and law enforcement centers. However, it seems the government is failing. The war of abuse continues to rage. I ascended the platform to make a clarion call through this guide. And hope you will take the fight further. The government appears to be addressing leaves and branches of abuse; we need to address the taproot through parenting. Take note, a family provides a basic environment for child development. It is a nucleus for informal and formal learning. A first platform to nature a child's development and a nexus to learn almost anything life entails. Marge Kennedy confirms; "The informality of family life is a blessed condition that allows us all to become our best while looking our worst." In early childhood, certain inclinations remain rooted to become worldviews later, especially abuse. Parents should know that children have never been very good at listening to elders but have never failed to imitate them. The lyrics in Dolly Parton's song 'Family' reiterate the importance of family: "You choose your lovers; you choose friends, not the family that you are in. They will be with you till the end 'cause it is family. And when it's family, you forgive them. When it is family, they are a mirror of the best and worst in you. When it is family, let me be all that I must be." Family is a building block of society. No family no society. If we address family, we address the nation.

The guide is a clarion call for action by parental organizations to delve deeper into the psychology that governs the mindset of young people. The government can actively help in this regard. Do not get me wrong, I am not saying they should tell parents how to treat or raise children. I am saying they can be an extension of help to those that cannot love their children because they were and or are still victims and products of abusive relationships. The subject of human abuse can be introduced in the Department of Basic Education; Government can promote the injection of continuous dialogue on this subject for parents on media platforms. Parents must also freely attend counseling sessions to break the cycle of abuse.

In resting the case of my introduction, I say, it is in taking small but persistent steps that a mountain can be ultimately destroyed. Yes, to demolish a mountain, we start with the removal of small stones. I am certain, by healing the scarcity of love and making it abundant within families we can untangle the scourge of abuse and gradually move towards an abuse-free generation. There is no better time to draw a clear line of distinction between animalism and humanity. It does not cost a thing; all it takes is a willing and courageous heart. My basic belief as a 'Porter of an abuse-free generation at work' is that I am molding 'Porters' that will be well equipped to stand against human abuse.

Remember, knowledge is power, but enthusiasm pulls the switch.

YES, WE CAN... WILL AND MUST OVERCOME!

2
STOP IT!

No amount of past pain can justify the cruel gesture of inflicting pain on another human being. I boldly highlight this statement for the mere fact that it has become the newly but progressively adopted 'scapegoat' of justifying the unacceptable act of inflicting pain to another being. It is detestable that some kill and still utter this statement as a means of justification. It is outrageously incredible, the comfort they resonate with, in saying this statement. All I can say, with a loud voice is STOP IT! STOP IT! And STOP IT!

Past traumas cannot be justified for further injustices, or are not to determine the future, but must be used to assist others as is the case with me. There is no amount of justification that is solid enough for you to inflict pain on others; it is unacceptable if not pathetic!

A mind is not a dustbin to keep anger, hatred, and fear, to randomly pass on to others willy-nilly, but a treasure box to keep love, happiness, and sweet memories. No matter where you come from, no matter what calamities you experienced during childhood, you can transform your mind for the better. No reason is enough for anyone to inflict pain on another human being. It is ignorance at its best and equates the human mind to that of an animal. Man is not determined by the past but is expected to learn from the negative past to embrace a positive mindset for the future.

To allow such worldviews to undermine human justice is more like equating a human being with primates, to be under the control of instincts in search of food, water, and procreation at the expense of others. Have you ever watched animals fight for sex? It is survival of the fittest. Surely, we cannot act like animals but behave like human beings. If past pain can be used to justify the act of abusing other human beings then all offenders roaming correctional centers for rape, murder, battering others, and theft must be freed from the confines of a prison. The unchangeable reality is that abuse is wrong, and the partaker should be dealt with accordingly and justice should fairly take its course. Necessary measures should be considered to protect and free humanity from the chains of abuse. The question is, "Is the law strict enough to deal with matters of abuse to all portfolios of humanity; (men, women, children, heterosexual, gay, lesbian, transgender, and other sexual orientations)?" The lack of confidence in saying yes to this question continues to grow momentum due to the ill-manner in which cases of human abuse are handled, think about it, putting the perpetrators behind bars and doing very little to educate and rehabilitate their mind-sets does very little to address the scourge.

To all authors and publishers on this subject, please be reminded 'Projection is vital'. The psychological effects of the titles we use for our content on abuse are enormous and venomous. It is not a wise approach to continue attaching neutral statements to matters of abuse. They defeat the means. The projection taken by some researchers is at times subtly promoting that human violence affects only a certain class of people. For example, titles such as: 'women abuse', 'child abuse' and 'men abuse' should be done away with. It is time we speak the universal language that speaks to human abuse or gender-based violence. This will in introspect facilitate the truth that abuse affects all of humanity despite race, status, gender, or sexuality.

There is a loud cry in communities that laments law agencies. Feels they are not doing enough. To an extent the yelling is justified, but what do we do on a personal level? Yes, justice should be a tool to protect us, but it continues to fail to achieve such a status. Taking into consideration statistics of gender-based violence on; the women, the girl, and the boy child who are raped, killed, and maimed daily we are left frustrated. The backlog in the South African justice system is nerve-racking, and cases of abuse continue to be on the rise. I have seen through my naked eye that the law is biased, especially on race, wealth, and social standing. For example, when a man reports an abusive case, he is treated differently from a woman. At most officers laugh at him. Similar discriminations abound for gay, lesbian, transsexual people, etcetera. Thus, I appeal to law enforcers, mental health workers, and community members, young and old to take into their hands in fighting the scourge. Together we can stop it. Let us learn from a fable of an Olympian championship for 10-year- Old paraplegics.

"The 10-year-Old Paraplegic athlete anxiously stood at the starting point of their 20m race awaiting the gunshot, ten in total. When the gun went in a struggle, they all started but one fell. To the amazement of a multitude of spectators - the athletes stopped, retreated, assisted the fallen athlete to stand up, and then took hands. They all completed the race on time."

We must all put hands on deck - If they could sacrifice their will to be the first by helping a fallen friend. Surely! We can STOP the scourge of abuse. We can do the same to pick up falling parents in their parenting role. Retreat - take hands

- stand together and fight the demon of abuse to our ultimate success.

Parents affect the spirit and soul of a child before and after birth. Hence, the saying; "Sins of fathers are revisited upon children." Parents influence children from an early age to think with the lower head – sexual satisfaction and material needs, or to think from a higher self – brain and heart. Parents must make children aware from an early age that there are no limitations in one's mind, except those that they acknowledge, to know from an early age that poverty and riches are an offspring of thought. And to do that requires buckets and buckets of love. Taking hands, we really can begin to make differences that will ultimately STOP HUMAN ABUSE.

To the law enforcers I earnestly appeal:
Please Mr. (s). Policemen:

Chuck away the classifications…We look up to you…Save us justly!

3
THE LONG-TERM SOLUTION

The guide appeals to humanity worldwide. Its objective is to create a positive impact on all humanity and to significantly challenge everyone to positively contribute to decreasing the raging war of abuse. I hope it is clear as daylight that this is a clarion call for everyone to actively show love, especially parents, to children of the world. By so doing, we shall be taking multiple steps towards a long-term solution to this monster. Remember, a distance of a thousand kilometers begins from a single step.

It is possible to eradicate the pandemic, only if we can act together, show concern, teach, and practice indiscriminate love, do away with gender, race, status, and religious discrimination. And accept any human being as a human being first. Love is the glue that holds the world together, and forgiveness makes us a united human species. For example, the practical application of love expressed in simple actions; like sharing or passing pleasantries, reporting criminal cases to law enforcers, being empathetic and compassionate, we can surely finish a huge elephant carcass. Remember, the best way to find oneself is to lose oneself in the service of others.

We are all potters at work, molding, forming, and transforming a generation that we can all be proud of. What is needed is a sharpened awareness and care, especially on nurturing children, and being able to instill in them the power of love. As potters let us unite, stand together, and take hands. We can stand together but do different things. So, standing together should mean having a common objective, not allowing manipulation to rule over dignity and self-worth. Standing together implies caring enough to know you are being abused, and being confident enough to walk away with pride, worth and dignity still intact. Remember, abuse is physical, spiritual, and emotional. As potters at work, the less sand in our clay; the easier for us to mold and build. The process needs commitment. Surely! Together we can.

Some individuals never realize what happens around them, move around, see nothing, hear nothing, and think of nothing, cannot even report instances of violence to relevant agencies. Yes, Bob Marley, the great Reggae singer, in trying to understand people confirms; "Some people feel the rain; others just get wet." Do you feel the rain, or are you one of those, who just get wet and do nothing or the one who wonders why and, seeks areas to protect one-self from getting wet? If you are one of those who just get wet, the guide aims to arouse a feeling of care in you.

Remember, an injury to one is an injury to all. If you are the one who gets wet and wonders why?

Take your cross and follow me, through the guide.

I aim to bring about a sense of conviction that will make you feel the rain and act. And cause changes to self and others. The bigger vision is to give birth to totally mind-attitude-behaviorally-transformed people. The problem is our short-sightedness and reactive mentality, we wait until abuse is experienced and then act, which is a very weak approach.

'Untangled' 'The Psychological Chains Of Human Abuse' will be our compass as we journey through this battle with the pandemic of gender-based violence. Let us allow the spirit of this guide to direct and lead us to a place of abundant love, peace, and happiness. It should reach deep within the very core of our being. It should revive the kind of love that we can all be proud of. It should restore hope where it does not exist. The spirit of the guide should fill the void in our souls – Emptiness that is a result of destructive parenting. With the submission of a greater will, nothing can hold us back.

In a time of so much upheaval, effective solutions may seem far out of reach. However, when all has been said and done, the one thing that humanity can rely on is a solution whose effects and impact are long-lasting. Like any other illness, the philosophy of fighting human abuse calls for the same approach – 'Prevention is better than cure'. Thus, introducing the vaccine of love at an early stage is a long-term solution that will ensure that the young blood is not contaminated by the stains of violent behavior. The vaccine of love at an early stage is not only fit for the present generation, but it is also a weapon that will be carried over to the future of the future generation. The key to finding the best solution that will wipe out the pandemic of human abuse lies in the sacred truth that; diseases and love have one thing in common, they are both contagious.

The organizations that are at the fore-front of curbing human brutality should be anchored on the firm foundation of a self-help guide such as '**Untangled**' '**The Psychological Chains Of Human Abuse**'. Think about the impact that is birthed, when organizations such as People Opposing Women Abuse, Brothers for life, and Out; start using the message of infectious love that is imprinted in this guide to untangling the psychological chains of human abuse that may be binding those that knock on their doors in search for healing, restoration, and counseling. Without blowing my own trumpet – I so hope, a self-help guide such as **'Untangled' 'The Psychological Chains Of Human Abuse'** is given accommodation on the bookshelves of these organizations. With an array of sizable topics that highlight the triggers of human violence, humanity cannot help, but cherish these life-giving words that are deeply immersed in love, hope, enlightenment, and restoration.

The best solution is to shift our focus to one that is long-term and building characters that are rich enough not to be affected before the reality of abuse kicks in. let us start to build bridges against abuse, let us make children and young people our concern and equip them with billions of love. If need be, take programs of awareness on abuse to all schools and homes, take advantage of their young-easy- to-listen minds and saturate them with the importance of love and increase activities that elevate self-identity, self-esteem, and self-worth, while emphasizing love and care of another learner. Knit together tasks that will expose the inhumanness infused in human abuse. Do not just preach to them but ensure that you are also living what you are preaching.

Believe me when I say, following this route is a long-term approach to absolutely annihilate human abuse.

4
IGOLIDE (GOLDEN)

Napoleon Hill reminds us of saying; "More gold has been mined from the mind of men than the earth itself." Love is gold. The best and most beautiful things in this world cannot be seen or even be heard but must be felt with the heart. Life without love is like a tree without blossoms or fruit. It is better to have loved and lost than never to have loved at all. Surely, love is gold, and it can only be mined deep within the minds and hearts of human beings. However, it can be blind; to take you anywhere ... to all amazing and forbidden places. If love is wrapped up in pain and pretense you may fail to realize that it is not real. Love can be presented as, affection and care without insecurity. Love is when you are happy for the other person's happiness even in their absence. It is when you are by yourself but can still hold great wishes for the other person. Hence, it is wrong to make your partner insecure in a relationship.

At times it takes a whole lot of strength, courage, and wisdom to clear up problems created by love, yet you fail to walk away. Be careful! You can be hurt if you love too much or live miserable when you love too little. Love has two sides and overlapping shades, unlike a coin that has clear distinct sides. As awesome as it can be, love can be the very reason why people choose to be subservient enough to stay and hold on to abusive relationships... being victims and or perpetrators of violence and abuse, all in the name of the gold inside ... love.

I am taken aback by the message that was delivered on the radio by a popularly known motivational speaker. His theme for the day was 'Push until something comes out' – Certainly, not only does it sound like a great theme, but it feels like an empowering theme. On the verge of giving up – such a theme can only produce endorphins of resilience and hope for a better day. In the light that this is a positive motivational theme, psychologically, it could trigger an attitude of holding on to an abusive relationship, because the victim may interpret it as a call of patience and hope for the transformation of an abusive relationship. Therefore, the motivational speaker should be wise enough to highlight the appropriate context that will allow for the application of this theme. Failure to properly contextualize may mean that victims of abuse continue to be tightly fastened by the psychological chains of human abuse. It could ultimately mislead humanity at large.

The lesson is motivational speakers should master the proper contextualization of their message and listeners should also master the proper interpretation and application of the message received.

The same applies to the analogy of gold-making. A motivational speaker may share the message that implies that for gold to be pure, it must go through the pangs of fire. Taken out of context this could ultimately mislead humanity into the belief that peace and happiness are sacrificial virtues that are earned at a price – pain. I strongly emphasize that it is vital for motivational speakers to properly contextualize their message. An impactful message is not ambiguous. A meaningful message is anchored in the roots of a positive and constructive interpretation.

Food for thought … its true love or circumstantial love that rules in an abusive relationship?" Hell-no! Surely, the gods must be crazy if an abusive relationship is to be paralleled with genuine love. If it emulates pain, it can never be true love! I say to the abused soul, "If your parents, guardians, and significant others never provided a mirror of true love, you will struggle to differentiate between genuine and fake love. If they adamantly showed you a reflection of true love, take a bold stand and seize to tolerate circumstantial love.

If love is from the bottom of the heart, other hearts will know that it is true love, especially if there are no terms and conditions attached to it. In relationships, the heart senses the type of love that is mutually exchanged. True love is kind, patient, and caring. It creates an open room for one to be authentically oneself and to genuinely express emotions without intentionally hurting the other party. Such must be the epitome of love, happiness, and joy. Such love is content. The more you give of it, the more it comes back to you. Oh...how sweet it is! On the other hand, circumstantial love is unkind, impatient, and uncaring; it does not create room for one to truly be genuine in expressing emotions without judgment.

Love is surely a piece of gold. It is not enough to talk about love. One must believe in it. And it is not enough to believe it. One must work on it and see it overflow to others. At most you get more joy out of giving joy to others; you should place a good deal of thought into the happiness you can give. Hence it is said, "To handle yourself, use your head ... think, but to handle others, use your heart ... the seat of emotions or feelings. There is no better place to display a clear line of contrast for open, genuine, fake, or conditional love than in a familial setting. A child should learn at an early age to distinguish between true love and circumstantial love. Let it be known to him/her that under human nature one is bound to make mistakes. However, love is not based on the number of flaws you make, but on ways, you correct behavior to confirm, exhume or compliment love. In religion it is said: "Faith without deeds is dead." Similarly, love without deeds is non-existent. In parenting, show through verbal and non-verbal means that children are loved regardless of weaknesses or flaws, while not necessarily confirming that it is okay for them to continuously-intentionally mess up. Remember; be objectively positive towards them, even when addressing negative behavior. By so doing, you kill two birds with one stone ... using the power of love, you can address unwanted action and at the same time use it to diminish fear of punishment and insecurity.

In a world where self-esteem and value are measured by the number of likes one receives from social media, one cannot be blind to the pandemic of insecurity suffered by young people in the 21st century. What we have ever enjoyed we can never lose or forget. All that we love deeply becomes part of us. So, the medicine of love is to instill a sense of pride in each one of them. To ensure each considers him/herself a piece of gold. Pure Love Quotes.com confirms: "For you see, each day I love you more, today more than yesterday and less than tomorrow." A status not measured through social media or material possessions. To ensure young people view themselves as pieces of gold is a work in progress to instill everlasting love in them.

Superficial love, looks, appearance, clothes, and sports cars cannot define self-worth, esteem, and identity, but unconditional love, genuineness, and caring of others do. Never doubt yourself. Every person has his /her specific vocation or mission in life; everyone must carry out a concrete assignment that demands fulfillment. Therein he or she cannot be replaced, nor can his /her life be repeated. Thus, everyone's task is unique as is his /her opportunity to implement it.

The medicine is in instilling a sense of pride that is not measured by the likes on social media or the amount of materialism one possesses. I believe it is a work in progress...one that starts in deeply affirming; "Likes cannot define your worth, you are uniquely beautiful young people"

Never doubt it – you are golden...IGOLIDE.

5
RELENTLESS SEARCH FOR MEANING AND BELONGING

If there is one thing that souls have in common, it is a relentless search for meaning and belonging, a search for unconditional acceptance and true love. Viktor Frankl says, "Love is the only way to grasp another human being in the innermost core of personality." Surely! Love runs deep and silent like water in a deep river; it travels far… goes beyond the physical and finds its deepest meaning in a spiritual being … the inner self. No one can become fully aware of the very essence of another human being unless he loves him. Through love one is enabled to see essential traits and features in the other person; and even more, sees that which is potential in him or her to actualize potentialities. By making one aware of what he /she can be and of what he /she should become, he makes these potentialities come true. We know what life is all about through others. Trust me; it comes with the territory of being human. It is because of the search for meaning and belonging that people are unconsciously taken advantage of, brainwashed, manipulated, and abused.

In search of an understanding or meaning of human abuse, a pessimist observes with fear and sadness what happens daily, may use his calendar record to follow a process, and for each occurrence tears a page from the calendar and throws it away, soon, all pages are gone, but does nothing, while an optimist, on the other hand, challenges the status quo. As he observes the abuse, he scribbles each day's intervention strategies on each calendar page, tears off each page chronologically, and files daily. Later manages to reflect with pride and joy the intervention made, validate progress, and improve strategies.

Brainwashers in the face of the earth know, the best loophole to address human abuse is to see nothing, hear nothing and do nothing, and what they present to the world confirms their views. Such individuals derive no meaning on what is happening; cannot stand against human abuse but use the status quo to further manipulate the world at large. Theodore Roosevelt bemoans such individuals, who at most never act on anything by saying; "To sit home, read one's favorite paper, and scoff at the misdeeds of men who do things is easy, but it is markedly ineffective. It is what evil men count upon the good men's doing." The extent to which human beings continue to fasten chains on the chained brains depends on the subjugated acknowledgment and acceptance of the prevailing status.

It is sickening to notice how people are attached to someone who promises them heaven, earth, and a sense of belonging while doing the opposite. Destroying everything they cherish to an extent of abusing them. It is like a toddler that goes for the cheese on a mousetrap and injures its fingers. So, teach young people the importance of genuine love at an early age. It is commonly said; "A stitch in time saves nine." Teach and show them at an early age that searching for the true meaning and belonging does not have to be a painful mission so that they become cautious throughout life.

Most people never consciously realize what happens around them, mostly say; "Thank heavens...it is cheese...a free meal...very nice," without considering the pros and cons, and for crying out loud, it is in a trap! So, in their quest to reach out for the cheese to satisfy their shortsighted immediate needs such as hunger and thirst, most people end up experiencing insurmountable pain and agony, pain that is greater than the sweetness of the cheese. Although it is said, "Pain teaches." It does not help if you never learn from it. The inferno within me blazes when I notice human beings trapped in self-made abusive prisons and inviting masses to the feast!

The ultimate result is spiraling levels of violence after violence without a sign of retaliating. So sweet is the cheese for a few, while the majority suffers. A cycle of mass-psychological suffering is established in the minds of abusers and perpetrators. And soon, it becomes a way of life, provides an erroneous sense of meaning and belonging. Not until it dawns on them that they are in chains and they need to let go of the cheese. They will be trapped until the gong of departure calls. I still accentuate; Teach and instill in young people a true sense of belonging and search for meaning through love, so that they cannot be trapped in the pleasures of tantalizing mirages in the future.

Search for meaning and belonging is a journey whose destination is oftentimes affirmed by the peace of body, mind, and soul. Different people have different ways of adhering to the needs of this journey. Some holistically devote themselves to an entity that is believed to have higher power and intelligence. Some, like me, surrender their lives to the Almighty God who is believed to be omnipresent, omniscient, and omnipotent. As an open-minded author, I must highlight, I am aware that the uniqueness of people implies that they will devote themselves to varying beliefs. There are Atheists, Christians, Muslims, Hindu, and those that have faith in ancestral worship. It is not in my capacity to critic either of these beliefs. Everybody has the right to choose and devote themselves to a belief that gives them peace of body, mind, and soul. The only time that I see it fit for me to criticize any belief is when it subjects its members to human abuse in the name of honoring, upholding, and recognizing the belief. Nobody should endure the pangs of human abuse in the name of a belief. Nobody should tolerate ill-treatment for the sake of a belief. Any belief should be anchored on the solid ground of genuine love. Any belief should stand on the firm pillars of tranquility.

Human abuse is human abuse despite the devotion of one to a particular belief. I am certain that the common thread that runs through these different beliefs is love and respect for another human being. As such, these virtues should always be highly esteemed so that ultimately no belief is an instrument of human maltreatment.

The abduction of young people in Nigeria by Muslims best exemplifies how belief may be used as a vehicle to perpetuate abusive behavior. It was inhuman for these young people to suffer the pains that are because of the conflict of beliefs. The conflict that lies between Christians and Muslims is one that I am not willing to tackle in this guide for personal protection. These are issues that continue to eat away at humanity's dignity while those in power continue to pour fuel to the fire by not creating channels that allow people of different beliefs to engage and understand each other.

Think about the churches that have been turned into money-making-schemes for the greedy that continue to prey on the bread of the poor. I am not against offering and tithing in church. I am challenging the head of the church to see to it that the finances obtained from offering and tithes are used for the proper upkeep and maintenance of the church. These financial gains should not be used for the personal aggrandizement of individuals, rather they should be used to feed the hungry, clothe the naked, and educate the illiterate.

I have heard so many Christians say, "I just pay my offering and tithe, but I care less what happens to it". This is a sign of ignorance. Start caring by enquiring how the financial affairs of the church, that you so partake in are dealt with.

In the light that I have highlighted the toxic nature of self-aggrandizement, it will be foolish to suggest that the Pastor of a church should go hungry when people are offering at the church. There must be a justified and properly administered financial system that ensures that the right amount of money, enough to take care of the Pastor is allocated to him or her. Like any other human being, a Pastor can also need food and other necessities. It is not wrong to help him or her - if it is done within the confines of proper financial administration.

In search of meaning and belonging, humanity should wisely and with awareness tread carefully, to curb human abuse that is experienced in the form of manipulation and brainwashing that takes place in the name of religion or belief.

Untangling and breaking free from abusive psychological chains, calls forth an understanding that all that glitters is not gold, to discern the 'what' and how of situations, individuals must not only know, the 'what' of that which promises them a sense of meaning and belonging, but the 'how' and 'why'. Deep interrogation and understanding of what we get ourselves into are but a weapon that shields us against storms. Do not just blatantly or ignorantly fall into a relationship because of the bling. Take your T...I...M...E to dig deeper into the realms of relationships before giving all of yourself in them. Instill an attitude of interrogation to your children and let them know that face value can be deceptive. It is by adopting this attitude at a young age, that psychological chains of human abuse can be untangled.

...This I am deeply convinced!

6
YOU ARE ENOUGH!

You are enough to challenge the status quo if your intervention will bring about improvements against human abuse. You must realize that greatness is the fruit of toil. For all of us is a greater call of action and duty; let us live in hope of harnessing victory, striving mightily; let us rather run the risk of wearing out rather than rusting out. You are more than enough to make a difference; you can no longer turn a blind eye to human abuse.

The emotional extremes brought about by love can make it very hard for one to reason well. Thus, my advice to those seeking to adventure in love is that do not lose yourself. Love should not rob you of your mental capabilities and individualism. Though I am not supporting the idea that you become selfish, I am of the idea that one needs to keep their interests, likes, and desires at heart. Succumbing to your beloved's interests with the hope that you will be loved, creates insecurity and dependence, and creates feelings of entitlement on the other person ... may think he or she owns you. Unless you stand up for yourself; all other mastery amounts to very little if you do not become a master of your soul. It is a principle to be instilled in young people. Let them become masters of their souls, to ensure that they will be able to protect their interests in the future even when the entire world turns its back against them. This will in introspect; equip them to walk into relationships with a secure sense of individualism.

If you find yourself having to choose between choosing yourself or your beloved, and oftentimes compromised or undermined, know that you are in for an unhealthy relationship ride. An abusive journey is disastrous, and it will in the long run drain every ounce of energy and passion in you. It propagates dependency ... makes you hang on straws of love. For example, today you become a punching bag, and tomorrow you are given an exquisite gift – Or – today you are showered with negative compliments directed to the fat in your body, and tomorrow you are given a meaningless apology. An abusive relationship gradually makes you less human and turns your lemonade into lemons. You ultimately find yourself without a face to wear a smile.

The wave fluctuations of the 'love and pain' episodes in an abusive relationship are unpredictable. With troughs coming in the form of fists, kicks, and negative compliments – the superficial crests come in the form of 'fake' love, gifts, and meaningless apologies. Smiles are short-lived. Happiness and peace become virtues that remain at the victim's arm's length.

It is one hell of a ride...

Be yourself and be enough ... stand your rights within the so-called relationship or marriage, or simply walk away. You often hear people speaking as if life was like striving upward towards a mountain peak, or that love requires tolerance at all costs. Love behaves similarly at times; in some relationships it feels as if you strive to reach a mountain peak or you are traveling a ridge crest. You have the gulf of inefficiency on one side and a gulf of wickedness on the other side, and it helps not to avoid one gulf, else you fall into the other. Maintain your balance and move through the two gulfs.

A healthy relationship is balanced. It is like a seesaw. It becomes a give-and-take phenomenon. A healthy relationship is complementary, supplementary - no one is at a receiving end. No one becomes the head or the tail. In relationships, people must have equal status. If you are forced to occupy an inferior position, consider yourself to be more than enough and do the noble thing ... walk away with your head raised high. Raising children to instill in them; boldness, impartial love, pride, and wisdom to be unique - Do not give them the fickle idea that by loving one person another person has to be hurt in the process. Be a symbol of impartial love, give it, share it, and practice it ... they will certainly root out the divisiveness nature presented by their adulthood affairs.

Avoid separating your children by rooting out the element of bias in loving them. Give them a fair share of equal and unbiased love.

In a world where strong relationship morals and principles have lost their essence due to the strong influence of media, making it easy for humanity to fall in and out of love like changing a pair of socks. It is easy for one to get lost in the relationship in the hope that they can keep their beloveds to themselves. Some go to extremes to please their loved ones, even if it means breaking the law. Some gradually start developing a dog personality. Take note, a dog is the only animal that loves its owner no matter what. You kick it today, but tomorrow it jumps at you like nothing wrong ever happened. This is a very toxic place for your soul to dwell. Love says, "You do not need to go to the ends of the earth to keep, maintain or prove me."

"You are enough...you are enough... you are enough!" - Tirelessly affirm your child. Endorphins of contentment are endlessly produced in the mind of a child that is constantly receptive to these words.

7
SYNDROMES OF ENTITLEMENT AND DEPENDENCY

Entitlement is a sticky word; parents today are at times terrified that what they say to children might make them feel that they are owned or force them to develop dependency feelings. A strong sense of entitlement and dependency is toxic. But hey if they have done something wrong, they surely, must feel bad. Young people with a sense of responsibility, not entitlement or dependency, who know when to experience gratitude and humility, are better at navigating social shoals of life when needed. However, I feel a sickening lurch deep down the pit of my stomach when I think about the sense of entitlement resulting as a by-product of abuse.

One can possess cars, houses, money, dogs, cats, and an abundance of materialism. The day one starts to possess other people, know there is something drastically twisted in that mind. Being in a relationship does not mean entitlement to that person. She/he does not own you. A misunderstanding of *lobola* which is primarily meant to be a bride price that helps to establish a relationship between two families - oftentimes breeds syndromes of entitlement.

For example, one who pays *lobola* strongly feels entitled to their partner whom they paid *lobola* for. This is a practical example of entitlement roots whose prevalence cannot be ignored especially in the African continent. *Lobola* is certainly not the enemy; it is the misunderstanding of the motive of paying *lobola* that is detrimental. It oftentimes forces the wife to be dependent and over-submissive to the husband.

It starts with owning someone and then it escalates to control, which further graduates to dominance. In the blink of an eye, one twisted abusive relationship built on the foundation of 'you either conform or feel the pain' is born.

Immunize any syndromes of entitlement that may be sprouting in your child. They must learn to differentiate between materialism and humanity. Make it crystal clear to them – they can own materialism, not human beings.

Anybody who thinks they are better than others or feels entitled to be above others transforms others into slaves, beggars, or paupers, especially if the dependency emanates from low self-esteem. Dependency is central in keeping people in abusive relationships. Dependency is birthed from parental inadequacies, which at times result from poverty, and creates in young people low self-esteem, confused identity, negative self-worth, and illiteracy which places these young people under the mercy of others, to be manipulated, ill-treated, harassed, and abused. The victim may develop fear tendencies that reinforce abuse. The best medicine is that parents must genuinely love, encourage, praise, pat the back, support, guide, and educate children. In so doing, you empower them to empower, be bold, and independent.

A sense of entitlement colors perception, at most leads to negative consideration of others, making them inhuman or objects. An object to be controlled - manipulated or moved as one wishes. Entitlement and dependency breeds 'power over' not 'power with' which quickly escalates to human abuse. The two when intertwined quickly elevates one into an abusive position, and the other a victim. Boss and slave relationship is soon established. The entitled position: and unjustified power over another being, leads to abusive tendencies. Blinds their reality and both think that abuse and being abused are noble behaviors in society. The reality to them is we are born unequal. What a lopsided and nonsensical view. However, the abusers use whatever power in their position to inflict pain in another being; manipulate, harass, batter the other person to dance to their music tune at all costs through; physical, sexual, emotional, psychological, financial, or cultural abuse. The abuser always demands respect. So, cultivate a culture of selflessness in your child; this I believe is the first step to ensure any form of entitlement is denied and dependency avoided from an early stage.

Reflecting on meaning and belonging; unfortunately feeling entitled to someone gives abusers a strong sense of meaning and belonging, the abuser feels a huge void in the absence of the person they 'own' - feels like a fish out of water. Can this be attributed to true love? No! True love recognizes no entitlement. Entitlement at most emanates from the scarcity of love felt in the early stages of the child. The void caused by the shortage of love in a child's soul manifests as a monster of entitlement in adulthood that demands love and respect through abuse.

Curb the sense of entitlement and dependency in your child by cultivating and nurturing in them a culture of sharing what they have. The process starts from sharing fruit, sweets, or biscuits. If they succeed in not developing a strong sense of entitlement to materialism, they will surely succeed in not feeling entitled to human beings.

Education is a critical key that empowers humanity to strip away syndromes of entitlement and dependency in people. Education is liberating. Bill Beattie confirms; "The aim of education should be to teach us rather how to think, than what to think – rather, to improve our minds, to enable us to think for ourselves, than to load the memory with thoughts of other men." Through education, one develops self-reliance, which builds a sense of inner security and strong character, which also removes feelings of entitlement and dependency in people, provides courage to move away from any form of abusive relationships. It is because of the importance of education that Dr. Nelson Mandela says, Education is the great engine of personal development. It is through education that the daughter of a peasant can become a doctor, that the son of a mineworker can become the head of a mine that a child of a farmworker can become a president of a great nation. It is what we make out of what we have, not what we are given, that separates one person from another." From an early age let your children know and understand the idiomatic expression: "Give a man a fish, you feed him for a day, teach him to catch fish you feed him for a season ... summer, but turn him into a fisherman, then you feed him for life. The decision lies upon us to best utilize and maximize opportunities that lie before us. Take it upon yourself as a parent, even when you swim in poverty to ensure that your children get an education. Opportunities might not present themselves to you, but it does not help to just sit and shift the blame onto anyone and anything around you. It is undeniable; that opportunities presented by the passage of time may not place you in a moral position to keep on blaming others or the state. Every child is born with potential and abilities, a clarion call was made throughout human history for young people to be tirelessly developed and instructed in lifesaving skills, to sharpen or hone their God-given abilities.

The greater call, I believe is to armor your child with a pen and paper. A well-groomed, empowered, educated, and skilled child, becomes independent, and has better chances to liberate themselves and others from psychological chains of abuse. Such a child understands the negative effects of entitlement and dependence and makes sure their roots are eliminated from an early stage.

Let us allow integrity and commitment to be the solid foundations of our opportunities. Knowing this that whatever that is built on commitment has a great deal of power to stand in an uncertain world. Isn't it amazing – the contagiousness that stems from a spirit of commitment? Not only telling them to commit but leading as exemplary figures sends a very powerful message for your child to follow in your footsteps.

Trust me...you need not say a lot...just lead as an example ...they will follow suit.

8
MADNESS

Madness does not necessarily mean being insane, extremely foolish, or ill-advised, but may also mean being very enthusiastic about something. For example, this young man is a soccer mad. You can be classified as mad if you do the same thing repeatedly and expect to get different results. To an extent, love also requires madness at times. There is always some madness in love, but there is always some method in the madness. If society applies the same strategies repeatedly to address human abuse and do not receive desired results, then it is a call to change methods and strategies, otherwise what is done constitutes madness. Surely, you cannot do the same thing again and again but expect different results.

When addressing a problem, be wise enough to ensure you, without a shadow of a doubt address the cause, not symptoms. Addressing symptoms is like destroying a tree, through cutting its branches, it does not help ... the tree will not die because forces of nature will cause the branches and leaves to sprout up again. So, cut out the tree's tap root, and the tree dies. Focusing on the root of a problem ensures the permanent elimination of the problem. It is like shooting at the bull's eye. Human abuse is a ripple effect carried over from an early age to adulthood and the baton is handed over from one generation to the next. What a self-defeating process. These are psychological chains of abuse that gain momentum daily. Positive means to untangle these abusive chains should be at most directed to the root cause to heal not just the present but the future of the future generation.

What will it take for the just act of imprisonment to be more effective?

The madness embedded in the seeming solutions that have long been implanted to deal with gender-based violence is becoming increasingly evident. At most, we see prison as the best place to put an abusive being. I am not against this idea; however, I am concerned about the failure to couple this act with more effective actions that include counseling the perpetrator so that, ultimately, roots of human abuse are uprooted from the mind of the abuser.

The approach of counseling the abuser is in acknowledgment that human abuse is a psychological illness that is carried over by pains that stem from gruesome struggles that one has had with abuse. It is an approach that will see to it that law enforcers understand the mind of the perpetrator and what drives them to violate other people. This approach will point at the proper way of dealing and healing the perpetrators of human abuse. It will suggest the attitude that should be worn by law enforcers when handling abusive people. A police officer may think beating up the perpetrator is a solution; however, violence cannot be fought by violence. Genuine love is the ideal fighter of violence.

Otherwise beating up the abuser does not facilitate change of the abuser's attitude - it only blows hot air to the already existing blazing fire.

Clearly understanding and having clarity of the mind and background of the perpetrator will propel humanity into a forward motion. Humanity will have taken a step if not multiple steps closer to the permanent elimination of the psychological chains of human abuse. It is this that will ultimately allow humanity to design mechanisms that will ultimately free the perpetrator of human brutality.

The problem is law enforcers are only interested in punishing the abuser and not in understanding their abusive background and families thereof.

Most parents are accustomed to investing in material things and money to ensure a brighter future for their children, but the 21st century requires us to do more than just material investments, we must invest seeds of genuine love. To build character, instill a sense of pride, self-reliance, and optimism in children. Remember, the words of O.J Simpson:

> "Fame is a vapor, popularity is an accident, money takes wings, and the only thing that endures is the character".

Tirelessly work on their character, and you shield all the other things you provide for them. Time progression may witness the disappearance of material possessions, but a strong character stands the test of time.

Character is like a waterproof umbrella in the face of a terrible storm. It is not easily swerved by the wind and it assures protection. A healthy character ensures that you do not only respect yourself but respect others too. A healthy character dissociates itself from all forms of abuse. Invest only materialism in your child, their future success is not guaranteed. Instill in them a strong character, their future success is like the wrestler Daniel Brian would say it – a big and bold YES!

It is the character, not their materialism that will take your children before the Kings and Queens of this earth. It is the character that will instill in them – discipline. The character will ultimately ensure that they are strangers to human abuse. The world longs for characters that will challenge and shake the unjust. It is in desperate need for characters that will see the need to stand in solidarity against the human abuse that is hindering the world from becoming a better place.

Let children wear characters that are fabricated in respect, honesty, love, and care for others.

By taking this step: the psychological chains of human abuse will be left without a choice but to unwind and break in the presence of these characters.

9
DARE NOT TOUCH ... ITS FIRE!

Children are flooded with don'ts from an early age. Just recall the many don'ts that were said to you by parents, guardians, and significant others: "Do not pull the tablecloth, don't talk while eating, don't talk to strangers, don't cross the street without looking left, then right and left again, don't, don't and don't." Dare not touch or the boggy man will get at you. These at times result in uncertainties, indecisiveness, and worry later in life. It at times happens that a fully grown man fails to decide unless someone supports and or acknowledges him. Failure to decide and uncertainty may result in you depending on someone ... husband, wife, father, mother, and friends.

Over time, tables are twisted, the person you relied upon, for assistance and assurance in life develops entitlement feelings, thinks he owns you, and you at the same time develop a dependency syndrome which makes you feel you cannot do or achieve anything without their support. In the blink of an eye, the person you depended upon for necessities starts controlling you heavily – leaving you without a choice but to conform to their orders lest you lose the bread. There is a thin line between a heavy hand of control and abusive tendencies. A position of dependency should be safeguarded so that it does not cultivate a syndrome of low self-esteem and insecurities as these are a ticket to an abusive field.

Sound decision-makers are not influenced so much by emotions in making thoughtful and good decisions. The decision to walk away from abusive situations calls for a fair share of soundness. In making this decision, it is very easy for emotions to get in the way and whisper misleading statements such as:

- "You are loved so much, that is why you get beaten up if you misbehave"

- "What are you going to eat if you walk away from this relationship?"

- "Who is going to support your child if you leave this relationship?"

- "You must fight for what you love, do not let go".

- "Do you think you will survive in this hostile world without him/her/them?"

- "My parents are the only ones that know what is right for me."

- "Without my aunt or uncle's support, this marriage will never survive."

- You are a fighter; never give up on your relationship no matter what comes.

The above misleading statements will cloud your judgment if entertained. Indecisiveness stems from a lack of confidence that is created by a failure to be self-reliant. A child that adopts an attitude of sound decision-making is not easily swerved by emotions to decide. Cultivate this attitude and your child stands a better chance of walking out of abusive relationships in their future love affairs.

I say the best solution is to walk out before you are carried out of the relationship as a corpse. I mean think about it; the number of deaths, disabilities, and bruises that could have been saved if humanity was equipped to be bold enough to walk out in the early days of toxic relationships. See above and beyond your circumstances and take a firm stand for your life. You are much better than getting beaten up and killed for love.

Fight yourself out of the relationship. It is not easy; hence equip their minds while they are still young so that their sound decision-making muscle can be strengthened enough for them to take a bold stand at a later stage in life.

Out of all the whispers that emotions whisper to the abused when faced with the decision to walk out of the relationship, there is one that I can relate to; "You must fight for what you love, you are strong enough not to let go". I have had to use it even when dealing with the hardest people I have come across. The more I affirmed myself I must fight for what I love. The deeper I fastened the psychological chains of abuse that were binding me. The more I convinced myself I am strong enough not to let go. The more pains I have had to endure emotionally, spiritually, and physically. The more I worked hard to prove myself worthy and capable of good positions in my career path, the more rejections I encountered and the deeper the pains I have had to endure. Not until I resonated with the affirmation that, 'I can only give of my best, I am much more than people's unqualified judgments of me' - that I began to attract more positive energy and the universe was left with no choice but to conspire in my favor.

Reflecting at my younger self I had to recall the lesson that: If it burns, dare not touch! You will get hurt.

That lesson still gives me the courage to walk away from painful relationships, to this very day.

10
THE POWER OF INTENTION

Intention speaks louder than action, and action speaks louder than words. Often-times, people are full of the 'what' and 'how' of what to do and not the 'why'. 'Why' is so vital because it provides reasons for your behavior. A clear understanding of purpose ensures alignment of mental and physical aspects ... aligns physiology and psychology - body and mind; it enforces unison of purpose and intention. For example, if you know the 'why' of your relationship is to support and positively grow together with your beloved. You will be challenged to put into action every behavior and action that will ensure this 'why' is achieved. In the same way, if the 'why' in your relationship is materialism, you will put into action every behavior that ensures this why is maintained. Deeply interrogate and find answers to your 'why' before-time, so that when you see the fruits of the relationship cropping up, you will not be perplexed. Do not just tell your children to brush their teeth, tell them why...so that they have an awakened sense of awareness in their relationships.

The human abuse encountered in relationships today can be attributed to the 'why' of the relationships. If the purpose of the relationship is materialistic, unrealistic, or pretentious, then it is easy for abuse to be the dominant notion in the confines of this relationship. My advice is: let the 'why' be firmly anchored on mutually beneficial results that are both productive and positive. By so doing, the mental attitude and behavior that govern these relationships will seek to build, instill trust and happiness in the parties involved. The ultimate result is the birth of healthy, sustainable relationships cultivated on the rich ground of integrity. Reprimand your child for the bad actions, more powerfully so, explain to them the consequences of those actions. Inform them about love, more impact-fully so, elaborate the reason to love. In a nutshell, I am saying – do not just tell them what they should do, give them reasons why they should do it. It well prepares them for a wise approach of elaborating the reason for their relationships.

A clear understanding of reason is what determines the zeal that one has for life. It is 'reason' that allows the alignment of principles and attitudes that will see the fruition and establishment of this reason. So significant is 'reason', it is like purpose. A life without a purpose is like an empty dinner table surrounded by hungry people. People are looking forward to benefiting from the special contribution that one was born to make. Therefore, misunderstanding or not knowing purpose simply implies that those that bestowed their trust on an individual are eventually disappointed at the failure of this individual to understand their reason. Reason gives meaning to life. A senseless life is a meaningless life. Life has got to be covered with the coat of reason. It is like a raincoat amid a terrible storm.

A reasonless life does not give one the drive to wake up and want to see the light of day. It drains the joy out of the gift of life. It serves as a deterrent that binds one to the psychological chains of human violence. I cannot over-emphasize the significance behind reason. It is the epitome of life itself. It is the heartbeat of life. Death is not just the stopping of the heartbeat. The worst form of death lies in the absence of reason. The ability to harness purpose or reason is the one that anchors one's dreams and aspirations. A 'reason' kept alive is productive and willing to put in more effort into the work at hand. It is like a torch that lights up the deepest and darkest of realms. The understanding of reason drives hard work and passion.
Strongly blinded by the psychological chains of human abuse is a human being that fails to answer the 'why' of their relationships and their life. It is easy to manipulate and take advantage of a human being that falls short of knowing the reason they are living. It is of high significance to instill a strong drive within young people to know and

understand their reason for living. It starts with asking them two simple, yet fundamental questions:

What do you want to become when you grow up?
Why do you want to become what you want to become when you grow up?

Engage young people in a dialogue that is actively aroused by the above questions. They must be explanatory about their reason. It is the ability to boldly proclaim their 'want-to-be dreams' that will ensure the high chances of success of that which they are involved and immersed in.

Even the court of law cannot rule justly without proving the intention of the action of the accused. So vital is 'intention', it can act as a determinant factor that lies between freedom and life imprisonment. Pure and good motives in a relationship, free us from the bondage of human abuse. It produces freedom within one's soul. In contrast; evil and selfish motives in a relationship, chain us to the bondage of human abuse. Only courage will determine the period of our sentence. The earlier the call of courage is answered, the shorter the sentence is served. The longer the call of courage is answered, the longer the sentence is served.

I speak of the courage to acknowledge and accept you are in chains. I speak of the courage to use your voice to scream your lungs out. I speak of the courage to reach out for the keys and walk away...

11
ROLE-PLAYING

I hate the sound and meaning given to the word 'role' when it is misused in relationships. For the mere fact that it enforces the idea that either you play your role, or you are useless, it further promulgates the idea that you stick to your lane or you are out of the game. Misconceived conceptions and stereotypes that suggest that work and roles are designated according to sex, strength, and gender, start propping up. The progression of time has taught us that this is not true. Anyone (men, women, transgendered) can carry out any chore or role if they are committed to it. Avoid assigning your child with chores and uttering… 'Because you are a boy' or 'because you are a girl'. The psychological toxin in this action is that it goes in to build a warped image of manhood and womanhood in your child's mind. It will in introspect; enforce the idea that as a boy you cannot carry out certain chores…I must say, I do not need you to agree with me on this view. However, it is my truth.

The world is currently experiencing diffused gender role activities across the spectrum. Role-playing has evolved to such an extent that technology in the medical fraternity has created sexual mechanisms that allow men to give birth and women to fertilize egg cells. Thus, the principle that there are no boy or girl activities must be made clear during the socialization of children. Socializing, training, or influencing your children into boy or girl child roles is detrimental. At most, it produces cowboys with inflated egos and kitchen aunties with deflated egos ... a basic recipe for entitlement and dependence, which soon hatches into abuse.

Role-playing is a phenomenon that has changed over-time. Humanity at large is starting to be open-minded about the term. From job sectors to house chores, people are beginning to appreciate the uniqueness of individuals. Masculine figures are starting to be involved in jobs that were largely dimmed as 'feminine jobs' such as hair saloon operations, house-cleaning, rearing up children, and tea lady jobs. In the same way, feminine figures are starting to get involved in jobs that were largely dimmed as 'masculine jobs' such as construction, truck driving, and painting Humanity might as well remove the word 'role-playing' from its vocabulary and replace it with a word more fitting such as 'character playing'.

Like any other noble phenomenon, role-playing should be used to empower instead of disempowering. It should not be used to strengthen the barricades that separate humanity such as gender and sexuality; rather, it should be an active tool to unify humanity at large. Role-playing should not be misused to highlight power over another being rather; it should be balanced in the sense that everybody has just enough power not to feel over-superior or inferior to anyone. Role-playing should therefore not be used to strongly fasten the psychological chains of human abuse. Rather, it should be used to reflect and celebrate the power of versatility and flexibility that is embedded in every being. Flexibility that indiscriminately allows human beings to carry out the tasks that lie before them - Versatility that indiscriminately enables human beings to tackle any career irrespective of the job description. (*Within the confines of respect, integrity, and dignity*)

I love the sound and meaning given to the word 'role' when it is used with an open-minded intention in relationships. An open-minded intention does not seek to belittle anyone in the process of role-playing. It is accommodating and it leaves the end open, in the sense that exchanging roles is still possible and fully acceptable in a relationship. Role-playing with an open-minded intention reduces the stereotypes that can be attached to it. Anyone can play any role if they commit to it fully. I am speaking from experience; the impact that it has had on me to perform all chores at home without classifying them, at an early age; has well-groomed me to be a very responsible person. It instills an attitude of self-reliance and self-dependency which nullifies the effects of human abuse.

An image of a boy that has been brought up to do only the chores mainly believed to be assigned for 'boys' from a young age, flashes in my mind. This young man is raised in gendered behavior. At a time, he is grown up enough to be independent or live on his own, the early teachings will start showing by the sense of untidiness that is radiated by his house. The boy finds himself without any choice but to enter a relationship for the mere fact that they need someone to help them cook and wash dishes. The purpose in this instance is not genuine love but the assistance that comes with the relationship. In the mind of the boy, the person they love should be able to perform all these house duties, failure to that, their perception, and the respect they have for that person fade away. It is indisputable that there is a thin line between losing respect and abusing another human being. The same psychological chain applies to a girl who has been brought up with an emphasis on gendered behavior.

The part of the human body that is most difficult to open is a closed adult mind. Open their minds while they are still young such that their main objective for a relationship is the love-game, not the chore-escape game.

These young minds should know the distinction between a worker and a lover. As confusing these two, is a sure way to human abuse…

12
IMPERFECT BEINGS

We are all sinners on the route of improvement ... imperfect beings on a road to better ourselves, but we never reach perfection, Marilyn Monroe confirms; "I am good, but not an angel. I do sin, but I am not the devil. I am just a small girl in a big world trying to find someone to love." One weakness related to the department of love affairs is that people tend to give all their hearts and mind to the relationship, overlooking possibilities of related pains. When one loves, one needs to be calculative of their emotions. Surely, the slow movement of a tiger is not a mistake but a calculated accuracy.

When things turn sour, the pain that comes with loving with all your heart is unbearable. My advice is, love that person, but leave room for brokenness. Do not be ignorant to the fact that, you are in love with a human being that has its flaws and weaknesses and the potential to break your heart as well. I am saying love them, but be conscious of the capabilities of getting hurt, do not be blind to them. Remove the blinkers that love can have on reality. Give your child an expectation that's very real about love. They need to be aware of the fluctuations that are brought about by love so that they do not break when it's at its lowest peak. For example, a parent needs to adopt a more realistic and less idealistic approach when teaching children about love. Do not just tell them the excitement that comes because of love. Tell them about the agony and pain experienced as well so that they have a sharpened sense of awareness. Bear in mind, telling them about the pain encountered in love is not in any way an insinuation that it is okay to endure the agony of human abuse.

Love is fire, but whether it is going to warm your heart or burn down your entire house, you can never predict. Love is a mother of all beauty and all evil. Without love, there is no evil. So if you take care of love, you take care of all evil that follows it.

Taking care of love simply means acting within the confines of what it means to genuinely love. It means straying away from hurting others. It means being selfless enough to humble oneself for others. As a passionate writer, I have made it my policy to cultivate and motivate young people. The circle of young people that have rubbed shoulders with me - be it from schooling, working, or living environment, see me as a selfless person because I am always encouraging them in their career paths.

I have rubbed shoulders with all of them, soccer players, actors, presenters, models, poets, and entrepreneurs. My consistent best piece of advice to them has always been:

- "Be the unapologetically, truest, and best version of yourself"

- "Do not allow your flaws to define you, learn from them, but most importantly rise above them – with just enough caution to shield yourself from self-hatred"

- "Do not be your own worst enemy, love yourself enough to be you, for you and do you"

Exposure to the realities of human abuse is made possible by giving away too much love and surpassing the realities of human nature. Tune in to the realities of human nature and shield yourself from the pain that comes with love. Human nature has flaws and weaknesses. Thus, expect these to be reflected by anyone who is fully human. Do not get me wrong, I am not saying you must tolerate abuse because of the nature of humanity. I am saying do not raise the expectation you have for someone too high. Be real and open to the fact that they have flaws and the potential to hurt as much as they love you. It is this sense of awareness that will ensure that one is not caught off-guard in the manifestation of the weaknesses of their beloved.

Weakness does not mean that someone is less of a human being. One must not feel less of a human being merely because of their flaws. It is when you feel less of a human being that you become vulnerable and exposed to human abuse.

The arduous journey of life requires one to fully embrace their flaws and not pretend as if they do not exist. We are all works in progress; we must fully accept this truth and not hide it behind the veil of perfection. It is in acceptance of this truth that the desire to abuse or inflict pain on another human being will be drastically reduced. Human abuse stems from the frustration and disappointment that we have failed to live up to the standards of perfection, which is humanly impossible. If we do not fully embrace our flaws, then we take out the weight that comes with acceptance and express it as anger on another human being.

Our weaknesses are a part of us; thus, we need not be in denial of them and we need not live up to the standards of the illusion of perfection. Love your children regardless of their weaknesses. They will hopefully activate the same power of love in their adulthood.

13
BEAUTY STANDARDS

One worst form of abuse is emotional abuse, where one's emotions are infringed upon and hurt by the other person. It is easy to see physical abuse; however, it is a challenge to even notice that one is being emotionally abused. Emotional abuse can be birthed by compliments that seek to lower one's self-esteem and confidence. Negative compliments that are directed to looks, character, and body are the roots that perpetuate emotional abuse. Thus, it is important to work on building self-esteem that will not be swayed by any negativity. Work on building confidence that stands firm while being challenged. Emotional abuse seizes to affect this kind of self-esteem and confidence. Give your child a platform that makes it possible for their self-esteem to stand firm. For instance, constantly remind your children - no one has the power to authenticate their confidence. They need to shield their self-esteem like a chicken protecting its chicks. This will in turn allow them to soar like eagles and roar like lions even in the face of emotional abuse.

I believe that contentment in your look is the first step to being fully human. Oftentimes it is a challenge to reach this place because of the nature of comparison that comes up with measuring up to the worldly standards. The world has its definition of what it means to be handsome or beautiful. One does not need to succumb to these standards, the moment one gives in to these standards. They will go to extremes to attain this standard. Unhealthy eating habits, use of steroids, and all kinds of body surgeries are carried out in the high hopes that these standards will be met. Only to leave more dissatisfied and broken human beings that have deep-rooted suffering self-esteem. Psychologically, the person who passes on negative compliments to the other person is suffering from a deep-seated lack of self-esteem. Due to the lack of courage to face their scars, they would rather impose them on the other person. It gives them a short-sighted sense of satisfaction.

It is crucial to rely on a kind of confidence that is not rooted in physical appearance, but one that stems from within. Beauty comes and goes. Beauty can be lost anytime. That is, burning off one's face with boiling water can accidentally occur anytime.

Ask yourself
"Assuming that you burn your face, and you are left with a huge scar on your face"
What will happen to your confidence level?
Does it decrease, increase, or remain the same?

My aim with the above question is to emphasize the fact that beauty alone is not enough to base our confidence. Let confidence emanate from the inside. By so doing, one's confidence is left standing on a strong anchor. Confidence that is not swerved by changes in physical appearances is ideal and attractive in an uncertain world.

May your confidence remain unshakable amid it all - Let it remain standing tall like a baobab tree. May its roots run into the deepest terrains and drainage systems – rejuvenating your strength so that it disposes of hurtful episodes of life with profound wisdom – Wisdom that will allow your strength to dry these abusive- episodes just at the right time before they become toxic enough to contaminate your strength; Move with anchored confidence.

The dilemma of 'social media trashing' needs to be met with some fair share of boldness and anchored confidence. Failure to have an identity that is rooted in anchored confidence will result in a lack of boldness and wisdom to handle negative commentary that comes from social media. The ultimate result is a lowered self-esteem, suicidal thoughts, and a growing momentum of the psychological chains of human abuse. To break free from these chains an introspection that deeply looks within to tap into the boldness that stems from one's character should be done.

Anchored confidence shields one from negative commentary.

We live in a world where the standards of beauty keep on mounting up higher. One cannot help but notice the newly progressing illness of low self-esteem that is birthed by these standards. Surgeries have become the popular way of attaining these standards. It is very sad the consequences that are suffered due to the surgeries. It is all in the name of attaining the beauty standards that the world has set for us.

Surgeries are not the enemy here; the problem lies in the motive that drives the decision to pursue surgeries. To a large extent, the decision to pursue surgeries is anchored in how we want the world to perceive us not so much in how we perceive ourselves. Self-image looks within oneself and not without.

A poor self-image breeds low self-esteem that in-turn exposes the human soul to the realities of human abuse.

One simple act at a young age can save a dissatisfied and meaningless generation. An act that affirms your child; they are beautiful and handsome just the way they are.

Superficial beauty is like chaff that is blown away by the wind, it is not worth pursuing!

14
HOPE FOR THE PERPETRATOR

Change is possible for a willing heart and mind. I speak of the kind of change that is required by the abuser. Hope is always available to change a willing heart and mind. The effortless change should begin on the inside and then manifest itself on the outside. It begins with a conviction that is greater than any fear. It begins with positioning oneself for it to be activated. Before giving your child a solution to the problems they may be facing. Teach them to acknowledge the problem at hand first and motivate them to have a greater will to be helped. This act is of utmost importance to activate the mindset that governs the healing process.

If you are an abuser or a victim, you can be taken to the best counselor or mental health practitioner, but you will never change if the change is initiated from outside and your will to change is absent. For instance, when an egg is broken by an internal force, life begins - a chicken is born, but when broken by an external force, life ends, whatever is inside the egg dies. It is often said; "If you look inside yourself for solutions, you receive answers, but if you look outside yourself, you dream." Take note, external assistance must be indulged to support a willing heart and mind.

In the abuser's quest to change and get help. The opposing forces enforced by ego will whisper; "You do not have a problem" or "Love is pain" or "They deserve to be abused". The decision greatly lies upon the abuser to either entertain or not to incline their ears to such whispers. It is in the abuser's courage to choose themselves and not their ego that the healing process can be activated. Ego says, "Succumbing to acceptance will devalue your esteem". Love says, "Succumbing to acceptance will in the long-run elevate your self-esteem". Thus, the abuser needs to choose wisely. Does he listen to the selfish needs of their ego or the greater call of love? The ball lies in their court. I am of a noble belief that effortless change is still possible...highly possible for a willing heart.

Oftentimes, the subject of human abuse becomes one-dimensional in the sense that it has been tackled in a way that provides empathy and solutions for the victim only. It rarely instills courage and hope in the human abuser. This is what differentiates this self-help-guide from other books that have been written on this subject. Plenty of books have been written on this subject; however, it remains an impossible mission to find one that instills hope and courage for the perpetrator. I do hope that both the victim and perpetrator of gender-based violence may find healing, hope, and restoration as they immerse themselves in **'Untangled' 'The Psychological Chains Of Human Abuse'** – a self-help-guide that promises, with the help of one's will, to unbind the psychological chains of human abuse.

It is my greatest hope to become an inspiration in the literature fraternity to start producing material that is two-dimensional when it comes to this subject. A balanced approach ensures that both the psyche of the victim and the perpetrator have the potential of becoming mechanisms that will drive transformation. Using the power of genuine love, both the victim and the perpetrator can find freedom.

A wide array of studies shows that victims of human abuse have the potential of becoming the perpetrators. Therefore, it would be wise to use a healing approach that is unbiased. Remember, this killer, abuser, and this monster that is scorned by humanity today were at one time hurt, bruised, and injured by other people. In the light that the abuser should not be tolerated – it is important to listen and empathize with their story if the theme of their story is: 'I was abused'.

Do not get me wrong, I am in no way insinuating the fickle idea that the perpetrator should not be punished. All I am boldly highlighting is that 'Objective punishment' is much better than Meaningless punishment'. The distinction is that; 'Objective punishment' does not only punish but, it leaves room for counseling, healing, and restoration to take place while 'Meaningless punishment' has the potential to increase the problem at hand because it is a form of punishment that cares less about the healing, counseling, and restoration of the perpetrator.

Let us support the implementation of a form of punishment that is rather constructive than destructive – 'Objective punishment'.

Taping into the will to change should be the driving force in the mindset that governs the abuser. They must be sternly warned; every opposing force hindering them to take the necessary steps to ignite change will haunt them down. The resistance of these opposing forces is the key that will open the doors to a change within. It also lies in their position; the abuser should firmly position themselves in faith, love, and hope. By so doing they stand a greater chance to reign victorious over and above the opposing forces that rage war against their will to change.

A child's will to become better should be greater than their weakness or flaws. Instill an attitude in your child that sees beyond the negativity and the challenges at hand. Shield your child with humility that will stand against the opposing forces of their ego in its ploy not to give them the courage to acknowledge their weaknesses. In case they find themselves entangled by the chains of abuse, they can reach out for the keys which lie in their crown of love and walk away with their character, dignity, and integrity still intact.

The future is unknown and uncertain, but you can armor them for these uncertainties…

15
THE VISION

"When I think of a vision, I have in mind the ability to see above and beyond the majority"

- Charles R. Swindoll

Vision is the ability to think with imagination and wisdom for the long-term. It makes a difference in one's life and interaction with others. Vision cuts across all spectra of life. We talk of a personal vision, an entity's vision, a community, and a country. It is important as a country to have a vision of ending human abuse. To think of a plan... vision to curb the scourge. It is said, "When God gives one a vision, He will give the person all that is needed to accomplish the vision.

Indeed, God has given us the gift of love, to accomplish the vision of eliminating the scourge of gender-based violence. Now, it is up to us to maximize this gift of love.

I cherish a vision that human abuse can be eliminated within families, communities, and the world at large. The majority of South Africans share the same sentiments. The literature on abuse haunts library and bookshop shelves. Everyone writes on the topic of abuse, but the war of abuse rages on. Why? We need to have a common vision as South Africans and take hands to challenge the scourge. The guide urges each one of us to develop visionary eyes that are capable to see beyond the present. Helen Keller, confirms; "The only thing that is worse than being blind is having sight but no vision." And Steve Wonder, the blind singer asserts; "Just because a man lacks the use of his eyes doesn't mean he lacks vision. Maybe South Africa does have a vision to adequately deal with human abuse, but vision without action is a dream pipe, just as action without vision passes the time. Vision is a destination ... a victorious point upon which all of us as South African citizens can focus all our efforts to reach as we dismantle human abuse.

Take note, a man or woman without a vision for the future always returns to his past ... to further perpetuate human abuse.

Powerfully so, a family is a prototype of society. If there is no family, there will be no church, no community, and no society. Parents, guardians, and all involved in raising children. Take note of Muhammad Ali's words; "Champions are not made in the gyms. Champions are made from something they have deep inside them ... a desire, dream or vision." So, learn to create personalities with vision in young people. This act will only lead to successful individuals in the future; it will produce future parents who oppose any form of abuse. As an adult, you are the now ... current reality, but your child is the future ... what is to be.

Help counsel the adult that was or continues to be a victim or a perpetrator of human abuse. More powerfully so, use the loopholes that are presented by abusive cases to knit together behaviors that will instill an abusive-behaviorally-transformed child. If it starts at an early age and it grows then the call for healing cannot exclude the behavior that governs the child. It is the abuse cases presented at adulthood that should be the guideline to what and how the child should be transformed in mind and behavior. If human abuse starts at an early stage and then graduates with time, then the call is for every one of us to cut-off the taproot at its early stages before it fully blossoms.

An abuse-free generation is possible. It will take resilient people to see to it that it is achieved. It will take very passionate and caring people to achieve this generation. The greater call is to work on the skills and qualities that will in the long run equip us to be the instruments that will guide young minds and show them the proper way. It is not easy...but a call that should be effectively adhered to.

Vision prepares the now for the future, it equips the present with the necessary weapons to fight the challenges presented by the future. The child is the now, the adult is the future. Let us, therefore, prepare the now for the future. Remember, people, perish not because they do not know but because of a lack of vision.

Vision remains a long-term foresight that never produces any fruit if it is not paralleled with the appropriate action. Many people have great visions; however, they fail to achieve them due to the inability to align the proper attitude and character. The appropriate attitude, values, principles, and actions should be in alignment with the vision. For example, a nation whose vision is to eradicate the pandemic of gender-based violence should see to it that it raises awareness, and it plants the seed of love within the heart of its people. An individual whose vision is to contribute positively to the movement of curbing gender-based violence should be responsible enough to report cases of violence to the higher authorities. A community whose vision is to promote an abuse-free society should genuinely treat its children in love and care.

As a visionary at work...I am knitting together behaviors that should govern the minds of young people so that ultimately - an abuse-free generation is brought to fruition.

16
THE BEST WAY OF WALKING AWAY

I would not have done justice to my writing if I don't highlight that the decision to walk away from an abusive relationship does not only lie in the hand of the victim. The perpetrator can make it difficult if not impossible for the victim to make this decision. The victim can decide to walk away, but the threats from the abuser can stand in the way of this decision. Threats, especially those that are directed to taking away someone's life can instill a deep-rooted sense of fear within the victim. The result is a human being whose consciousness is under deep oppression. Fear leads them into making miscalculated decisions that are toxic to both their well-being and freedom. Only a safe strategy will assist the victim in this case.

Confidential reporting of the case to the police is the first most vital step; Police must always be alerted of the threats made by the perpetrator. The day that the law starts taking its course, the victim must be always protected from the abuser. Contact with the abuser should be always avoided by the victim.

Walking away from someone you still love is the bravest thing you can do. It means that you were strong enough to disregard your feelings, despite how strong they were. It means that you were strong enough not to listen to your ego because you knew it could mislead you. If you were dependent on the perpetrator for necessities, it means that you were bold enough to face the short-term pangs of hunger than the long-term scarring effects of gender-based violence.

One of the truest signs of self-love is when you love yourself enough to walk away from things that are not good for you. This includes relationships too. ... If their energy is not aligned with yours, if they are not giving you the love that you need, then it's time to walk away. It can be a very difficult decision to take however it is necessary.

It is one of the selfless acts that one can do because an abusive relationship does not only hurt the victim; it terrorizes the friends and family of the victim as well. The noble act of walking away from an abusive relationship is a selfless act that is significant not only to the abused but to those, like me, who are at the fore-front of cultivating an abuse-free nation.

Keep in mind; when you love deeply and intensely, you won't easily leave someone you love. Do not allow superficial love to blind you. Love yourself enough to protect your life and the lives of those that you love.

Lillian Glass, a California-based communication and psychology expert who says she coined the term in her 1995 book 'Toxic People', defines a toxic relationship as:

"Any relationship [between people who] don't support each other, where there's conflict and one seek to undermine the other, where there's competition and where peace has no room.

Walk away from anything that preys on your peace, walk away from anything that undermines you. The act of walking away is a bold statement that sends a very powerful message to the young generation. A message that suggests to them that they should not in any way tolerate a relationship that compromises their self-worth, identity, dignity, and self-esteem. Merely preaching to them will not work, it is important to ensure that you do not preach to them, but you lead as exemplary figures. It is this that holds substance and will in the long run bring about a positive revolution to this struggle with human abuse.

Why walking away is attractive?

The first reason walking away is extremely attractive is because you immediately elevate your self-worth and dignity. Again, there are high chances that any person you get into a relationship with will respect you for this.

The victim of abuse should ensure that they do not in any way disclose or give the impression that they have reported the abuser to the police. This should be observed until the day that the law takes its course. The abuser must not be made aware, to protect the victim from possible escalating levels of abuse that could ultimately lead to death. The strong-hold of fear should be uprooted by the enforcement of not only harsher but safer measures.

The law should work together with the victims so that justice can take its course at a speedy pace. Procrastination should at all costs be avoided, to counteract the unjust actions that can be taken by the abuser. Delays can only increase the damage that can be done to the victim by the perpetrator. Therefore, they should be avoided at all costs. Some level of sensitivity and some sense of urgency should be applied to cases of such nature. These are all lessons that are vital for young minds. It is of high significance to promulgate knowledge that speaks to dealing with human abuse to the young minds in schools.

'Perishing' is at most a product that is birthed by a lack of knowledge. Failure to follow necessary steps to deal with human abuse can result in horrific actions. Some degree of confidentiality and sensitivity must be rightfully applied to cases of such nature. I strongly appeal to the law enforcers at large to ensure that the intricate delicate attention that calls for such cases is put into practice and action. I concur that the implementation of the correct measures by law enforcement will have a greater impact on the call of curbing human abuse. It is that golden weapon that humanity is in desperate need of.

A time that has objectified human beings to punching bags calls for noble and just law enforcers that are not afraid to move mountains to see to it that humanity's dignity is restored.

17
CHECK YOUR POSITION

While preparing for war, some warriors look fierce but are mild. Some seem timid, but are vicious, the position they assume before war becomes very important. The same happens in relationships, look beyond appearances, and position yourself for the advantage, do not place yourself in a position that forces others to overlook you. It is true; the position can restrict or elevate vision.

Without any shadow of a doubt, I am certain when standing at the bottom of the mountain the view is different from the one that appears when standing on top.

At times, the way we position ourselves blinds vision and provides limited reality. By changing positions, views can be adjusted for the better. In the same way, positions in relationships can blind our view of what is taking place in our relationships. It is only when we take it upon ourselves to elevate our vision within a relationship that we begin to have a better understanding of situations.

As one that has been spiritually abused; it was not until I elevated my position that I had a clear vision of reality and was courageous enough to walk away.

Learn to observe other people in similar situations; it helps in elevating your position. Be open-minded; observe what happens in other relationships, intending to broaden knowledge, listen to their stories and incorporate lessons, without ear dropping or sinister motives, because you aim to position yourself in a better position because if you place yourself in a position where you are required to stretch out of your comfort zone, you expand your consciousness. It is critical to realize that a position of self-centeredness can be very toxic and blinding. It is like standing at the bottom of a mountain, your vision is obscured and limited.

The same occurs in relationships, to an extent that one cannot even detect that one is being abused. Positioning yourself adequately enough in a relationship offers you the ability to detect when matters are getting south.

You do not have to be compulsive or suffer obsessions, ensure your relationship is open for discussion when necessary. Ensure it is not one-sided; else you will be placed in a position of obscurity, where-in you see or hear nothing until someone wakes you up. You must at times asset your position without harming others in the relationship. Let your position allow you clarity and free communication. Let it not be a hindrance or obstacle to reality. At times one must reset one's sails to take advantage of changing winds within relationships. In relationships, it helps to position yourself in the center of genuine love, to be elevated to a position of clear vision in that relationship, marriage, or situation.

Like visionaries at work, it is vital not to settle for the position of just embracing and hugging others. It is high time that we strive for an elevated position. A position that allows one to uplift others and put them to the noble elevation they were destined to reach - A position that empowers one to raise proper awareness and education to bring about radical transformation to the psychological illness of human abuse. I challenge all facets of humanity to put into place all the necessary tools that will see to it that everybody is anchored in a position that empowers and elevates others. For example, the educational fraternity should knit together programs that are specifically designed to address the pandemic of gender-based violence. These programs should be facilitated by the acquisition of qualifications in the form of certificates, diplomas, and bachelor's degrees.

Those that acquire such qualifications should not just sit on them but put them to active use. They should be the active mouthpieces of communities. They should be the psychologists and counselors in broken relationships and families. A qualification in the psychology of gender-based violence should empower humanity to empower others.

Keep in mind:

A qualification remains a piece of paper unless there is a practical application that is in alignment with it.

Lack of awareness is very toxic - All that you know about relationships is an experience of your situation only, you do not have any insight that allows you to determine how healthy or unhealthy your situation is, you do not know whether it needs a shakeup or not. You may not even know whether you are correctly positioned or not. You may behave like a harnessed horse that is just moving, unsure where it is heading. So, position yourself in such a manner that you are open to learn from others in similar situations, and engage others. Do this and the result; you can easily detect when something in your relationship heads south ... gets out of hand.

A practical example is to create a dialogue with young people after watching some series that depict non-abusive and abusive relationships. Where possible discuss the pros and cons of such relationships. It provides young people atop of a Mountain View or elevated position on relationships.

Instill in young people the ability to assume positions that elevate them in relationships, not to harass, manipulate or abuse others, but to ensure they can assert themselves and be respected.

Make room for your children to practically make a comparison between good and bad relationships. This will place them at the top of a mountain peak where their vision is not obstructed but as clear as daylight.

18
THE POWER OF TOLD-STORIES

If you are an internet browser, you might have seen an old story floating that states; "Those who tell stories rule the world." Even though there is no neurological research to prove that telling stories is the best way to capture people's attention, bake information in memories, and forge close personal bonds, the power of telling stories continues to do just that. Humanity has always known that people crave and seek out stories almost as much as they seek food and water. Thus, people and brands who tell the most compelling stories command the most influence within communities and the world.

Telling stories is our obligation from generation to generation, and the purpose has always been rooted in deeply arousing engagement and opening meaningful dialogues within communities, societies, and nations.

By listening to other people's stories, you become more whole, more aware, and more informed. Stories to a large extent, add on to what others know. We are all pillars to one another forming an enlightened chain of the human family. We learn from each other's stories. It is by sharing our light with others that we remove darkness from other people's lives. All it takes is a good story told in hope. Good stories surprise and force people to feel and think. At most, told stories stick in our minds and help others remember ideas and concepts. It is not a one-way street, but a holistic approach like raising a child. Remember, it takes an entire village to raise a child that knows the meaning of true love. Listening to a story is as loyal as reading a book. Ernest Hemingway confirms; "There is not a loyal friend like a book."

Stories are based on life experiences from time immemorial. History is one of the best ways to inform and share all that is necessary for human life. However, one must understand the paradigm in each story. Although most stories matter, it is critical to place yourself in the shoes of the teller or writer. Some stories are told to dispossess and malign; some to encourage and motivate, empower, humanize, break, or build.

The common denominator is that human beings want to listen to interesting stories to broaden knowledge. Thus, no story lives unless someone wants to listen. Stories we love best live in us for eternity. So, whether you receive information through a page or mouth, there is always something you achieve. However, it is time that we become objective about stories, so we can prefer those that improve our knowledge on fields that are essential for harmonious living. Or topics that increase our understanding of things that bug human beings like human abuse. Stories in books or told by way of mouth on problematic human life issues like gender-based violence, crime, diseases become learning curves, beacons of hope and light to broken souls, but if you never listen to stories or read a book you place yourself in an obscured position that limits your view of reality and your vision.

One powerful way of experiencing and living a story is to listen attentively and create a mental picture of what is being told. You can further publish such stories on media and create platforms for worldwide consumption. Untold stories seize to have an impact on humanity. Let us be encouraged to harness the skill to convey stories with a long-lasting impact on humanity. So, parents cultivate in a young person's mind, a culture of telling and writing stories and empower them to nurture that skill.

I share my story in the guide, so you can see fragments of yourselves in it and take necessary corrective actions. I was spiritually abused for years by those who thought they loved and protected me. I was taken to traditional healers, prophets, and fortune-tellers. This was all done in the hope that my sexuality would be changed. Myriads of people, young and old, irrespective of gender, have been abused, and are still abused as I write. I appeal to them to shake loose from the trauma, dust themselves and share their stories.

A story that always holds a place in my heart ... that seeks at best to highlight the scourge of human abuse is that of Tyler Perry's Temptations ... *'Confessions of a marriage counselor.'* Every time I listen or watch the story, I have a refreshed revelation of the character of an abuser, their background, and what drives them to behave in barbaric and hostile ways ... how they inflict excruciating pains on other people. And feel pity for the abused innocent souls. The journey presented in the story reveals the inner qualities of marriage ... its pros and cons and it is mind-boggling.

Briefly:

It starts with Bryce and Judith, a happily and recently married young couple that moves from a village to a city for better life prospects. They get along very well. They were excitedly content and deeply in love. You would swear that the flames of love they ignited for each other were powerful enough to burn the entire house to ashes. They were the perfect epitome of the obedient Adam and Eve.

A handsome and rich guy comes into the picture of their marriage. Little do they know that this city guy by the name of Harley never knew the meaning of true love; he perpetually, emotionally, and physically manipulated young women. He was always influenced by lust rather than love - a serial sexual abuser. Through his persuasion ability - Judith falls for one of his fishing angles. He convincingly promises Judith pearls and gold until she gives all of herself to him – body, heart, and soul. Blinded by material things she starts to cheat and neglect her husband. Deep insecurity and dissatisfaction scars start to show in her relationship with Bryce.

Her behavior towards him changes as she guiltily transfers her love to the young, rich, and handsome guy. However, Bryce remains supportive and caring. An argument between Judith and Harley opens a can of worms - it turns out that the guy is a psychologically manipulative and serial sexual abuser who used material things to lure young ladies. On becoming aware, Bryce rescues Judith who is on the verge of being killed by Harley. This was not the first time, that he rescued her from the fangs of death. The first time, his helping hand was painfully rejected, but now the intervention to prevent death is embraced.

The above is a breath-taking love story, where two kinds of love are presented to an individual who has a poor self-image.

Bryce is a good guy - honest, genuine, dull sense of humor, poor, handsome with a 'not so appealing sense of style', but content in himself and the little that he has.

Harley is the kind of guy that most ladies would call phenomenal – extremely smart, handsome, great sense of humor, very rich, popular, in-genuine, dishonest, and discontent. These two guys present two contradictory kinds of love, but surprisingly enough they are both irresistible in the eyes of ladies.

Judith is the typical 'church girl' from the dusty streets of the town, smart, hard-worker, ambitious, poor self-image, discontent, and still on a journey of self-realization. If Judith was content, she would have never allowed the critics she got at her workplace for putting on flat shoes to persuade her to extremely change her sense of style. She would have resisted Harley from luring her into an intimate relationship using the very things that he thought she lacked - money, sexual satisfaction, and fame.

It is Judith's discontentment that propelled her to leave a poor man that loved her genuinely for a rich man that in-genuinely loved her. She had always longed for recognition and power – something that she was deprived of by her religious background that emphasized that she must always be the tail to her husband.

Think of the impact created by this story. It presents both sides of a coin in marriage. Practical sides' that people can identify with ... the lovely and enjoyable side of marriage and the dark defeating side that may end horribly. The story highlights issues of intimacy, true love, care, insecurity, low-esteem, greed, and lack of appreciation in marriage. Most significantly the psychological chain that attracted Judith to the handsome rich man came in the form of material needs and sexual satisfaction. Was she able to attain this? Yes, but it all came at a very agonizing price ... a near-death episode.

Reflecting on the background of this couple, I realized, they came from a solid religious background. Bryce's mother-in-law portrays this to be an undefiled truth through her prayerful attitude. I do not know about you, but my final analysis is that Judith's mother propped up insecurities in her daughter by not being openly complimentary to her beauty, looks, body, and personality. 'Remember the long dress and the flat shoes she wore on her first job in a corporate environment; these should certainly say a lot about Judith's poor self-image.

Shout...shout...let it all out...your story and my story, have the power to untangle the psychological chains of abuse that are binding humanity at large.

19
THE POWER OF A COMPLIMENT

A compliment is simply a polite way to express appreciation, praise, or admiration to another person, who on receiving it feels special, appreciated, or loved. Nice and thoughtful complimentary comments boost self-esteem and build self-love in people. Robert Brault confirms by saying that there is no effect more disproportionate to its cause than the happiness bestowed by a small compliment. So, to make someone, especially your children to be able to take themselves seriously ... begin to love themselves and feel wanted, start to compliment them for little errands done well. It helps them to handle bigger issues with confidence.

A compliment may appear small, but its ripple effect goes far. It snowballs to reach each area of the body. A strong self-image in young people is crafted from constant positive compliments. Please note, do not flatter ... be genuine. I strongly recommend that parents must give children a fair share of compliments to build and anchor their confidence and self-security. It is undeniably true that people are social beings, and regardless of the good in them, they still need a fair share of external affirmations in the form of compliments. At times children may not be aware of the good they do and through appreciation and praise, they begin to appreciate themselves. Often-times it is compliments and external affirmations that build a strong sense of conviction to what they already hold.

At times, conviction seeks to fight for us in the face of fearful, confidence-testing, and heart-sickening situations, but to overcome, one's positive conviction must be greater than any discouraging situation. Positive convictions should be greater than any lie told. Thus, a conviction that one will surpass problems may not be that convincing to the individual unless if it is supported through compliments. So, without external appreciations and compliments, a conviction that is deeper than the ocean may not assist an individual to achieve goals unless it is supported by compliments. Statements like the following dig out courage and power in others:

- "Thank you for your presence."
- "You are the best thing that ever happened in my life."
- "You make me see the world in a way no one ever has."
- "I love the way you make me think."
- "I appreciate the way you challenge me."

- "Around you, I'm the best possible version of myself."
- "I love you so much it hurts."
- "Your energy is infectious."
- "You are my entire world."

Compliments are the fastest and easiest ways to make someone feel better about him or herself. There is always a bonus in complimenting others. Parents who genuinely, persistently, consistently, and constantly compliment their children are soon amazed, at what happens to their personality. The power of a compliment soon intricately builds conviction and an attitude that says, "I can." That allows an individual to fly and soar like an eagle amid negativity, doubts, and impossibilities.

Like fuel for an empty tanked vehicle, compliments keep us moving. On the verge of giving up, there is that compliment that upholds us. You are the best cook, you are caring, you are beautiful not just physically but in character, you have an infectious passion for people, and you are a hard worker. These compliments mine the best treasures in us. They give us hope for a better day. They keep us safe and sound amid discouragements.

Psychologically proven - sick patients that are positively, constantly, and genuinely complimented by their caretakers have higher chances of overcoming their sickness than sick patients who do not receive any compliments from their caregivers. The power of a compliment goes in to activate positivity and a healthy state of mind which in the long-run speeds up the healing process.

There is a psychological effect that is carried by the words:
"You are healed"
If said genuinely and persistently – it goes in to produce healing enzymes and endorphins in the mind. It is a matter of time that the healing toxins produced in the mind can begin to manifest on the problem that is experienced on any part of the body – it could be a headache, backache, or sore throat.

Trust me; the mind is a very powerful tool that can be used to heal any sickness. All it takes is persistent affirmations infused in genuine love that is uttered in faith, hope, and positivity.

I am not in any way encouraging anyone to neglect medical instructions for the affirmation of healing words. I am saying, while using the recommended medicine, healing affirmations will add to the effectiveness of the medicine.
It is a deep sense of conviction that resonated in the hearts of great leaders, that they were able to give their best to the

world. There are numerous leaders in this regard, but it will be sufficient to mention a few like Abraham Lincoln, Nelson Mandela, Theodore Roosevelt, and Mother Theresa. Without compliments from their countrymen, some could not have reached their goals. There emerged, in most of them the power to move mountains. An unknown author confirms: "Some people are radiators; they make you feel warm when you are around them.

They offer complements to lighten up your path.

Parents are encouraged to compliment or appreciate their children daily.

Let it be known:

They don't just have the right to be individuals; they are obliged to be one.

20
THE UNIVERSE APPLAUDS

It takes courage to love again when you have been hurt, it takes strength and strength again to chuck it all away. Somewhere, somehow, somebody must have the courage to use the power of genuine love to untangle the psychological chains of human abuse.

The energy of the universe cannot direct how our efforts are channeled. It is the ability to resist the power of discouraging energy; that will see to it that our efforts are always applauded. I must say, life has a way of putting us in spaces that are painful and hurting. The power lies in not allowing these toxic spaces to determine our passion for life. The power lies in not allowing these poisonous experiences to determine our zeal for love.

If you have been hurt or scared by an abusive relationship, I empathize – in the same light; I am challenging you to look at the beauty of love that the universe has stored specially for you. Have the courage not to allow the past unfortunate experience to detect the lifespan of the current experience. Clear the haze of the past traumatic experience that may blind you from seeing and feeling the joy of the present experience.

The present love experience needs your undivided attention. Lose yourself in what the present experience has in store for you. Enjoy and wholeheartedly cherish this moment. Do not rob yourself of the now-moment of genuine love. Feel it with every fiber of your being – the tickles, the smiles, the gifts, the rides, and the intimate conversations. Do not entertain thoughts of the past traumatic experience. Safeguard these thoughts so that they do not turn the gold in the palm of your hands into shit. Love without boundaries and trust without borders (*within the confines of dignity, respect, and integrity*) – loosen up!

Believe me when I say:
"The universe is behind you now".

I am of a noble conviction that everybody is born for a purpose. Nobody is useless - we all have a special contribution to make, it is certainly not a coincidence that we are all born with our hands closed...we are born holding this purpose in our hands. Please discard every thought that is a product of being told otherwise. So many people have missed their mark in life because they have only listened to voices that tell them they will mount up to nothing. The human injustice encountered today can be attributed to these negative and discouraging voices. The task is for everybody to do an authentic introspection deep within the realms of their soul and nurse the scars that are a result of being discouraged.

The scars of negativity, failures, and discouragements need a doctor that is armored in a coat of positivity to renounce all the negative words with encouraging words that are saturated in hope. Words of encouragement should be sung like praises at childbirth. Psychologists have proven that uttering loving words at birth has an enormous effect on child development; the echoes of these words are loud even in their stages of growth. Loving words are the building blocks of a beautiful palace, the builder who is the parent must be cautious of the quality of the brick so that the final product is strong to withstand any strong forces.

Gone are those days when motivational speakers only spoke 'feel-good' words to their audience. It is high time that through our words, we challenge the audience to not just 'feel-good' but to see tangible changes in their lives. Shake the audience, if it means making them feel uncomfortable, so be it, if it is for their good. After being told you will mount up to nothing, do you just sit on these words, No! You look at yourself and do everything it takes to nurture your talent and skill. Our actions must speak louder than our words in redeeming ourselves from discouraging words. Silence these limiting words by acting not wording, the impact is much greater. Make children aware that they have a special contribution to make while they are still young. It becomes their goal to search for this special contribution and cherishing it for the greater good of humanity. More powerfully so, see to it that you fully support their talents. They will grow up knowing their contribution, they will not experience the agony that stems from being told, they are nothing or useless in life.

I say the greatest asset you have in life is yourself. Nobody knows how you feel except you. Nobody can take you out of the pit of depression and frustration except yourself. Self-pity will only make you feel better, but it will not create any impact. It is when you tap into the courage to try to act in creating something out of your nothingness that the universe can start cheering you up. It is when you take a stand to better yourself amid the discouragements that a fence that shields you from the realities of human abuse can be erected.

You just need to believe it:
Take a bold stand:
The universe applauds our existence.

21
THE POWER OF REFLECTION AND INTROSPECTION

To reflect is to reconsider or to look back into past experiences and actions. Introspection is the deep self-reflection of those thoughts and inner reflection of the self-within, both engage body, mind, and soul. The two, when infused together provide a powerful message of evaluation of one's thoughts and actions that foster and ignite the desire to seek change. Reflection and introspection are not just merely 'looking back' and 'evaluation of thought,' but being mindful enough to pay attention to lessons learned from past experiences and applying them for future growth and well-being. It is an inward introspective inquiry with oneself. The process implies looking back and forward and adjusting one's current behavior and activities. At most, we are busy trying to earn a living and keeping up with our lifestyles and it is so hectic that we hardly find time to do justice unto ourselves ... to reflect and introspect.

Bear in mind, by reflection I am in no way insinuating that one should remember abuse-triggering events. Rather dwell and focus your energy and mind on the precepts of positive reflection and introspection.

Reflection and introspection are vital; allow us to sass out the journey that we have taken so far, and to implement changes where needed. Through reflection, so much can be revealed in our character, attitude and how these contribute to the current state of our relationships. The problem is we tend to tirelessly go-go-go in life, even if it means going with unnecessary baggage that will affect us negatively in the future. It is only wise to reflect on the journey so far traveled if need be, leave unnecessary baggage, and move forward with lighter souls. In reflection and introspection, we rise above fears by facing them. We can do that because we are not the fear, the thought, or pain that we are reflecting on.

Reflection and introspection are gifts of our spirit, these allow the deeper parts of who we are to come forth and be discovered. This makes it possible for us to create something extraordinary out of the ordinary. Positive self-reflection and introspection is a balance of how we see ourselves now and whom we see beyond the now and allows us to blend who we are with whom we want to be.

A moment of reflection is the key to tapping into the unexplored realms of one's character, the solution to finding a lost identity. Reflecting on compliments and positive affirmations like "You are an overcomer" certainly anchors an individual that is on the verge of giving up. Reflecting on acts of kindness and care assures one of his or her identity amid discouraging words and bad influence. Like a chore, one has got to allocate time for positive reflection and introspection.

It is reflection and introspection that give room for one to adjust and improve attitudes that can make them vulnerable to human brutality. Teach your child the significance of introspection. Let them reflect on the good and positive experiences they have had so far. In so doing ... I am convinced they will reflect and adjust even in their adulthood. On reflecting, learn to open the ends; do not box your soul.

Reflect on self-esteem, insecurities, confidence, abilities, and hopes. Try to apply positive changes where there is a need. Consult external parties for professional advice and incorporate this advice into your daily interaction with others. I am fully aware that reflecting on your insecurities and painful experiences can be traumatizing. However, demons avoided only strengthen the magnitude of their toxic-ness. It is dangerous to live in denial of our past because peace can only result from honestly facing the past and make resolutions to move forward, denial cannot make you authentic, acceptance and courage to face the pain will build up an authentic muscle within you. Of course, you cannot do it alone, some hands are willing to pull you up and help you. If you don't have one, this guide is a friend whose impact, motivation, and presence are much greater than that of any friend.

It is of paramount significance to not just reflect in thought but to write down these reflections so that they become secured archives of hope, inspiration, and strength. Creatively diarize your reflections; it could be poetry or the audio recording of these reflections so that they become meaningful reminders of the road so far traveled.

Reflection and introspection are giftings that curb humanity from falling into a pit of ignorance. They give room to improve the now for the future. It is a failure to reflect that causes one to fall into a pit without even noticing it. Failure to reflect cannot see the need to improve and apply changes to the unexplored realms of a relationship. Think about it - the abusive actions that could have been avoided if only a moment of reflecting on the dire effects of the past abusive actions was taken. Teach children reflection and introspection skills so that they can consider past experiences and consequences of their past actions so that they can adjust and implement changes if necessary.

Self –introspection looks deep within and not without. It deeply interrogates the happiness, satisfaction, and value of being in a relationship. It is after self-introspection that one can have the answers that speak to their happiness and satisfaction. If self-introspection suggests that one is not truly happy or satisfied – it is a call for changes and improvements to be made. If it costs you your happiness, it is not worth investing your effort in it. Adjust and if there are no noticeable changes, walk away before your unhappiness graduates to depression. Walk away before the depression escalates to suicidal thoughts.

I emphasize,
Walk away before you are carried out of the relationship as a life-less body.

22
THE POWER OF POWER

The purpose of reflection and introspection is to gain the power of balance on the past, the future, and the present. Just like standing on the bank of a flowing river, and watch the river flowing; the past, present, and future are interlinked. The water is not disjointed but flows as a unit. That is a balance of power, and such power determines a healthy and an unhealthy relationship. However, absolute power becomes poisonous; it is unbalanced and soon feels entitled to own others. Soon, the skewed power causes manipulation, undermining, ill-treatment, and abuse of others. Power, I must say; is great, sweet, and satisfying in and of itself. So many leadership struggles encountered today are a result of power struggles. It is true that too much power is destructive, it can corrupt. Yes, power needs to be balanced, if not, it corrupts. Mahatma Gandhi confirms; "The day the power of love overrules the love of power, the world will know peace. And Abraham Lincoln takes it further; "Nearly all men can stand adversity, but if you want to test a man's character give him power.

Absolute power is evil and corrosive. It is like acid, corrodes the vessel in which it is contained or stored.

The danger of excessive power has been displayed by great Nations that have crumbled in the hands of leaders that could not let go of the sweetness of power. Absolute power is the root of manipulation, conflict, and an unhealthy sense of title-ship. We have seen them all, those that steal from the nation's pocket, those that brainwash the disadvantaged, and those that use the power of money to manipulate the voting system of a country so that they remain in power. I intentionally did not include examples of these leaders in this guide for the mere reason that I do not want to turn it into a political battlefield. My objective is to advise, heal and transform.

What is a balanced state of power?

A balanced state of power seeks to achieve an equilibrium state between parties in a relationship. Equilibrium in this case means that no one feels that they have power over another person. Everyone has just enough power to live without feeling over-superior or inferior over anybody.

This kind of power is attractive and influential because it assumes the accountability and responsibility of the leader. Leaders that have a balanced state of power do not just send orders, instead, they find great pleasure in leading as examples.

It is awfully surprising the extremes to which humanity can go, to gain more power. If humanity can go to the lengths of killing, destroying, lying, betraying, and pretending to gain more power...it should only be befitting that human abuse should form a part of this nasty package. Human abuse that is fueled by the unbalanced state of power seeks to see to it that the victim feels greatly inferior. It aims to silence the voice of the victim at all costs. It is at best, a form of self-satisfaction. One that is very addictive, controlling, and manipulative...oh how distasteful it is! Meaning is added to human existence only if this state of power is achieved through hurting others. It is only when the power is balanced that respect, integrity, and order can form the foundation of the relationship. Balance, in this case, is a state in which no party feels over-superior or inferior over the other party, I emphasize!

The subject of leadership should be taught in such a manner that it does not in any way promote the fickle idea that leadership is designed only for the few special people that have been destined by blood. Simply because it is this approach that triggers misconceived behaviors in those that are in power.

Leadership should be taught in a manner that captures the essence of the message that everybody is a leader. Everybody has the potential to tap into their leadership spirit – A spirit that is granted by birth – authority that is granted by God who said, *"Let us make mankind in our image, to be like us. They will reign over the fish in the sea, the birds in the sky, the livestock, and all the wild animals on the earth, and the small animals that scurry along the ground"*.

Despite one's background, race, status, and gender, everybody has the potential to lead. The only distinction between followers and leaders is that leaders have captured their leadership spirit and followers have not or they are still in the process. But ultimately this is a spirit that is given to everybody by birth.

The power struggle does not start at the adulthood stage; it starts early and grows within an adult. Believe me; the effect of power is evident from childhood when one is given charge over another young child or an activity. It is in how you groom them to take charge of the little things at an early age that molds them into the adults that will justly take charge of greater things in the future. That is if they are showing signs of being too bossy or controlling at an early age. Chances are great that they will turn out to be controlling and too bossy adults that will seek to satisfy this need at the expense of their loved ones.

Curb this attitude from a young age. It can only lead to a greater sense of hunger for power.

Let us change our language:
It is power 'with', not power 'over' that will heal humanity from the deep wounds of the psychological chains of human abuse.

23
THE HERO WITHIN

"Are we truly free?"

We all long for 'Freedom,' it is what our forefathers painfully fought for...the works of their sweat should never be taken for granted. They should be highly revered and always honored. "We salute you!" To me, freedom is having the ability to act or change without constraint. Something is 'free' if it can change easily and is not constrained in its present state.

Some of us are still fighting for this freedom. Deep in the lines that run through this writing is an unrelenting fighter that will not rest until humanity is truly freed from the entanglements of the psychological chains of human abuse. I might not be carrying an AK47, but I would be honored if I am remembered as a fighter even at my time of rest. One of the lines in that final speech should read... "Her writing is a weapon that fought and won the battle against human abuse". My objective is to create an impact, so great and deep in the mindset that governs the human family to start investing so much care and effort into raising an abundantly loved child that is a pioneer of a human-abuse-free generation.

The question that is always food for thought for all humanity is, 'Are we truly free?' If someone sees it fit to inflict pain on another human being be it physically, emotionally, or spiritually, then our definition for freedom should be thoroughly revised. Freedom can never be inclusive of pain and agony. It is not manipulative or brainwashing. It seeks to see the reigns of peace ruling the human soul and the upholding of human respect and integrity regardless of our differences. It appreciates our uniqueness as a people; it never condemns but cherishes the special contribution that everyone was born to make.

I am of the ideology - it begins deep in the psyche that governs the human mindset. It is only when one begins to think and act freely, that the true meaning of freedom can be truly known and felt. A young free mind is possible only if the adult can understand the huge responsibility that lies in loving their child and acting within the confines of what it means to be free.

All parents are to be guided by Nelson Mandela's words; "For to be free is not merely to cast off one's chains, but to live in a way that respects and enhances the freedom of others."

Talk about love being the absolute compatibility of two completely different but complementary human beings - The sprouting flower will not grow if a stone is placed on top of it; the freedom of the flower is curbed by the force and the properties of the stone. On the other hand, if fertile soil is placed on top of the flower – the flower has no choice but to grow at a fast pace. The freedom of the flower is upheld and promoted by the force and the properties of the soil.

The above analogy simply implies that for love to mutually benefit all the parties of the relationship without curbing the freedom of either of them there must be compatibility. That is, the qualities and personality traits of both parties should nurture and nourish – not imprison or curb growth. For example, qualities like honesty, integrity, and care can only nourish the other person, however, qualities like selfishness, un-care, and neglect are like the force of the stone on the flower – they eliminate freedom and growth. The joy of being in a relationship implies that there is room for growth. Without growth, one is as good as dead. Life is about embracing growth.

Growth and freedom are vital in any relationship; this is facilitated by compatible qualities and personal traits. An abusive relationship is suffocating; it does not leave room for one to breathe, it preys on one's freedom. Like a prison, one who is abused gets told, what to do, when to do it and how to do it. Failure to abide by these orders is followed by a series of punishments. One is kicked, slapped, scolded, and even killed. The freedom of choice and expression is limited by the demanding nature of an abusive relationship. An abusive relationship is like a bird that attempts to fly on a broken wing. The bird can crawl, walk, and jump but it cannot do what it was originally purposed to do – which is flying. It is impossible to fly on one wing.

To be truly free,
One has got to find a compatible wing that will allow them to soar like an eagle.

The freedom I speak of respects another human being regardless of differences. I despise a chained mind; it just seizes to be free. It is ruled by the fear to think and act positively. It is saturated with the consequences that come with thinking or acting positively. A chained mind is a pit that can only lead one to devastating destruction. It is at best - a prison state of mind that is surrounded by thick walls and chains that are not willing to let it see the full light of day. I cannot fully express how toxic it is for humanity to continue finding shelter within the confines of such a mind.

It is this noble reason that keeps me restless until I am convinced that mind-freedom is achieved. I will not stand aside and watch others fight and die for me.

Leave the spear and shield for King Shaka Zulu. With my pen and paper, I will fight till the final curtain falls.

24
SELF-ESTEEM AND SELF-WORTH

"Don't touch my hair!"

Self-esteem as used in this guide refers to a person's beliefs about his or her worth and value. It also has to do with feelings people experience flowing from the inner sense of worthiness or unworthiness. Self-esteem is important and critical in a person's life; heavily influences one's choices and decisions and well-being. Psychologically, self-esteem is used to describe a person's overall sense of self-worth or personal value. That is ... how much a person appreciates oneself? Self-esteem is often considered a personality trait; it has much to do with loving yourself. People, who love themselves, do not hurt or abuse others. However, those who do not love themselves or who hate themselves tend to hurt or abuse others. Thus, to untangle psychological chains of abuse in others, let us start with the individual; instill in your child positive self-esteem. Wayne Dyer confirms the importance of self-worth by saying:

> "If you do not love yourself, nobody will ... and not only that, but you will also not be loved by anyone else. To love; start with the self."

The problem with scars is that they tend to prey on the perception that we uphold of ourselves. A captivatingly beautiful gift, if not properly taken care of, it gets worn out with time. In the same way, if self-esteem and self-worth are not properly upheld, they get worn out with time. Taking good care of self-worth involves so much - from the thoughtful consideration of our relationships to the compliments that we entertain and the people that we converse with.

The power of choice is the best gift that life has to offer – no-one should be robbed of this power; it is an affirmation of 'individualism' respect - an attribute that is a vital element of freedom. Without respecting the power of choice, individualism is lost, and self-esteem is suffocated. One has got to have at their disposal, the power to choose relationship partners, the compliments to be entertained or discarded and the people to engage with.

The naked truth is everybody is born with self-worth, it is not earned, and it can never be measured by our possessions, it is everybody's birthright. Unfortunately, the progression of time, growth, and worldly standards blind us to this truth. Our minds as we grow up are just channeled to believe that the more possessions you own, the more self-worth you gain. This is one long psychological chain that binds our thinking and acting.

Prone to human abuse is a human being that has no self-worth. A sure fact is that the absence of self-worth exposes one to the realities of human abuse. This calls for minds to be adjusted, let us claim the birthright that is rightfully ours. Materialism is a short-sighted fickle way of equating one's self-worth. Accentuate endlessly while they are still young, their lives are worth more than a barrel of gold. Nobody and no situation should convince them otherwise.

To emphasize this, I still say, even in one's nakedness, self-worth is one garment that can never be stripped away. Even at death the corpse still radiates the self-worth that a soul possesses. Unfortunately, self-worth today fluctuates with the status of our possessions; when it should be stagnant, firm, and unshakable regardless of the different situations that we encounter. Let the strong winds come and the storms arise but these should not at one time strip us of our self-worth. It should always be kept intact, deep in the realm that governs our soul; our self-worth should always be kept alive. It is that vital.

Nakedness is not in the absence of our clothes; true nakedness is in the absence of our self-worth. Not even our weaknesses or failures are enough to rob us of our self-worth. It is the greatest asset that humanity has the responsibility to always uphold. Affirm them there are worth more than the powerful currencies of this world.

Problems should never convince them otherwise.

It is a position of unrelenting self-worth that channels the mind to have the respect and integrity that is unwavering and willing to respect another human being. One cannot give what they don't hold. It is when one recognizes and upholds their self-worth, that they can recognize and allow others to uphold their self-worth. In the palm of their hands, let them firmly hold on to their self-worth, knowing that, saying yes to self-worth is in introspecting saying no to human abuse. Challenges will always shake the roots of our self-worth, but if it is firmly anchored, it will be left untouched.

Young people have seen the radical dialogues that are directed to the upholding of self-esteem and self-worth in countries such as South Africa and the United States of America.

It can only make sense to bear this cross, seeing to it that colonization, racism, and slavery are prevalent calamities that are still experienced in the 21st century; Movements that have preyed on the self-esteem and self-worth of young people for such a long time must be eliminated from humanity.

It starts now, in the way a grow-up person treats a young person; as a grown-up person, deviate from adding on to the list of the injustices that have for a long-time stripped humanity of its esteem and worth. Support the positive endeavors of young people. Do not pull them down. Do not discourage them. Cheer them up and persistently motivate them.

I earnestly appeal to grown-up people:
Give room for young people to lead without feeling threatened by their success.

To the Solange of this world, we need to start singing...

"Don't touch my hair
When it's the feelings I wear
Don't touch my soul
When it's the rhythm I know
Don't touch my crown
They say the vision I've found

Don't touch what's there
When it's the feelings I wear
Don't test my mouth
They say the truth is my sound"

25
H-A-B-IT

Habit is the continuous repetition of an action. What distinguishes a good habit from a bad habit is the nature of the repeated act. Repetition of bad actions builds up to what is referred to as a bad habit. Repetition of good actions builds up to what is referred to as a good habit.

Like an addiction, overcoming a bad habit is only possible if there is will. I have come to deduce the phenomenon of a habit as something that you cannot live without. It could be a cigarette, alcohol, food, and energy drinks. Breaking free from the pangs of addiction calls for resilient people that will be courageous enough not to allow their emotions to be controlled by these intoxicants. Addiction simply implies that one's feelings are controlled by the strong desire to use the above intoxicants. One should master the ability to be able to control these intoxicants and not to be controlled by them.

The strong grip of addiction could be self-defeating; however, the courage to practice self-control will be instrumental in loosening this grip from the victim. Self-control is designated for those that have been able to rise above their desires and emotions for a greater and noble course. I must highlight though, mastering self-control has never been an easy discipline. It takes a whole lot of maturity and serenity to harness the precepts of self-control. It is a process – a journey that starts with self-realization. One who becomes aware of their identity with maturity has the potential to master self-control.

The day that I was able to master self-control is when I was at a point in my life when I was fully aware and unapologetic about who I am. All the while, I felt controlled by my emotions, but with experience, growth, and maturity – I was able to gain the power to control my emotions and not the other way around. It may take time but keep on working with your soul. It can be done.

I was astounded by the fact that greed for food can be paralleled to addition. A gluttonous human being has the greater potential of being an addict and a perpetrator of human abuse.

Therefore, considering the above psychological fact, the most effective solution to uproot the struggle of addiction in young people is to properly rationalize their food. Make sure that they do not bite more than they can chew.

What is the one habit that one who wants to pursue their dreams is bound to be engaged in, in quest of achieving their dreams?

Some lie, some cheat, some give of themselves, some manipulate, and some make decisions based on a hungry stomach.

Do you relate to any of the above-listed?

Dreams should be pursued; accolades should be won, and visions must be fulfilled as long as these do not compromise on our self-worth. As glittering as these may appear, they may be the very driving forces that can lead us to the realities of human abuse if not trodden carefully and wisely.

It is when in desperation, we consciously give of our bodies and hearts to those that promise to help us achieve our dreams and accolades that we render ourselves vulnerable to human abuse. My deep sympathy is extended to those who are forced and threatened to give of themselves in return for favors. My advice is that you seek the safe channels to speak out, seek justice, and save a lot of other people from falling into the same pit. Big ups to encouraging our young ones to achieve their dreams, just keep in mind it can be a very long arduous journey that calls for them to always tread carefully and wisely.

If the dream is going to cost you, your self-worth and dignity, it is not worth pursuing. Walk away with your self-worth and dignity still intact. A place of desperation can be a short-sighted and blinding space to think and act from. Eliminate desperation, always think, and act from a place of abundance. Not the abundance of materialism but the abundance of love, joy, peace, and contentment.

The effects are amazing, it automatically propels you to make sound and bold decisions that seek to keep your self-worth secured. It may sound easier said than done...but it takes a lot of practice to master this. 'Practice' is good, but practice-practice-practice is best.

Remember:
It is not so much in the huge leaps but in a series of small consistent actions taken in faith that will mount up to huge improvements and fruitful results. It starts by cultivating a soul that radiates an abundant love and contentment to the young ones.

Overcome the habit of basing your decisions on a hungry stomach. I will tolerate it if you think I am not being realistic but think about it. It is sickening; the number of amazingly talented people that have fallen into abusive traps because of making decisions based on a hungry tummy. It takes a meal to feed a hungry tummy, but it will take a whole lot of effort, strength, and courage to untangle oneself out of the psychological chains of human abuse.

My mentor Cecil Robert Jordaan taught me the analogy behind the word habit, you eliminate the 'h', you still have a bit; you eliminate the 'a', you still have the bit, you eliminate the 'b', you still have it.

Lesson is:
Run away from it before it matures into a HABIT!

PART TWO

26
SCARS UNTOLD

The perpetual cycle of abused human beings gets passed on from one generation to the other, from the great-great-grandmother to the great grandmother, to the grandmother, to the mother, to the daughter and the son –

I choose to break this cycle now,
I choose courage,
I choose love,
Nightmares...no more!

You might have heard from others or read a passage that says: "Wounds are healed, but scars remain." Unlike physical wounds, mental wounds leave a lasting impression on the minds of carriers to haunt them for a long time. At most, external wounds are completely cured through modern medical procedures to remain as painless scars, but emotional wounds, especially those that result from lack of love from those that are supposed to love and nurture young people into successful and worthy people; sink deep into the soul, remain there at most suppressed and turns into emotional scars that are carried anywhere the person goes and may end up determining the person's future behavior. Deep hidden scars may change a person into a perpetrator of human abuse or a victim of abuse, in one's quest to handle reality.

Scars are the tattoos of torment and trauma that remain imprinted in the realms of one's mind or they may come in the form of physical bruises and injuries. These remain imprinted in the core of every being. They are the very concomitants that make it hard for one who has moved from an abusive relationship to a loving relationship to genuinely enjoy the fruits of the present relationship and let go of the pain. Pains that plot the manifestation of endless nightmares become the order of reality, the reality that continues to gain gross momentum. Breaking the cycle of a scarred family genealogy is a call that needs to be adhered to. As failure to untangle it from an early stage may lead to a generation that is far from curbing the scourge of human abuse. The breaking antidote lies in pouring the young one with lots of genuine love.

The previous experiences may have robbed humanity of so much; however, these painful episodes are not that important. What matters now is what lies in the palm of humanity's hands. It's a child – a child that must be nurtured differently – a child that must be cheered – a child that must be affirmed "They are genuinely loved" despite differences in gender, status, race, culture, and background.

Scars come in various forms; they can be un-forgiveness, isolation, rejection, and any other negative experience that one has encountered with time. If not dealt with properly, these are most likely to be expressed as anger, frustration, and cruelty that seek to harm another being. Venting the emotions onto another being comes with an artificial sense of relief. I must say, it is a warped and intolerable way of dealing and healing deep wounded scars. The human instinct knows that the law of gravity is inevitable unless you are not on the planet earth. Karma is embedded deep in human nature. Our human nature will always resonate with Karma connotations that suggest that what goes up, must come down. What goes around must always take its turn back. This is the very reason that one who gets inflicted with pain will always want to see to it that another being feels the same if not a greater magnitude of the same pain.

Venting our pain onto another human being may seem like the relief pill. However, it only adds salt to the scar. It is like healing pain with more pain which is at best a toxic and deadly journey. It is toxic not only to the abuser but the surrounding people as well. Some form of mind-transformation must be activated in the mind of the abuser. It begins with deep acceptance and acknowledgment of their wrongdoing that the healing process can begin to be at work. Acceptance is a gesture of surrender. It is like wide open arms that are welcoming the help that comes into one's life. Until one genuinely surrenders, it is impossible to overcome their mind. Genuine surrender holds into captive every thought that seeks to wrestle the healing process. Absolute surrender fights the opposing forces of the ego that will always try to fight the force of love. It is a place of deep acceptance that energizes the enzymes for healing.

Instill in your child an attitude of speaking-out about their pain, regardless of how small it may seem. Discard the stereotypes that suggest that a certain gender is stronger than the other gender, thus more attention should be paid to one party. Treat them all with the equality of human love. Give them room to cry, shout and laugh their lungs out.

Their small pain should not be allowed to progress into the agonizing deep wounded scars that will later manifest as a form of brutality imposed on another being.

27
AN IMAGE OF GOD

Assuming there was a sculptor, and everyone can choose the image they want to be:

- What would you choose?

To remain as you are or to be redone completely or to be polished up a bit

- What would be your motive for the decision taken above?

To be seen by others as beautiful or to see yourself as beautiful or to attain happiness

The world's standard of measuring appearances (handsomeness and beauty) can be misleading and at best pressurizing. I feel a sickening lurch deep down the pit of my stomach when I think of the pain that humanity must endure to fit into the worldly standards of a good-looking image. It is this standard that is a root cause of many inferiority complexes and discontentment. An inferiority complex can undoubtedly make one prone to the realities of human abuse.

Think about it; some must unnecessarily lose a lot of weight, some must take steroids, painful surgeries, and strenuous exercises as a part of the process that one has to take to fit into this standard. Do not get me wrong, I am not against any person who does this. All I am objecting to is that like anything else, the intention should be deeply interrogated when going to these extremes for an image. The intention will always speak louder than the action taken. If it is an overly external stimulated intention, I can only be certain that this individual is heading to one miserable life whose happiness is anchored so much on other people's views and opinions. It is best and much safer if it is an overly internally stimulated intention.

It is important to interrogate and have conversations with ourselves. It may sound insane, I know, but it is very healthy and affirming of one's existence. One of the questions that we need to self-probe is:

- Where do we draw our inspiration from?
Inner qualities or outer qualities

It is very limiting to draw inspiration from outer qualities because these can fade away with time. If they fade away, are we going to be left as empty vessels? Surely, our inspiration must stand on much firmer ground than an outer quality - something that can be corroded by acid.

Drawing inspiration from outer qualities exposes one to the realities of human abuse because these are easily lost.

Inner qualities such as a positive character and strong self-worth are worth drawing inspiration from. These protect one from the realities of human abuse because they cannot easily fade away.

We all have kept that checklist of the person that we think is going to fit into the category of being our life partner:

- ✓ He must have a good smell
- ✓ He must be caring
- ✓ He must be honest
- ✓ He must have a great sense of humor
- ✓ He must be a good listener

This is my ideal checklist because it is made up of more inner qualities than outer qualities.

You can write down your checklist and deduce if it is made up more of inner qualities or outer qualities. If it is made up of more outer qualities, then chances are very high that you will be in an abusive relationship – and vice versa.

One best lesson that humanity has taught me is that you cannot please everybody unless you are money. Happiness should be anchored in how you see your image and not so much in how other people see your image. The lesson is to shift from external intention to internal intention. The same people that can be applauding you today can be the very same people that can criticize you tomorrow. Thus, one needs to act with the intention of inner and not outer approval or intention. Opinions are just that, wavering views that can never be consistent and always pleasing to the ear. Do not base your happiness on people's opinions. A cat has nine lives, but you only have one precious life. The joy of this one life should be deeply rooted in how you genuinely feel about yourself, never in how they feel about you.

Young people should be aware:
If your drive is an internal one, I say go ahead and do the surgeries, darken your skin, lose the weight, and take the strenuous exercises. However, if your drive is to please the world and not yourself, I strongly recommend that you stop it. All you need to do is to have the courage to take a mirror, genuinely reflect on your image and shout out loud with conviction...

I AM FEARFULLY AND WONDERFULLY CRAFTED IN THE IMAGE OF GOD, and so is every person I come across irrespective of their gender, race, age, status, and color.

28
THE COMPARISON DISEASE

One noble lesson that has kept me anchored is:

"Focus on your lane and run your race"

The time wasted in looking at other people's lanes curbs us from positively running our race and making it to the finish line with the least number of obstructions. The problem is we tend to focus on other people's lanes, and we become blind to the hurdles and the stones that lie ahead of us, the result is – we slow down or at worst we fall. These stones could have been avoided and well noted if we only took time to focus on our lanes.

In life, we are often guilty of unfairly comparing ourselves to others. It always happens that grass appears greener on the other side, but if you consciously look around you, you will realize that the grass is equally green. When you look with envious eyes at things you think you are lacking, they appear nicer. You may think that you are not perfect, because you want to be someone else … no, no, and no, you are unique and perfect, and you are enough. An unknown author advises you; "The only person you should try to compare and be better than is who you were yesterday." So, never compare yourself to another person, because you have no idea what his or her journey is all about. The ultimate danger with comparison is that you always feel either better than someone else or worthless to someone else. So, be who you are and say whatever you feel, because at most, those who mind do not matter, and those who matter do not mind. Do not allow the disease of comparison to cripple your life or happiness.

The disease of comparing is so deadly, it takes away contentment which is a quality that is most needed to attain happiness. Discontentment is one sure way that leads to unhappiness and miserable life. We are unique people with different ambitions, mindsets, gifts, goals, and efforts. Thus, it does not make sense to sacrifice our happiness because of comparison with others.

The problem is we tend to live in a scarcity mindset, a kind of mindset that limits us into believing that one's achievement will take away space for other people. I can assure you, there is just enough room in this world for achievements, accomplishments. and goals. One's achievement does not take away anything from anybody. It inspires and unconsciously propels others to be inspired enough to want to pursue their dreams and vision. I emphasize:

There is enough room for achievers, dreamers, and visionaries in this world.

Do not allow anyone's achievement to suffocate you...rather focus on your lane and run your race.

Untangling the psychological chains of human abuse calls for people that will be courageous enough to genuinely reflect, deeply accept, and fondly love themselves for who they are. The young minds should be convinced; one should measure oneself against their standards and not against the world's standards. Do not doubt it...YOU ARE ENOUGH.

Comparison is healthy if it challenges one to be better, positive, and determined. On the other hand, it is toxic if it makes one feel inadequate, incompetent, and envious. As much as 'comparison' has the potential to build, it can be the root-cause of inadequacy, insecurity, and incompetency.

This is slowly but surely progressing into an illness in the human family. Every day a lot of people are becoming carriers of the comparison syndrome; they are suffering from it and only true introspection will allow them to note it. It can be very difficult to be aware that one is suffering from the comparison disease.

Thus, genuine introspection is the key. Sadly, a lot of people have gold in their hands, but they cannot see it because their eyes are too fixed on the gold in other people's hands. It is not until they take the effort to tilt their head and change their view that they will be able to see their gold.

The comparison disease makes it impossible for one to reach a place of satisfaction and contentment. I despise the comparison disease for the mere fact that it de-motivates the human spirit. If it becomes an obsession it has the potential to mount up to unnecessary envy and jealousy. It is vital to be in alignment with one's uniqueness, potential, strength, and capability. I strongly believe that we are unique people with varying capabilities and potential, it is so important for one to fully embrace this truth. Failure to do so on the ground of comparison will surely rob one of the special contributions they were born to make. It will in the long-run taint the scale of one's performance. One will find themselves always chasing to attain more for the mere reason of wanting to out-compete the person they compare themselves to. I emphasize, do not allow the comparison sickness to cloud the judgment and verdict of your ability. Compare healthily and positively...

The effective pill to this comparison disease is in first acknowledging human uniqueness. Fully embrace that human beings are different, first self-evaluate your performance based on your capabilities only and constructively build yourself. Only after you have authentically self-evaluated, can you positively compare with others and strive to better yourself. The problem is as soon as one obtains their results, the first thing that comes to mind is to compare the results with other people. A good example is that of school performance and how it slowly escalates into a battlefield, with learners wanting to be the best of the best in class. This is not wrong if the objective is positive and healthy.

Teach the scholars,

First, genuinely self-evaluate based on one's strengths and weaknesses because vulnerable to the realities of human abuse is a human being that struggles to find satisfaction and contentment in oneself due to comparison.

29
IDENTITY

Identity is who you are, the way you think about yourself, and the characteristics that define you. Identity is something people are born with or given. However, it can become something people create for themselves as they interact with life and discover their purpose. Experiences shape us to be what we are today. Gabriel Garcia Marquez confirms on saying; "Human beings are not born once and for all, the day their mothers give birth to them, but ... life obliges them to over and over again give birth to themselves." Thus, identity is at times acquired directly or indirectly from parents, peers, and role models. Psychologically, identity formation is a matter of 'finding oneself' through matching one's talents and potential.

In agreement with Marquez, life obliged me to give birth to a real identity, as an open-minded proud African black child. I always had to fight for my identity without coming across as arrogant but confident and bold. I can safely say that I have not only found, but also cherished my identity. Identity is a prison you never escape from, but a way to redeem your past without running away from it, but to try to understand it and use it as a foundation to grow.

Remember, I was spiritually terribly abused as a young person. My family took me to Traditional healers, Prophets, and Spiritual healers simply because they never acknowledged my identity, I used that traumatizing and scarring experience to develop and cherish my identity ... I chose to become 'A PORTER OF AN ABUSE-FREE GENERATION'.

Like peeling an onion, one's identity keeps on unfolding and turning with life's experience. The world longs for your core layer and most people are still on the outer layers. The inner layer is for the few that have been courageous enough to be authentically true to their identities despite people's opinions and views. These kinds of people are bound to be successful because they dare to be themselves regardless of people's views. It is not easy for inner layered people to be tangled by the psychological chains of human abuse. The power of staying true to their identity is a sign of self-love that fights for them. It is like a weapon that shields them amid discouragements, challenges, and disappointments. Strive to be an inner layered being.

If you have your own identity and cherish it as I do, you will keep on doing what you think is right for you and others. And you will also understand the next step you want to take in life. Unlike a drop of water which loses its identity when it joins the ocean, once your identity is well established like mine, it is never lost irrespective of situations you find yourself in. You not only develop yourself but also develop the society at large. Considering my experience with abuse, my identity was never fabricated but emerged within because I dared to use my abusive past to fight for the emancipation of all suppressed people.

Within my confidence is the greater respect that honors everybody's identity. It will be arrogant at best to disrespect all other identities that make up the human family. Identity is an endlessly unfolding aspect of humanity. What makes up our identity is still food for thought for some. Is it our roots, background, influence, religion, career, or status? One way or another, part of being holistically human is our need to identify. It is the failure to identify that opens the door to not knowing oneself and what one stands for. It is in the failure to identify that one is easily swerved by opinions because one is not anchored on any identity. An absence of identity is like an absence of being. If you come to terms with your identity, you put yourself in a position of self-awareness that will seek at best not to expose your mind to the realities of abuse.

The law is that one can only give away what they are holding. An awareness of one's identity gives room for them to be aware of other people's identities and therefore honor them. I envision a world where all identities are truly unified, where there is no room for hatred among the array of identities that the universe holds. The abundance of love should be the common thread that runs across the bloodline of these identities. In a strong-like sense, I envision a world in which these identities complement one another. Looking at the status quo, this may sound like nothing but a fallacy of mine. However, I still believe that it is possible to raise a racism-free generation; if only the abundance of love, human will, and mind-transformation-power can work in unison. It is a journey, one that begins by teaching young minds to love and respect all humanity regardless of race, gender, sexual orientation, or status.

The human brutality that is encountered today, due to the failure of respect for all facets of humanity is shocking. It is arrogant and unacceptable for humanity to feel superior over another being on the grounds of race, gender, sexual orientation, or status. After all, take away all the connotations that we have set for ourselves, what remains is a human being. Therefore, we are all part of the human family regardless of our differences.

The complexion of one's pigment should never empower them to abuse or subjugate.
The truth is… YOU ARE HUMAN FIRST.

30
THE POWER OF SPOKEN-WORD

As social beings, it is a norm for us to raise compliments and talk about other people's lives. We verbalize the thoughts we have of other people's lives, even if it means directly approaching them and telling them. The eye to see and compliment just comes with the territory of being fully human. The problem is when these complements start becoming the concomitants of emotional abuse.

A revelation that has always been so profound is the power of spoken words. Some of our lives are a product of the spoken words that were uttered in our lives. 'Spoken-word' can kill, give life, destroy, and empower. If such is the case, then humanity should use the power of spoken words as a tool to untangle the psychological chains of human abuse. It has always been my aim to not only engage with the people around me but to ensure that the conversations I have with them are always uplifting, motivating, and meaningful.

There are different people in the circle of life. After a conversation, some people drain every ounce of energy in you, and some people add substance and energy to you.

The difference is the ones that drain your energy are the ones that you always find yourself having to encourage and motivate while they are silent. There is no mutual sharing of information. You become the tanker of information while they listen. An absence of mutual sharing of information will certainly drain every ounce of energy for life in you because you are the one who is always at the giving-end. On the other hand, those that add substances to your life are the ones that engage with you while you motivate them. With them, there is a mutual sharing of information. You do not feel drained around them. You give and take from them as well.

Xhosa people will agree *Ina ethe (give and take)* is healthier than *Ina (give)* only.
Stick with mutually beneficial relationships, they give life.

Never make the mistake of begging for a relationship, let the love come to you naturally and affirm you of your significance as well. If you beg for it, chances are very high that you will end up in an abusive relationship. Respect yourself enough not to beg for love.

One lesson I have learned to adopt is not to allow everybody's compliments and views to rule my life. Everybody has a mouth to speak and compliment, however, the power lies in us to allow these compliments to rule over our lives, emotions, and thinking patterns. Consider the convenience of social media that has made it easy to shower others with compliments just at the click of the button. It can be very haunting and challenging to turn a blind eye to compliments. It certainly can be a process to master the act of ignoring and shutting out the mind to these compliments; one that takes time, commitment, and consistent practice to get it right. Some people's characters are just strong enough to by-pass negative complements. On the other hand-for other people, it takes time for them to allow their minds not to harbor such. It is a process, one that calls for unrelenting dedication and commitment. It begins by saturating and affirming the mind with positive thoughts from a young age.

Show your children, they are not just human beings filling the family gap. Show them they are significant and valued as well so that they do not make the mistake of under-estimating themselves in any relationship.

I am of a noble belief; one should be careful - who speaks into their life. Not everybody who speaks in our lives has the intention to build us. It is the intention that has the after-effects that one suffers long after the words have been uttered in their lives. It is sad, the decisions that are taken out of the compliments that take root in our mindset. Compliments uttered with impure intention can build a false image of oneself in the mind. As powerful as the mind is, processing these compliments can ultimately destroy an individual's confidence, self-worth, and self-esteem. The result is an emotionally abused human being that is drowning in a pool of negative compliments. Considering these negative compliments - The mind must reflect on at least one positive compliment; it can be a compliment from your parent when you were young. Draw strength from reflecting on this compliment. Allow the force of this positive compliment to fight the force of any negative one. This is what the power of the mind can do for us if we can just learn to consistently exercise and trust it.

The above simply implies that the words uttered by a parent to a child have the power to build or destroy that child. Saturate their young minds with positive and constructive compliments. It is at a time that they are showered with negative compliments that the parent's compliment will be the weapon that will see them through their battle with negativity. A stitch in time saves 9.

The power of spoken word implies that everyone should:

'ENGAGE THE BRAIN BEFORE THE SPOKEN-WORD!'

31
THE POWER OF BALANCE

"We come into this world headfirst and go out feet first; in between, it is all a matter of balance."

- Paul Boese

The rapidly changing lifestyle of today makes it a challenge if not impossible to attain a balanced state of life. Not to say that it must be perfectly balanced, but at least striving to attain a balanced state of life should be the goal. One may wonder what a balanced state of life has got to do with untangling the psychological chains of human abuse - Let me save you if you are beginning to drown in a pool of confusion. If human abuse can have an immense impact on the human mind, then it will only make sense for the fighters of human abuse to pursue a healthy state of mind. Thus, a life that is balanced, physically, mentally, emotionally, and spiritually will make it easy to untangle the effects that human abuse can have on the human mind.

Attaining a balanced state of life calls for one's commitment, it means paying attention to all the small elements that can make a positive difference in one's life. I am not a fitness doctor, but it is my pleasure to give a fair share of some useful advice. Physical balance can be attained by being on guard with your diet, exercising regularly, and attending check-ups, for psychological and physical wellness. Remember to always practice safe sex. Mental balance is made possible by taking some time to refresh the mind, to just be free and not be thinking about work. It helps to 'now and again' be still and not get lost in thought because a cluttered mind cannot reason well. Emotional balance is attained by not allowing life's situations to restrict you from fully expressing your emotions. Cry and speak out about the pains you are feeling – be vulnerable with your emotions. Spiritual balance is attained by creating the time to surrender to a higher power; it is relying on power and grace that surpasses human limitation. Armored for the battle of human abuse is a mind that sees the value of practicing a balanced state of life.

With the highly demanding and pressurizing life, we see today, it is easy to fall into a pit of extremes. Extremely work-hard, extremely exercise, extremely drink alcohol, extremely eat, and extremely spend. It all goes back to contentment and comparison. One who is discontented with their life is bound to compare their life with other people. In their quest to prove a point they extremely spend even if it is out of their means. The cycle is they extremely spend to impress, run broke, get into a relationship for material acquisitions, become dependent, and get abused.

This is a psychological cycle that continues to gain gross momentum. The only cure to break this cycle lies in dealing with the root-cause which is to uproot discontentment that stems from negative comparison.

Balance means that a fair share of time is allocated to all these vital aspects of life. It is the consistency of the effort that is most vital. Detecting the psychological chains of human abuse becomes a very easy task for a human mind that is balanced. Dealing with the reality of human abuse is not so much a challenge for such a mind. A cluttered mind that knows no refreshment can be a playground for abuse. A body that knows no fitness and a healthy diet can be an easy target to human abuse. Unexpressed emotions can be toxic at the time that they are vented out. A life that has no spiritual experience is dead to me because it only relies on the limitations of human power.

A balanced state of mind leaves room for self-reflection and introspection. It sees the value not only in working but the pausing and the moment of silence as well. A mind that is constantly pushing becomes the playground of fatigue -

fatigue breeds frustration and at the blink of an eye, an angry person starts throwing tantrums at everybody. Some abuse, merely because they are frustrated and tired.

The solution for such minds is resting and easing the pace of the mind.

Teach them the value of balancing out all spheres of life, they must learn to take a bite out of life such that when the juices come running down, everybody licks their lips. They are to experience life in all its forms - The making of friends, playing with friends, socializing with friends, going out for lunch, taking a tour, taking a drive, meditating, taking a walk, exercising, and healthy eating

This approach will shield them from the realities of human abuse.

Remember to inform them humorously, but seriously:
'All work and no play make Jack a dull boy' and all play without work makes Julia also a dull girl."

32
A TWO-WAY STREET

As promulgated in the previous chapter:

Any relationship should be anchored on a mutually beneficial foundation. That is both parties need to be selfless enough to let go of their ego and give room for true love to take root. A mutually beneficial relationship simply means that both parties benefit from the relationship. It is a two-way street that calls for the efforts of both parties to be channeled in making it possible for the other party to be happy and feel loved. If it is a one-sided relationship whereby only one party always gives and the other party always takes, then disaster should be expected down the line. Ultimately the party that always gives will reach a climax, a point of frustration. This point of climax is most likely to be vented out in the form of human abuse. It is an inappropriate approach to always receive in a relationship, make it a priority to partake in the giving as well, to revive a kind of love that is appetizing, meaningful, and satisfying.

A relationship that seeks to always take from an individual is one dreadful and draining journey that calls for restoration. To me, it seizes to be a relationship because it is deeply rooted in selfishness. A never-ending taker in a relationship is prone to the realities of human abuse. The value of giving oneself in a relationship is the key to all the conflicts encountered in relationships. Giving in this sense does not mean materialism. It means giving profound virtues such as love, care, sympathy, and happiness. The effect of giving of these profound virtues is huge.

The young mind should always be challenged to always give profound virtues in the relationships that they engage in. By so doing they stand a better chance of closing the door of human abuse.

Love is certainly a two-way street. It is the selfless act of giving oneself to another. Like an egg that completely dissolves with the other egg yolk if gently scrambled. One cannot even tell how many eggs were mixed because of the oneness that they become. It is a tricky one as well because the act of selflessly giving oneself so that you become one with the other person should not in any way insinuate that you melt or disappear in the other person. As much as you give of yourself, it is important not to be lost in the other person's world. It is important to keep one's individualism intact even in the oneness of a union.

A complementary relationship is appetizing, meaningful, and satisfying. It is not dreadful and daunting. The force of this kind of relationship cannot be easily broken by enemies or jealous people because of the magnitude of strength presented by two unified energies. Two unified energies have the distinct power to oppose any force that may plot evil against it. Unlike, a relationship in which only one person gives while the other receives; this kind of relationship is easily broken by enemies and jealous people.

Two unified energies are far much better than one.

A unified team is certainly much better than a million divided people.

The battle with the scourge of human abuse cannot be fought alone. It is a two-way street. The victim of abuse needs the police officer to intervene, the community for support, the counselor for therapy, the friend to cry on, the author for restoring words, and the social workers to provide means of survival. This is a chain of people that are involved in a noble course. Everybody in this chain is of paramount significance. The one element that should govern all these parties is genuine love.

This element will speed up the recovery rate of both the victims and the perpetrators.

If it is not a mutually beneficial relationship it will have a tilted happiness scale, which is unfair and should be corrected. It is selfish and can only be the root cause of unnecessary disputes and arguments. I emphasize that I am not speaking about giving materialism but sharing qualities such as love, care, and happiness. All the parties of a relationship should give and receive a certain magnitude of these qualities. Succeeding in giving and failure to receive can be very destructive and dissatisfying. It can never be a relationship if it is not mutual. Even a child responds in love, care, and sympathy for the parent who makes the provision of these qualities. Children that understand the value of mutual love will always enquire about the parent's needs. It is rare for them to abandon or neglect their parents.

If it is not mutual, there is an element of dependency that rules the relationship. An element of dependency empowers the psychological chains of human abuse to hold into captive the human mind.

Please do not just receive in a relationship-kindly give of your qualities as well.

We all must know and instill in our children the notion that; Love is a two-way street. One who gives of love should receive love in return.

So never tolerate abuse, no matter what, because human abuse is never an alternative route.

33
A BALANCED STATE OF CONFIDENCE

Confidence is good but like any virtue, it needs to be balanced, as extremes of confidence can have drastic consequences. Extremes refer to over-confidence, low-confidence, and no-confidence. These extremes can be attributed to the realities of human abuse.

There is a very thin line between over-confidence and arrogance. It is indisputable that over-confident people can oftentimes be mistaken for arrogant people. Like anything else, it is important to keep a balance. Overconfidence that is anchored in arrogance can be attributed to human abusive behavior. This kind of confidence can blind one to reality; it seeks only to see its way and nobody else's. It chains the mind into the making of a false image. An image that radiates the fickle idea that it's either my word goes, or nothing is done. It sees the effect of one's voice and nobody else's...oh how selfish and self-seeking it is! The mind needs to be flexible enough to respect and value other people's voices regardless of one's confidence. As failure to strike a confidence balance can easily escalate to abusive behavior.

Over-confidence is a kind of boldness that leads one to the pit of self-destruction. Oftentimes, this kind of confidence is bound to lead many astray. Human beings love to be controlled; it is the nature of humans. Therefore, an over-confident person stands higher chances of being highly revered by many while they are led into a pit of destruction. Many have been brainwashed to believe that leadership is only for a few destined by blood and a charismatic character to lead, which in and of itself is misleading. This is the reason why many people have a sheep attitude when it comes to life. They just follow ignorantly.

An over-confident person takes advantage of the power of mass-persuasion and manipulation to ensure that his or her ego is propped up by followers that do not interrogate the reason and meaning behind the following. These are masses that continue to be led astray daily by an overconfident person and they sheepishly follow without questioning.

Furthermore, it is very limiting to walk in a state of low confidence. This kind of confidence belittles one's voice. It values other people's voices more than its own. It is easy for people to walk over a low-confident person. Oftentimes it is the main reason that bottles one's special contribution and gifts within. It seizes to create an impact in this world. Gifts that are kept within due to low confidence are useless.

Many souls have died with special gifts kept within them due to low-confidence, gifts that could have even saved them from dying or pro-longed their lives. Believe in yourself enough to have the confidence to let your voice be heard, it is liberating. Low confidence can expose one to the consequences of human abuse. It seeks to give power to other parties by always conforming and not having the confidence to challenge. It is easy for a human soul that has low confidence to suffer and to be entangled by the psychological chains of human abuse.

The total absence of confidence is the worst form of human existence. Humanity has been subjected to the realities of slavery due to the absence of confidence. Low confidence can be improved if there is a greater human will to improve. Like a process, one will have to transcend from a state of having no confidence to low-confidence and then a balanced-state of confidence.

Activate just the right amount of confidence within them while they are still young. Let them be consistent to carry this confidence up to their adulthood. It is like a golden shield.
In an uncertain world that can be very insensitive and unsentimental to people's emotions. Everybody has the responsibility to uphold their confidence. Life situations have the potential to strip away the balanced confidence

that we have worked hard to maintain. It is therefore a huge responsibility to always keep one's confidence at guard.

Untangling the psychological chains of human abuse calls for people that will be courageous enough to uphold their confidence. Life's situations are inevitable at times, people will always speak in our lives, materialism will take wings, and the only thing that endures is the confidence of our character. Let this confidence soar through the winds and storms of this life. Without confidence, life is but a void place that is not worth adventuring.

I cannot imagine life without my confidence...even this guide would never have become a reality. It is the inspiration that is birthed by unrelenting confidence that has made it possible. Of course, my confidence was and still is challenged; however, firmness of character has seen me through.

Saying YES to a balanced state of confidence is in real terms saying NO to human abuse.

34
THE KINGDOM WITHIN

"The Kingdom of Heaven, oh man, requires no other price than you. The value of it is you. Give yourself for it and you shall have it."

- Saint Augustine

What if you have been abused to such an extent that it becomes, in your own eyes, the new 'normalcy' of life?

It becomes a challenge to even note the difference between a non-abusive and an abusive relationship. People around you notice it, but you don't. They tell you, "You look like someone that is under a lot of oppression, but you have become so used to the pain of abuse – you think everybody is just bruising in the same way.

If you ask me – I certainly can relate.

It takes a whole lot of self-analysis to pinpoint if you are unknowingly living under the belt of human abuse. It is genuine moments of reflection and introspection that will show you where you started and how it all escalated to abuse. If the revelation that you are entangled by the psychological chains of human abuse comes to you – there will be a greater magnitude of the force that propels you to want to be on the move and get to a place where you start again, clear your mind, and forget about it all.

Some escape to another country, some commit suicide and some go to the streets – they would rather be beggars than inhabitants of an abusive environment.

At most, we do not know who we are, because we oftentimes are not aware that the Kingdom of Heaven is within us. Take note, in the animal kingdom, the rule is, eat or be eaten; in the human kingdom, the rule is, define or be defined. It is through abuse, that we ignorantly continue eating one another as human beings.

As a person that has experienced a series of disappointments from my career. I have had to be thrown under the bus at the expense of the people that were less skilled and capable than I was. The pain became more real because of some of these people that I had to teach how to do their jobs. I have certainly had a fair share of my kindness abused by those that I trusted and looked up to.

To survive and truly let go, I had to do a deep introspection, this is what I discovered:

The Kingdom is within you, only you are the key holder to this Kingdom. The power lies in your hands. I speak of the power to decide whom you allow access to this Kingdom. I speak of the power to decide who can exit and does not have access to enter the realms of this kingdom. Treasures of happiness, contentment, confidence, and love are intricately forming part of this Kingdom. Be mindful, the maintenance of these treasures is determined by the people allowed to enter. These people cannot be granted the opportunity to abuse this Kingdom; they can only positively uphold it.

As much as life has the potential to present an array of situations, it is up to us to allow these situations into our Kingdom and therefore breeding destruction to the treasures in our Kingdom. The key is to be mindful of the people that we allow in our lives and the impact that they have on us. We have the power to activate the meaning in our relationships. If a relationship does not benefit one in any way, I suggest that some revision of intention must be done. If it drains one's energy it is not worth keeping. Only you have the power to decide what you allow to rule your life. Use intention as the main point of reference to make a decision that suggests whom to keep, trust, love, and delete. A Kingdom that is not well governed will uphold even those that abuse it. Take great care of the kingdom's keys...only open the Kingdom after some thorough searching has been done.

I say thorough internal and external searching must be conducted first before you open. For the mere fact that all that glitters is not gold. So many times, one gives people access to this Kingdom based on outer appearances and lovely meaningless words. Only after opening the present box can one truly and certainly know what the present box holds. Do not use face value to open the Kingdom. Take your t—i—m—e to search before you use the keys to open the Kingdom. At times human abuse is a result of just opening the Kingdom, without taking the time to search that which wants to enter.

Do not rush or allow the external voices to be louder than yours. I am not saying be arrogant, I am strongly objecting that you open the Kingdom based on your voice

Kingdom in this case represents one's life. Everybody is blessed with the gift of life. The keys represent the power of choice. Everybody has the power of choice to decide whom they allow in their life.

The greater lesson of this chapter is,
Human abuse can be curbed by the application of wisdom in using our Kingdom keys

35
CAUTIOUSLY LETTING GO

What can be done to shield the value of forgiveness?

In the light that I am aware that letting go of pain is a necessary step to healing humanity, there is one thing that I have always intently observed, and it makes me sick.

I am worried that with forgiveness becoming as easy as changing a pair of socks, the value of forgiveness is becoming worn away. The meaning behind forgiveness is no more. People continue to intentionally and purposefully hurt others without care while harping on meaningless apologies and the cycle of life continues.

One who is forgiven is obliged to recognize the meaning behind this act and stop intentionally and consciously hurting others – this is the only way, at the disposal of humanity that will shield the value of forgiveness.

I have found the value in letting go of all the hurt and pain that life has presented to me. If I dared to let go, I strongly believe everybody can tap into the same courage. It may be hard, but the after-effects of letting go are the beginning of so much peace and liberation.

I cannot argue that the hurt and the pain can be so much to take in and let go of. This is the main reason I speak of courage. Not every soul can have courage; it is for the rare, which have chosen to sacrifice their pride and ego for a greater course. A course that is much greater than the pain that has been encountered. Pride and ego will always plan to create a ploy against the veil of courage. Ego says holding on to the pain is meaningful. Pride says letting go is a very scary and exposed place to be, you will be left with nothing to hold, it is meaningless. Pride further whispers that what goes up must come down, vengeance is the only way to be truly free.

Courage says letting go is liberating and meaningful, it says to forgive and forget so that you can be truly free. Therefore, courage is the sacrificing of pride and ego within so that one can be truly free.

Un-forgiveness can be equated to the psychological chains of human abuse that are deeply fastened by the pride and ego within. These chains can only be untangled by the courage to let go, forgive, and forget. See - un-forgiveness has the potential to greatly influence one's behavior and attitude. It is very toxic to the human soul and can in the long run be attributed to the psychological illness of human abuse. Brutality becomes a channel to vent out deep-seated un-forgiveness. It brings about a sense of short-term relief. The harmful effects of un-forgiveness are evident in relationships today. It is a bitter pain embedded within the heart that seeks to blind our view of reality. Clouding our judgment of the present is the goal of un-forgiveness. Only those who dare to murder pride and ego can truly forgive and forget...the ultimate result is TRUE LIBERATION.

The courage to forgive is the definite answer that activates the enzymes that will speed up the process of untangling the psychological chains of human abuse. It is worth it to kill our pride not only for the now but for a generation after us. One thing that Christianity has taught me is to practice what I preach. If I do not practice what I preach, it is better to keep it unsaid. I am appealing to a parent that is struggling with un-forgiveness. Deal with your un-forgiveness as a parent before you preach the word of forgiveness to the young mind. The effect is it is a powerful way of informing the young mind. Words are just words, but if they are coupled with practice then the impact is much greater.

The young mind needs to know the value of letting go. It is this approach that will cultivate a generation that will root out un-forgiveness and be truly liberated from human abuse.

However, in highlighting the value of forgiveness - I believe there is a limit to forgiveness simply because some cruel human beings are bound to take advantage of one's kind heart and so they continue to intentionally hurt others because they have high hopes that they will be forgiven. The value of forgiveness can only be kept intact if those that are forgiven can stop continuously and intentionally hurting others. I do not know about you, but life's experiences have taught me that, for me to protect the value of forgiveness, I need to armor my forgiveness with terms and conditions.

Like kindness, forgiveness has the potential to kill as well. Therefore, it is important to build a mutually beneficial relationship with these virtues. One, who gives of kindness and forgiveness, should experience freedom and peace in return. Not the opposite.

To all the perpetrators of abuse – I say:
Stop hiding behind the veil of forgiveness.
Stop hurting others.
Stop Gender-Based Violence

36
CHEERS TO THE UPLIFTING OVERCOMERS

I am taken aback by the truths about positioning oneself, but an interesting take on it comes to mind. What is seen and possible to be seen is determined by one's position. The analogy of steps makes a room in the realms that govern my mind. A person cannot reach out their hand as a gesture of uplifting other people if they are all standing on the same surface level and the same view. The only thing that is possible in this case is dragging, embracing, and comforting, but not uplifting. Uplifting others is only made possible by a human being that has dared to take an upward step. Not only is it physically conducive to achieve this, but the view of the person who has taken an upward step facilitates the act of reaching out their hand to uplift others. It's like the new surface level and the new view both play a role in equipping the person to uplift others.

I speak to all the over-comers of human abuse in all corners of the earth. These are the people that have dared to take an upward step. They are standing on a new surface level and their view is much clearer. Apart from me, a good example of a person who has not only won the battle with abuse but has used his experience to uplift others is my mentor Juan de Beer Odendal who has demonstrated his strong will to heal abused humanity through his book Magic Mirror Mind.

An experience of over-coming is just that, an experience. Unless it is shared it seizes to create any impact on anybody. Experiences of over-coming human abuse should be documented and given the power to influence, empower and change mindsets. These are the very experiences that will reprimand even the abuser. To all the over-comers of human abuse, I appeal that you make use of the new view and surface level that you are standing on now. Use the new position to uplift others so that they stand on a new surface level with a much clear view. It is only in cultivating an attitude that is willing to uplift that will make it possible for everybody to stand on a new surface level with a much better and clearer view.

I am so honored to be among the influential young voices that refuse to remain silent on the issues of gender-based violence. I do hope that I may inspire and persuade other young people to come and join me in this fight against human brutality. They can do this by merely respecting their elders and spreading love to their peers and sharing the information that is imprinted in this guide to uplift and motivate their peers that are affected by abuse.

Young people are highly observant beings; it is easy for them to notice that their friends are entangled by the psychological chains of human abuse. I do hope that they may be courageous enough not to stand in the background or behind the scenes. They should put on their crown of genuine love and using the power of this love. They must be instrumental in exposing and therefore dealing with the burning issues of human abuse.

Ultimately, they are the epicenter of these issues.

Thus, hiding them will not work.

The experience with abuse can be used as a drive to help those that are struggling with abuse. Giving of one's knowledge and positively contributing to the breaking of the human abuse cycle may be rocket science for introverted people; it may take time to be able to harness the skill of expressing one's emotions and experience – it needs practice. Like public speaking, the first time will be nerve-wracking, the second time, it will be much better. Keep in mind; this may be a necessary step that will speed up the healing process for the victim.

What is the worse that could happen if you stand in front of an audience for the first time to deliver a speech?

As the first speaker of my team in a debate contest with Providence College – I was so nervous - I peed myself.

The second time felt like I have done it for years. In a matter of 3 years, I became the official President of my high school's debating club.

The lesson is: Practice, practice, and practice, you will succeed!

I have not only found the sharing of gender-based violence information as a vital step to protecting the victim, but it is an ideal step for healing my deep wounded scars. As I untangle others from the psychological chains of human abuse, I am both consciously and unconsciously liberated as well. It is this that has birthed, within me, growth and unrelenting hope for a better generation and a better tomorrow.

For me, the solution to the pandemic of human abuse is simple but long-term; it lies in the abundant love that is genuinely extended to the young human soul.

To all the uplifting over-comers of human abuse,

I SALUTE YOU!

37
THE FAVORITISM POISON

The effect of the 'bias nature' or for a lack of a better word the 'favoritism nature' embedded in humanity is strongly felt at a young age. It is just human nature to like one person over another person. It comes with the territory of being human.

The only instance where this becomes toxic is when a parent is biased towards their children. A child that has been favored over another child tends to have a warped view of life. It is destructive because they go through life expecting the same favor from humanity. If they do not get this special treatment, they are most likely to substitute it for the total submission that they can receive from their beloveds in a relationship. Failure to receive this total submission will lead to desperate measures such as human abuse. A child that has suffered favoritism over another child has the potential to suffer from low confidence, low self-esteem, and a sense of outside approval. The progression of time can cause this child to suffer from an Attention Deficit Hyperactivity Disorder. Such a child is more vulnerable to the realities of human abuse.

Given the limitations of human nature - It can be a real challenge to instill an attitude of impartiality in all their children. However, it is a necessary aspect of parenting that can never be neglected. It takes practice at times, but I am certain a parent can instill impartiality in all their children. It is awful that favoritism can have so much influence in the molding and shaping of adulthood characters. If only parents could open their eyes to this influence, careful consideration would be considered in the treatment that is rendered to the children. Bias screams out subtly to the child that is not favored, "You are unlovable!" This child goes through life seeking approval that they were robbed of from an early age. This child can easily and strongly attach themselves to a person that promises to dearly love them. That love goes in to fill the void that was created at an early age. Against all odds, this child will hold on to the cheese even if there is a trap, all this is in search of meaning. Something they were robbed of at an early age.

Favoritism is toxic; it cripples a child that is preferred over the other children. This child goes through life with a 'special treatment' mentality – a superior mentality that demands that they be treated with extra care than anybody else. A warped mindset that they are better than others and should be treated like they are the cream of it all – For someone like me who has had to break a leg for my dreams and success to be realized. I do not like a person who thinks they are better than the other person; I detest a human being that wants to be treated with extra-care from other people. I never gained any special favors for anything that I have achieved. I have had to toil very hard for my success. Therefore, I can only motivate all young people to avoid short-cuts when it comes to success.

The long route may be arduous, tiring, and terrifying, but it is the noble way that can lead and direct one to the treasures of heaven.

Short-cuts may be very easy and attractive; however, they do not challenge one's character. Virtues like patience, contentment, and maturity cannot be seasoned by short-cuts. These are virtues that are cultivated by hard work, commitment, and resilience in performing tasks and orders, and instructions. Short-cuts defeat the means; they can only prop up unseasoned young people.

The firmness of character can never be cherished by unseasoned young people.

The world longs for seasoned young people; Young people that will commit and focus on the task with all their effort and strength; Young people that will rather take the long noble way by not imitating others – but by trusting enough in the value of their uniqueness to be original; Young people that do not see themselves as special and separate from others; Young people that do not need undeserved favors – who would rather work hard for success.

A golden caliber of young people is ideal for a desperate world.

As a parent, it is vital that you become aware that you are a potter at work. Be informed; you are a potter that is actively at work - molding characters for the future. A potter will never instill impartiality in their work for the fear that what they create with their hands will break. The ability to withstand pressure is dependent on the amount of clay that is used. The potter needs to use just the right amount of clay in molding the creations that are not going to break during pressure and storms. Impartiality in the use of clay should be applied to all their creations so that they have the same magnitude of strength.

Isn't it interesting to know that - the person who is to be blamed if the creations break is always the potter?

So, parents are warned, to start to annihilate favoritism as they nurture their children. The child that you under-estimate may turn out to be the Queen that determines whether you enter heaven's door or not.

38
BE AUTHENTICALLY YOU

'Authenticity' is all about being real and genuine with no stint of imitation. It is about your presence, living in the moment with conviction and confidence, and staying true to yourself. It is derived from the word authentic which means not false or copied, but real. That is, representing one's true nature, values, and beliefs. Trying, no matter what and always to be nobody but yourself in a world that is doing its best, day and night, to change or mold you to be somebody else. Thus, to sum up; becoming authentic; means living your life according to your needs and values rather than those that family, friends, and society expect from you. Such a life offers you several benefits, including respect from others and the ability to realize your uniqueness, true potential, happiness, and wellbeing.

I have to say that one of my biggest role models goes to the hard-working and successful designer David Tlale. Simply because of the attention to detail that is attributed to his work of art. It has taken him before the Kings and Queens of this earth.

I must be honest though; it is one thing to look up to a role model - it means one draws inspiration from the qualities displayed and the achievements acquired by their role model. It is another thing to live under the shadow of a role model. It means extremely finding pleasure and meaning in copying the qualities and personality of the role model. It's like dying to your own life and living the life of your role model. This behavior is disastrous in the sense that one becomes blind to one's potential, uniqueness, and voice. Such a behavior stems from a lack of confidence and exposes itself to the psychological chains of human abuse.

It is great to look up to a role model, but that does not mean that one must go through life striving to become their role model. Mind you I said 'becoming' not 'becoming like' their role model. For the mere reason that the desire to become has a toxic effect on one's self-image, it is like for one to become fully human, they need to constantly put on the mask of their role model. Happiness and contentment should not be anchored on how close one is to 'becoming' the role model. This approach silences one's voice. It kills the one precious life that one must make a special contribution to all humanity. It is like one who goes through life putting on a mask of their role model. Confidence deeply revolves around this mask, if it is lost then lack of confidence starts showing up. If the masquerade is removed, then one feels naked and weak.

This is a sure insult to one's self-worth. It can only tightly fasten the psychological chains of human abuse.

Loosen the psychological chains of human abuse by boldly proclaiming your existence, worth and uniqueness before anybody else. Look up to your role model but remember to be you and not your role model. Sadly enough, the mind can be lost in becoming the role model such that it can be lost in a world of illusion. Living under the shadow of somebody else is an insult to the creator who gives us life. It is liberating to be fully and authentically true to oneself. With all the weaknesses and failures, one must have the drive to be nothing else but true to oneself.

Loosen the pangs and attitude of imitation from the young minds. They would rather settle for less if it is their genuine effort. They would rather run the risk of failing than excelling using another person's efforts.

To the scholars:

Do not copy that homework from another learner. As hard as it seems, do the right thing and do it on your own and do corrections if you must.

To the aspiring authors:

Value your own words, restrain from copying another author's work. Find value in your uniqueness and shine it on the world.

BE ORIGINAL.

Originality is the first compliment I received as a book-review of; **'Untangled' 'The Psychological Chains Of Human Abuse'.**

It made sense because I love originality, I love authenticity, I love being true to myself, strengths, weaknesses, and all.

Life is too short to be fake – be real, be original, be authentic, be you, be lovable.

With all the superficiality and faking going on around the world, it is refreshing and powerful to walk in the shadow of nobody else but oneself.

Untangle the psychological chains of human abuse by staying true to yourself –

BE AUTHENTICALLY YOU.

39
THE POWER OF HUMAN-WILL

Remember the saying; "Where there is a will, there is a way." Indeed, those with a greater sense of will-power can unchain themselves from any abusive thoughts. However, those with a lower sense of will-power fail ... they find it difficult to move away from whatever is destructive to their lives; they even fail to walk away from abusive relationships.

One of the captivating lines in Madea's Family Reunion by Tyler Perry is when Madea probes a question to Lisa's sister, who was stuck in an abusive marriage with a rich man - a relationship she was forced into by her selfish mother - it goes:

> "Does your friend want to walk out from the abusive relationship?"

The above question is directed to human-will. It is a question that seeks to know if one is confident enough to take a bold stand for their lives against all odds. It is a question that calls for answers before a helping hand can be extended to the victim. Only the victim can pick up the call of responding to this question... I call it the power of human will.

So vital is the response to the above question, it will be the one that determines whether one continues to suffer or is liberated from the pains of mistreatment. Often-times the response to this question is the one that is attributed to the deaths, burns, and brutality that is long - suffered. If the response continues to be a very bold and firm 'no', it can only bring about more damages to the victim. The more one stays in an abusive relationship the greater the magnitude of abuse and pain that has to be endured. Maintaining 'no' as an answer to the above question is the very reason that keeps in bondage, one who has been tangled by the psychological chains of human abuse – over time, the small insults that are taken lightly will soon escalate to bigger scars such as acidic burns and cutting of one's body.

The reason Madea is asking this question simply shows respect and reverence for human will, which is vital. The decision that someone takes for their life deserves some fair share of respect. It matters less if the masses think it is a good or a bad decision.

A turning point emanates from the self-within. It is not imposed or thrust upon the shoulders of an individual. The power of a turning point lies within oneself – It must be activated by one's free-will.

A turning point that is imposed or thrust upon the shoulders of an individual is ineffective. It is a matter of time, the one who is forced to walk out of a relationship has higher chances of regressing and going back to the hands of their abusive partner.

I have seen the victims that are forced to come into an abusive relationship. It does not work. One who is forced has not had their conviction and personal revelation of the danger that lies in an abusive relationship. It's not until a strong conviction is birthed within the victim - a conviction that suggests that they need to walk out of the abusive relationship because of the dangers of such a relationship – that the victim will move away and never look back.

The three equations of walking out of an abusive relationship are:

Conviction + Genuine human will = walking-away success
Conviction + Imposed opinions = walking-away failure
Conviction + Suggested opinions = walking-away doubts

Effective human-will has to emanate from self-within

Unwinding the chains of human abuse calls for a people that will have a greater will to timely give a firm and bold 'yes' response. A 'yes' response empowers the helping parties to help the victim. Such a response gives energy to the hand that is extending a gesture of help. Sadly, most people have had to delay this response. They have to say it only after losing a part of their body. They have had to say it only after enduring the worst of pains. The reason for this unreasonable attachment to the abuser is often infused in the hope that things will change with time. Another reason can be the circumstantial love that one has for the abuser. For example - the fear of losing support and shelter. It can also be the threats from the abuser to the victim that breeds fear to walk away from the relationship.

Do not waste time. Abstain from hoping for changes while in pain. Timely respond with a firm and bold 'yes' if asked whether you want to walk out of an abusive relationship or not.

I applaud the parent for teaching the young mind to never give up in life. However, the context of this statement should be clearly understood.
To the young minds, I say,
"NEVER GIVE UP ON YOUR DREAMS, GIVE UP ON THE ABUSIVE RELATIONSHIP".

40
THE POWER OF PERCEPTION

Perception is the pre-conceived ideas, beliefs, and opinions of a human being, an experience, or an object. These can be misleading because they are mostly based on opinions and not facts. Within these pre-conceived opinions - If the good overlap the bad, then that is a positive perception, however, if the bad overlaps the good, then that is a negative perception. Perception comes and grows with maturity. I dare you to choose to walk within the precepts of positive perception. It is healthy and it works for the greater good of untangling humanity from the psychological chains of human abuse.

Pre-conceived ideas enforce attitudes, behaviors, and level of passion that is directed to the energy of life and its relationships. The root of our perceptions deserves some fair share of being revised and if needs be, changed and removed from our minds. Things that influence our perception include our beliefs, background, level of education, and experiences. These, in the long run, build up the preconceived ideas that are kept in the mind.

Life evolves with time; this evolution implies that there are changes in the religious and educational fraternities – note that these are the two elements that have strong power in shaping and molding our perceptions. The problem is that some human beings fail to adjust their preconceived ideas with these changes. The result is that their perception remains, outdated and dull. For example, the preconceived ideas about sexuality have radically evolved with time; churches are beginning to change how they treat people of different sexual identities. However, some deeply religious churches are still not adapting to this radical evolution of sexuality.

The pre-conceived ideas that are held in mind for a person are determined by the attitude and the behavior of that person. If it is a partner that we once perceived as uncaring; and the same partner adopts an attitude of buying gifts the perception we had of this partner has high chances of changing. If it is a parent that was once perceived as dishonest; and the same parent adopts an attitude of encouraging others, to tell the truth, the perception that a child has for this parent may change.

Perceptions cannot change if there are no changes in attitude and behavior. Changes in attitude and behavior initiate changes in perception.

Perception has the potential to build or destroy. It is the perception that directs our attitude. If positive perception is withheld in the mind consistently, it has the potential to allow the right attitude governing the core and inner workings of the relationship. Everybody is wearing an attitude-the power lies in the hands of all humanity to decide on the attitude costume that will best fit them for the sustaining of a healthy and non-abusive relationship.

Relationships have their ups and downs - I am interested in shedding some light on the causes that can be attributed to great relationships that slowly suffer the pains of human abuse with time. Ever wondered what happens to a relationship that was at one point great but has gradually progressed into an abusive field over time? One cannot help but begin to wonder – "What went wrong?" - It could be that the power of negative perception was much greater than the power of positive perception. The perception that one has of someone will determine the attitude one decides to give to that person. Maintain a positive perception of your beloved and stand a better chance of keeping the status of a healthy relationship by applying the right attitude to it. The right attitude – loves - cares and gives room for pillars of joy to surround and anchor the relationship. The right attitude is self-less, patient, kind, and forgiving. It knows nothing of inflicting pain on to another human being.

It is not my objective to paint an unrealistic image of a relationship. Realism suggests that conflicts will always surface in the relationship. Conflict can have a major impact on the sustainability of the relationship. I strongly believe dealing with conflict is in essence seeking to unify and not to separate. Thus, it is of vital significance that the voices of all the parties in a relationship should be valued. Human abuse can be a product that develops from the minor conflicts that are encountered daily. It is interesting how small things can gradually develop into greater things especially when it comes to human behavior.

Deal with the conflict carefully and wisely while it is still a small prevailing case. Bigger conflicts will potentially give room for devastating end-results. It starts with fighting over a remote control and escalates to criticizing behavior and the battlefield becomes more real and agonizing. Failure to resolve the conflict of the remote control is a ticket to a disastrous relationship that is tangled in conflict.

Positive perception of our beloveds will channel us into the right frame of attitude that seeks to respect and honor those that we love. Cheering up our beloveds and supporting them anchors the relationship. It is not easy for such a relationship to be entangled with the psychological chains of human abuse.

Young minds should know this kind of love so that it infectiously guides their adulthood love – life. I am not Doctor Love, but I have experienced what it is to truly love and be authentically loved.

It is not just awesome but meaningful...

41
SINGLE-PARENTING

"I am the mother and father of the child"

The above statement has become music to our ears, and it is disturbing how society is gradually accepting it as the new norm of life. The number of single parents in South Africa continues to be on the rise making it a rare privilege for children to grow up with the balanced support of both parents.

The parenting department is quickly taking a new turn - the number of single-parent house-hold-headed families today is appalling. The challenge with single parenting is the lack of balance that it presents. Parents are unique and it is in this uniqueness that helps form a complete human being. So many reasons can be attributed to being the contributing factors leading to the escalating levels of single parenting. It could be intentional abandonment and or rejection by the other parent. It could also be the death of the other parent.

Experiencing single parenting can be so drastic to such an extent that if not handled wisely it could progressively lead to a warped view of gender and roles in the child's mind. This can quickly escalate to the human abusive behavior that is experienced today. The child who is subjected to single parenting due to intentional abandonment and rejection by the parent will find it hard to have peace of mind until they understand the reason behind the rejection by their other parent. It is an immensely sad situation. No child deserves to be subjected to one parent.

A South African author who writes immaculately well about single parenting is Patrick Neo Mabiletsa in his book 'Chronicles of a fatherless son' - he delves deeper into the life of a child who grows up in the absence of the other parent.

The role that parents play in the child's life is an experience that can never be replaced or taken away. Without a shadow of a doubt, it has long-lasting effects on the adulthood life of the child. The adults we see today are the reflection of the role that the parent has played in the child's life. It is for this reason that any child deserves to have the presence and support of both parents in their life. Failure to have the presence and support of both parents is a serious problem today.

South Africa is one of the leading countries where single parenting is prevalent. Sadly, most of the single-parent cases are not attributed to death but the intentional abandonment of the other parent. This means that a balance must be brought to the light, the single parent needs to at least be well versed with how they are supposed to raise their children. Workshops and education should be brought to light and single parents need to have access to single parenting education.

The current situation calls for a resilient parent that will have the courage to equip oneself with proper parenting skills. Failure to properly parent children is the main factor contributing to the escalating levels of human abuse that are immensely experienced today.

It is irrational for single parents to continuously assume the role of being superheroes to their children. It is practically impossible to be everything to your children – a male figure and a female figure.

Parents have their personality traits and qualities - the mother of a child can never be the same as the father of the child. These are two completely different human beings with unique personalities. The presence of these personalities is of paramount importance to the proper growth of the child.

I am not saying, the single parent cannot play-role the missing parent. It is possible to play-role. However, role-playing does not in any way replace an absent person. It may try to fill the void, but ultimately an absent person is an absent person and only their presence can replace their absence.

I, by no means, do not intend to make a child that has been raised by a single parent feel bad...I wrote this chapter because I deeply empathize with them. They must not be discouraged – They must not allow the absence of a parent to define their worth – We are all golden young people despite our challenges and hurdles.

The lack of a parent should not cost the child's peace of mind. Some sense of sensitivity and knowledge must be applied to how the child's mind is approached and made to feel at peace with the single parent they have. It is not easy. It is a battle. It is a battle that will need resilience and patience. Failure to have the courage to face this battle is a sure way of raising children with human-abusive tendencies. Failure to have the courage to face this battle is a definite way of raising adults that are incomplete and filled with a sense of thirst to know more about the reason behind the rejections by their other parent.

If the child was rejected, chances are high that they will end up rejecting their child because of the bad experience they have had, which continues to give them a warped reality of what parenting is about. This is a cycle of single parenting that continues to build strong momentum. Breaking this cycle is a call that begins with you; Choose to embrace the parenting responsibility today and you are assured that your child will do the same to their child.

To all the single parents, abundant love and wisdom are the keys to raising a child whose mind is liberated from the chains of human abuse. Do not pretend that you know it all and do not assume the role of being everything to your child. Seek professional advice and stand a better chance of raising children that will make you proud.

42
THE FLAWS OF MEDIA

I am not your intimate partner, but I will undress you.
I am not your friend, but I will keep you company.
I am not your job, but I certainly will keep you on your toes.

What is my name?

In a world where technology is rapidly developing, it is inevitable for one to wake up to a post of their naked image making the rounds on social media pages. As much as media has had an impact in helping to curb abusive behavior, it has also led to escalating levels of human abuse. The question that is worth debating is, "Has the media contributed more positively or negatively in curbing human abusive behavior?

The media remains a very instrumental tool whose impact upon our lives is solely dependent on how we use it. Some use it positively by, learning from it, promoting their business, reporting abusive cases, and educating humanity. Some use it negatively by negatively commenting on other people, posting other people's pictures without their approval, and reporting false news to the world.

The positive or negative influence of media remains in the way humanity uses it.

The power of media cannot be ignored in all fraternities of human life. News, entertainment, and lifestyle are the cornerstones that pillar us, and the media is a platform that has facilitated the acquisition of the most current and updated information about these pillars. Taking advantage of this platform, humanity continues to be manipulated, brainwashed, and deceived by propaganda.

Using the influence of media -masses of humanity can be programmed to act, behave, and think in a certain way. Propaganda refers to the spreading of false information to mislead and persuade humanity to behave in a certain way or to have preconceived ideas about a figure, a place, an experience, or a political party.

Propaganda is at least another prevalent form of human abuse.

Now, enemies have a platform that they use to attack their haters, the social media pages have become platforms of conflict which are used to address a clash of personalities.

The amount of corruption that has been fueled and propelled by the influence of media remains huge. Some spy and hake into other people's lives – again, these are all psychological chains of human abuse that continue to gain gross momentum – reinforced by media.

We have seen and witnessed the clash of celebrities on social media pages that remain well archived to be retrieved by the young generation. The young generation must refrain from the negative connotations that are birthed by the conflict of the celebrities that remain on public platforms such as Twitter and Facebook. Young people must be encouraged to rather focus their energy on stories that are immersed in positivity and inspiration.

They must positively use media.

Imagine an individual that wakes up to a post of their naked image making the rounds on social media pages. It would be traumatizing. It can even lead to suicide. It's like stripping one's dignity to the core. It is not human at all. The effects are at most deadly to the human soul. Harboring the pain and humiliation that stems from this incident will break one's confidence. Low self-esteem will be birthed from such an incident. Low confidence reduces self-worth and one's dignity which in the long run will lead to a soul that is vulnerable to the pains of human abuse. It is not easy, but one must have the courage to seek justice and move on. Deep within the realms of a human being is the courage to let be and let go.

People have different ways of dealing with such a situation. Some would choose suicide as the best solution. The courageous ones will choose to allow positivity to triumph over negativity, sacrifice their pride and ego, forgive, forget, and let go. Harboring the pain only breeds more pain. You cannot recover water that has been spilled, but you can investigate the person who is responsible for spilling the water and thereafter seek and find justice.

This is a simple analogy yet pro-found; water has been spilled and it can never be recovered. However, justice can still take its course by bringing into captivity the person that is responsible for the irresponsible act of posting another human being's naked pictures

The above simply means that the image has been posted it cannot be recovered, given the strong development of social media that will only facilitate the widespread of the image and not the eradication of the image. However, justice can still take its course because the person that is responsible for this act can be investigated and be charged guilty for this irresponsible act.

It is how humanity decides to use the instrument of media that ultimately deems it as toxic or good for human usage.

43
THE SPOTLIGHT

The one time that I was completely convinced that the spotlight can be dangerous is when I came across a young man that was willing to sacrifice their child for fame and riches. After a prayer session, the man publicly confessed this sick desire that kept on taking a bite of peace from his conscious. I was not only perplexed but terrified of this confession. A deep sense of relief came from his courage to tell nothing but the truth. Consequently, the truth did set him free.

The life of being in the spotlight can be very satisfying and meaningful. It is a life that most people aspire to. One cannot be blind to all the competitions that seek to promise to put one under the spotlight of fame. To name a few I love these competitions; singing (South African Idols), dancing (So you think you can dance) and talent (SA's got talent) competitions. The noble drive of these competitions is to look for that one person that outshines the others and shine the spotlight of fame on this person.

Those in the spotlight are often considered to be influential and famous people. They can easily motivate and inspire others. They have at their disposal the opportunity to be role models to other people. This could be pressurizing – at most depressing. It is important not to succumb to this pressure. One has to move at a pace that allows them to breathe and live a healthy lifestyle without succumbing to any pressure. It becomes a form of mistreatment to allow the desire to please others to control the very life of the one who is in the spotlight.

Respect yourself enough not to be abused by the need to maintain the profile of a social media hero or heroine.

I at most appeal to those in the spotlight to drive social cohesion platforms that will wipe out the concomitants of gender-based violence. The power of influence means that one stands in a position that makes it easy for them to effortlessly convince and persuade others. For example - if an unknown person pushes the message that says stop gender-based violence on social media, the number of likes they are going to receive become far much less than when the same words are spoken by the South African president – Cyril Ramaphosa and or the world's first Human 1st author – Brightwell Dube.

Influence is power; however, we must strive to work towards reaching a place where everybody's voice is valued despite their influence, popularity, or status. If positively maneuvered; it could bear fruits of genuine love that will allow humanity to untangle the psychological chains of human abuse.

As much as the spotlight can be this fulfilling it may come at a cost of being abused if not trodden carefully. Maintaining it might as well prove to be a challenge thus exposing one to making them prone to the realities of human abuse. One cannot deny, in a literal sense, the spotlight has a very clear view. Everybody that surrounds the spotlight cannot ignore the view of the spotlight as it is appealing and attractive.

Some will fight their way to the spotlight no matter the cost, even if it means they must be abused. Maintaining the life of being in the spotlight can be very pressurizing. It means the upholding of an image that your fans will always like. The intention of bettering one's image begins to shift from internal satisfaction to external satisfaction. This can be a very toxic place to be, it seeks to take a person into an abusive cage. Freedom will mean one must have the courage to reach out for the keys and walk away if their soul feels caged by the limelight.

As much as one is in the spotlight, it is vital to keep a sense of separateness. Strong attachment to fame is misleading. It is a notion that keeps me anchored - knowing that; not everything is about me - has helped me to easily detach myself from hurtful people. 'Not everything is about me' is a notion that says you do not need to go to the ends of the earth to impress, be accepted, loved, and approved by other people.

It is a powerful notion that helps one to eliminate attachment that stems from the pressure to impress and be approved by others

Fame is a vapor, it comes and goes anytime, it is never guaranteed. Therefore, one's happiness and purpose for life cannot be anchored within the reigns of fame. Subtly, fame says that one's life is not theirs anymore but it's everybody 's life. One cannot live life along with the parameters and confines of pleasing the world and upholding an image for the world to aspire to. It puts unnecessary pressure on a person. Fame is certainly the root cause of the never-ending surgeries, darkening, and skin lightening schemes that are becoming more popularized.

Again,
Do not get me wrong I am not against anybody who sees it fit for them to perform such. I am strongly against the intention that seeks to please the world and not oneself when they perform such. There is nothing as hard as living a life of pleasing the world. One forgets to please oneself

and is pressurized to be what the world deems to be good, acceptable, and pleasing.

Fame certainly calls for one to be anchored in a strong character - A character that will know how to balance the life of pleasing others and oneself. Such a character will certainly shield one from the realities of human abuse.

He was no angel, but his words certainly left an eternal mark:

"Fame is a vapor, popularity is an accident, Money takes wings and the only thing that endures is the character"
O.J Simpson

44
THE HUSTLE

The notion of breadwinners is gradually taking an interesting turn. It is shifting from the shoulders of men to be cherished by independent women and young children. The progression of time has seen to it that the participants of the economy are not only masculine figures. Equality continues to fight to see to it that women are as equally active participants in the economy as their counterpart. To me, this is impartial justice simply because it discards the participation of the other sexual orientations.

It is high time that we start supporting movements that polarize every sexual identity. The LGBTQI+ community deserves a fair share in the active involvement of the economy. After all, statistically speaking a huge portion of breadwinners is made up of the LGBTQI+ community. If they can have the capacity to help keep families alive, they surely must be allowed to take care of the Nation's affairs.

Considering all the atrocities, injustices, and pre-mature deaths suffered by the LGBTQI+ community. It is time we qualify the question:

How about an openly gay South African president for a change?

Food for thought...

On one hand:
It is not surprising that some breadwinners see abuse as fitting towards those that they take care of. In a world where the levels of unemployment are skyrocketing, it is empowering to find a job and earn some money. It is this power that propels other breadwinners to abuse and violates the very same people that they take care of. It comes with a sense of superiority that can easily escalate to the perpetration of human abuse. Breadwinning is good; however, it does not in any way put the breadwinner in a position of violating those that are on the receiving end.
Fend for them but do not abuse them.

On the other hand:
Some dependents show a lack of appreciation for the work of the breadwinner, by wasting that which is provided. Bear in mind, appreciation, in this case, does not in any way imply that the dependents should bow down and worship the breadwinner; it simply means that the dependent must show some sense of gratitude by not wasting that which has been provided by the breadwinner. If the dependent was in the shoes of the breadwinner, they would have asked for

the same. Gratitude is simply effectively utilizing that which has been provided by the breadwinner. For example, it is shown in simple but effective actions like not throwing away food unnecessarily.

Receive the bread but show some sense of appreciation by not wasting it.

Wasting food does not in any way give the abuser the right to abuse the dependent. They can sit down and talk about it to come up with solutions and suggestions.

I emphasize,

A lack of appreciation or accountability cannot be used as an excuse to justify the atrocious act of violating the dependent. The bottom line is violence is inhuman and it should be curbed.

The pressure that breadwinners must face to be able to put food on the table can be insurmountable. Only if dependents could understand this pressure, they will be very careful how they utilize the resources that are hardly earned by the breadwinner.

The pangs of human abuse that some breadwinners must endure to be able to provide are uncalled for. The nature of a breadwinner is that one must provide and put food on the table for the family. However, it is in the varying ways that the different breadwinners provide this bread that can be abusive. There are different kinds of breadwinners; there is one that seeks at all cost to see to it that they provide regardless of the cost. This kind of breadwinner will do whatever it takes to provide even if it means their dignity and integrity are shaken. Their main aim is to see to it that provision is made possible for their beloveds. It cannot be argued that their action stems from a place of love for their beloveds. However, it is this unrelenting desperation driving them to provide that will make them prone to mistreatment. They can be the abuser by forcefully taking from others in the name of provision. They can be the victim by taking in pain and submitting themselves to abusive actions in the name of provision. One should never aspire to be this kind of breadwinner.

The other kind of breadwinner will look at all possible ways to look and find the bread, without compromising on their dignity, self-worth, integrity, and value. It is this approach that blesses their hustle. They can never be exposed to the realities of human abuse. They are hustling within the spirit of love not only for their families but for their providers as well. This means that the actions that are channeled to their hustling will be pure and well calculated. This kind of breadwinner will find the bread and keep their dignity, self-worth, integrity, and value untouched. Everybody should aspire to be this kind of breadwinner. It draws humanity closer to untangling the psychological chains of human abuse. Cheers to breadwinners that hustle within the confines of love and respect…I SALUTE YOU!

I will not turn a blind eye to the realities of unemployment and poverty that face a lot of individuals. At the same time, I am convinced that, no amount of suffering can be attributed to the atrocious act of using abuse as a way of hustling or succumbing to abuse as a way of finding the bread. Provision is good, if it is within the confines of one's dignity, self-worth, integrity, and value. It should never be attributed to inflicting pain or succumbing to the infliction of pain.

To the dependents,
Well note:
Before wasting the bread, one should take their time to ponder upon the effort and hustle that was used to attain it.

45
THE CRYING BABY!

It was on this fateful day that the sound power of a crying baby became so real to me. I was on my way to my workplace which was only a km away from home. As I advanced along this deserted road, I first thought I heard a strange sound, but the sound became so real and loud as I was moving towards a litter bin that was left in the middle of a highway road. I recognized it was a human sound and with great and much-anticipated curiosity, I opened the litter bin only to open my eyes to a cute baby boy that was wrapped in heavy blankets. The boy had been dumped by a heartless person in the middle of the street.

Had it not been for the cries of the baby, I would not have taken him to a place of safety.
Had it not been for the cries of the infant, I would have by-passed the litter bin.
Had it not been for the cries of the cute little boy, he could have been killed or hurt.

The cry of the baby was certainly a call that saved the one precious life of the child.

The burden of an unplanned pregnancy can be a lot to take in. Human life is not a joke – a child needs food, clothes, toys, milk, pampers, and education. If one is not able to provide these needs, they may resort to terminating the pregnancy, killing the child, and abandoning the child as a solution.

The decision to abort a child is a personal decision and I am not in a capacity to inform the parent not to abort or to abort the child. However, it is important for one to carefully weigh the pros and cons of such a decision. Abortion is not the only option if you are in a position of not being able to take care of the child. You can keep the child and give the child to social workers – some people are in a financial position to adopt children – you can give them the child. That is if you will be able to handle the emotional detachment that comes with this decision.

The option of killing the child is a crime and the partaker should be dealt with accordingly... No negotiations and no exceptions!

The option of abandoning the child is a crime and the partaker should be dealt with accordingly...no negotiations and no exceptions!

A crying baby can never die of hunger and neglect. It is the cry that ensures that even a neglected baby is given some shelter. It's like a human being that is living under the heavy burden of abuse. Only the cry of the victim can alert other people to lend a helping hand. Only the cry can save the victim from the psychological chains and physical pains of human abuse. If the abuser has not killed the voice of the victim, there is still great hope for the victim to use their voice as an instrument of raising awareness and educating humanity at large.

Isn't it amazing that the power of creation lies in every human soul? With our words, we are always breathing life into the human characters and attitudes we see. It is not earned; it is just a gift that everybody is given at birth. It comes with the territory of being fully human. Even the cry that is produced by an infant is creating a bond with the parent that has long-lasting effects. Imagine the trauma that goes through a parent that gives birth to a silent baby. It can never be life; this is death, and it is terrifying. Crying at birth is an affirmation of life, it says to the parent; love me, embrace me, and bond with me…I need your affectionate embrace. The baby's cries can only be affirming the parent, 'I am a soul that longs for some embrace and love. Apart from all the sounds I have heard, the sound of a crying baby takes the cup for me. It is affirming of life; it is courageous enough to say 'help me' – I am in need.

If there is one thing that the art of speaking and writing has taught me, it is the power of words. The effect of words is felt in a strong-like sense long after the words have been uttered. The impact of spoken words can make a King, a President, a Slave, or a CEO. The positions and titles that one holds are so much a product of the words that were uttered in the early stages of their growth. In a nutshell, words can create. That is the power embedded in words.

This truth can only mean that careful consideration must be taken when uttering words or writing words for someone. If they were to be scaled, the number of the negative words that are uttered in an abusive relationship far much outweighs the number of the positive words. I am certain the un-reckoned force of spoken word has the potential to prop up a perpetrator or a victim of human abuse. Early stages of growth that are saturated with more negative words will ignite misbehavior and a bad attitude to life that then mounts up to an unattractive character. Negative words seize to encourage and motivate a soul in need of hope. They fail to cheer up the big dreamer within everybody. They are an enemy to happiness and peace. One of my strongest desires is for humanity to comprehend the value of speaking positive words. In so doing, the human language will change for the better and the greater course of all humanity.

To the victims of human abuse, I say - if you can't say the words:

CRY OUT LOUD...HUMANITY WILL SURELY COME TO YOUR RESCUE!

46
PASSION

One of my personal life mottos is – 'If I do not have a passion for it, I do not touch it'.

Nick Williams writes in one of my favorite reads – 'Powerful beyond measure':

"Passion is taking such a bite out of life, such that when the juices come running down the face, everybody licks their lips".

Humanity should be given enough room to experience life in all its forms along with the different phases of life...The toddler phase, the growing phase, the teenage phase, the young adult phase, the grown-up phase, and the aging phase. All these stages of growth have certain behavioral tendencies that are attributed to them. A toddler cries for milk. A teenager makes good friends. A young adult starts dating. A grown-up takes care of their family. An aging person needs care and family support. A human being should not be robbed of the experience that comes with these different stages of growth.

When it comes to intimate affairs, the conflicts that are experienced by the parent and the young adult can be outrageous. For some parents, it is a pain to let go of their child —no matter the age – the parent will always punish the child for dating John. It all goes back to control – if not trodden carefully, the hand of control imposed by the parent on the child has the potential to harm the child.

It is not wrong for a young adult to have an affair, if they have the emotional capacity to handle such relationships. The fact is, someday the child will be a grown-up person that has to choose marriage and having their children. It does not make any sense to curb young adults from gaining experience that will teach them how to handle the pressure that stems from intimate relationships.

Remember:
They will not remain forever young.

After genuinely socializing with them and informing them what life and relationships are about – the consequences of risky behavior such as over-usage of alcohol and drugs and unprotected sex. Do not chain them, let them be free and experience life in such a manner that their growth and maturity is not curbed by your heavy hand of control as a parent.

Informing your children about the dangers of risky behaviors is the best thing you can do as a parent. It is effective enough to untangle the psychological chains of human abuse from your child's mind because risky behavior exposes one to the realities of human abuse.

Sit back and relax - stop being anxious about the unknown.

It is a fact that there is a time for everything. One cannot expect a 50- year-old to behave like a 10-year-old. It is humanly inappropriate. Part of being fully human means that one must do certain things at a certain stage in their life. Failure to do this can be detrimental to growth and maturity - it can open the doors to abuse stemming from the need to experience what should have been experienced a long time ago.

Live and experience life in all its form at the right stage in time. There is a time to play with other kids and bond with them. There is a time to make friends. There is a time to focus on one's studies and goals. There is a time to intimately love. There is a time to be with family. There is a time to just sit down and rest. There is a time to let loose on the dance floor. There is a time to go to work.

There is a time to rest - I call it rest because I don't believe in retiring. You will be amazingly surprised at the experience that the 'retired' people can bring if allowed to be in a working environment. They are truly a wealth of experience and wisdom. I for one have had the pleasure to tap into the wisdom of the grey-haired...Cheers to all the grey-haired...I love you.

If one is robbed of the opportunity to experience life in all its forms, they can open their souls to the detrimental effects of human abuse. Think about it - a child that is not allowed to play with other children. This child will have a hard time bonding with their beloveds in their adulthood. Bonding is a by-product that is manufactured from the early stages of life. The manufacturing process is the friendships that are created by the child from the early stages of their lives. Thus, if they can be able to love, care and bond well in their friendships at a young age. They will be able to love, care and bond well in their adulthood affairs and relationships. If it is the right stage and time for them to play and make friends, let them be, never stand in their way.

The best that a parent can give is the support they need in carrying out their playful activities and making friends. Do not just tell them, but practice what you preach to them by now and again involving yourself in their games. It can be a chess game. Take your time to take off the tie and put on the golf shirt and play with your child. Show them the value of playing.

Do not host a party for your child, if they do not have good friends to grace it. Let them know that the only condition that you can host a party for them is when they invite some of their good friends to the party.

Life should be adventured, there are no short-cuts and there is certainly no jump- cuts...one should take their time to walk and FULLY LIVE LIFE TO THE FULLEST.

47
LIFE SEASONS

A series of heavy rainfall is stimulated by a series of hot weather conditions. Without intense heat, water cannot evaporate to refresh the dense air. As refreshing as rainfall can be, it is impossible to experience it without first experiencing the agony of heat. The abuser harps on the fallacy that - happiness and peace are qualities that are birthed after episodes of painful experiences. This may be the ideal cycle for nature, but not for human beings. Human beings are pricelessly destined to live in happiness and peace. They are not to be misled into believing they must pay a price for peace and happiness.

There is no price tag on one's peace and happiness.

Seasons of life are inevitable. They make up the game of life. Creationism suggests that humanity was created after the light was formed from the darkness. This means for humanity to exist, there first had to seasons. Without seasons humanity could have seized to exist. The existence of seasons is an affirmation of the 'normalcy' of life. It would not be normal to experience summer throughout the year.

In a literal sense, seasons refer to the varying situations experienced in life. These are inevitable - they certainly make up the heart and soul of life. The good times, bad times, challenging times, and celebration times are the essence of what life is about. Imagine life with only one season - winter. I for one will not want to experience this kind of life. Life is meant to be adventurous. It is what gives it meaning and purpose.

It is in humanity's response to these seasons that determine the maintenance of the happiness and misery that comes with life. Humanity should be well-equipped enough not to succumb and break amid any season encountered. The effect of seasons on humanity can be heartbreaking. As much as seasons can give humanity an abundance of refreshing fresh air - They also have the potential to create pressure and heat that one cannot stand. Without the necessary support, suffocation can be the result. During the pressure and the heat, it is most likely that one can resort to the chains of human abuse in the hope that they will be rescued from the heat and find some comfort.

With time, we inevitably face heat and pressure. However, this does not necessarily mean that one must endure the agony of human abuse in the hope that there will be a change. Run-away and seek fresh air, not from those that promise it at the cost of one's dignity, self-worth, and integrity. I have found that abuse can deeply reside in the way religious tools such as The Holy Bible are misinterpreted.

Let us explore the book of James chapter 1verse 2 to 4; it reads:

2 My brethren, count it all joy when you fall into divers' temptations.
3 Knowing this, that the trying of your faith produces patience:
4 But let patience have her perfect work, that you may be perfect and entire, wanting nothing.

Misinterpretation of this verse will suggest that one must persevere in all the problems, afflictions and trials faced. The misinterpretation lies in the inability to specify the problem that one encounters. It will be inappropriate to give this word to a victim of human abuse because it will mislead the victim into believing that abuse is just another trial, thus they must not let go of an abusive relationship, and instead, they must be joyful through all the anguishing pains experienced. The continuous misinterpretation of this verse will see to it that many will ignorantly continue to suffer and continue living in silence and denial of their suffering. Let's face it, the number of Christians that continue to suffer while hiding behind the veil of their faith is appalling.

Perseverance is a good virtue; however, the application of this virtue should be appropriate. On one hand, one who is born in dire poverty should persevere while they are working towards building a stable life. However, one who is in an abusive relationship must not hold on to the agony of such a relationship. They must do the noble thing which is to seek professional advice from counselors, psychologists, and police officers. People perish not because they don't know, but because of lack of knowledge. Seek knowledge and find life.

Persevere in achieving your dreams
Do not preserve in abuse
Do not persevere in silence
Do not persevere in injustice

Serving God and reading the Holy Bible is good, however, it must be done in wisdom, knowledge, and truth. Christianity or any belief cannot be used as a vehicle to continue fastening the psychological chains of human abuse. The basis of any belief should be anchored in genuine love.

48
THE BLAME-GAME

As I immerse myself in this chapter a humorous movie scene quickly flashes in my mind. The chocolate cake that had been recently purchased had gone missing in this house of three people – the mother who is a detective, the father who is also a detective, and the daughter who is a scholar. With chocolate cake cream that had found a home on top of her mouth and nose, the daughter sternly refused that she ate the chocolate cake. She even used her head as a body language that emphasized, she did not eat the cake. Not until the father decides to take some of the chocolate cake cream that was on her daughter's mouth and puts it on a white paper – that makes the daughter regrettable say the words "I did it!" in response to her parents' earnestness and intentional enquires.

Had it not been for the chocolate cake cream that had made a home on the mouth of their daughter; the mysterious chocolate cake eater would have remained anonymous to the parents. They would have been left with an unfinished case. At worst, it could result in a conflict between these two parents, because chances are - they could be each other's suspects.

The lesson is: A sense of accountability serves a lot of conflicts.

Some blame gamers would even choose to take the fight further and blame hunger for eating the cake. I have witnessed some who, upon being asked "Who ate the food?" Their response is "I was hungry".

Blame gaming is not cool:
Save humanity from a lot of confusion and just admit that you did it.

In a world where uncontrollable forces such as weather, time, money, hunger, and thirst can be easily blamed for humanity's irresponsible actions, it has become golden to have an attitude of ownership. As much as the forces are uncontrollable, we certainly can counteract the damage they cause by acting responsibly. A persistent latecomer at work cannot continue to shift the blame on the weather and watch. It is completely irrational.

Life is a pain to adventure with blame gamers. I detest blame gaming. It is a waste of time. God knows the time that could have been saved if only John admitted to stealing Sipho's calculator. Now the whole class must stand in a long straight line and get their precious body parts and bags thoroughly searched. Only to find that the teacher will find the calculator deeply buried in John's long new pair of socks. Those were some of the humorous incidents from my schooling days. As humorous as they may sound, there is certainly a profound lesson to take from these incidents. Heaven knows what goes through John's mindset when the teacher suggests that everybody should stand in a straight line to be searched.

If fear was to be measured, that would be the highest degree to break the world's record of fears.

The above scenario briefly shows us:

As young as John is, an attitude of unaccountability has already taken root in his heart and mind. If this attitude is not brought to a halt from the early stages, John will grow up to be a kind of a human abuser that will abuse and cover up all the tracks even if it means threatening the victim not to speak out. Upon redemption, one would not be surprised if John, grows up and confesses to secretly abusing a beloved. If at a young age John saw it fit to hurt someone's feelings by taking their calculator and still not own up to his action. Then it is only fitting for him to grow up as a hideously abusive person.

The only weapon that could curb John from growing up as a hideously abusive person is how the teacher deals with this incident after recovering the calculator from John 's pair of socks. If I was the teacher in this case, I would have subjected John to a very good punishment. The punishment will not only see to it that John stops this behavior, but he also adopts a sense of ownership and accountability. I could have told John to stand in front of the class and convincingly say the words…I DID IT.

State resources are wasted by blame gamers who keep on financing court rulings that could have been curbed by a sense of ownership; the above three little but effective words of accountability can save so much effort, money, and time.

If you abuse someone, be brave enough to admit – do not cowardly shift the blame on circumstances, the past, and a clash of personalities.

Ownership and accountability are vital. They save a lot of precious time in trying to find the main culprit. They instill a sense of responsibility and acceptance of one's weakness which is a necessary step in untangling the psychological chains of human abuse.

To all the naughty young minds, if you do it, do not be ashamed to convincingly say out loud…
I DID IT!

49
THE SEESAW

The analogy of a 'seesaw' is that it can only be enjoyed if there are two people whose weights complement each other. One's force is required to uplift the other person. One person must be willing to go down for the other person to be uplifted. If no one is willing to go down, then it is impossible to enjoy the pleasure of riding this board.

This is a perfect portrayal of how a relationship should function. Both parties must be willing to humble themselves and use the best of their effort to see to it that their beloved is uplifted. I love that it is a two-way street, as both participants will have the equal pleasure of being uplifted by their beloved. It selflessly seeks to balance happiness and pleasure using humility and effort from both parties. This is a perfect portrayal of a selfless relationship...I must admit that I love this analogy.

This is certainly not a 'sacrificial act', rather a 'meet me half-way' act of showing selfless love. It's an act that says, "Meet me halfway by letting go of some of your weight so that I can lift you meet me half-way by using some of your weight to lift me". It is not a forceful act, rather a cheerful act from one party to the other.

If either party is not willing to be humble enough to use their effort to see to it that their beloved is uplifted, it is impossible to enjoy the pleasure of riding the seesaw board. An example of a healthy relationship implies that all parties are willing to be humble enough to share a unified kind of happiness. In other words, the absence of a balanced force in the seesaw analogy implies that all parties in a relationship will always be down. It is not until they reach a point where they are both willing to use their force that uplifting can be attained for both. This analogy should be eye-opening to today's relationships that just struggle to strike a selfless balance.

It is inevitable that in a relationship of two people, there will be a clash of interests, likes, choices, and decisions. If I am a vegetarian, it does not necessarily mean that my partner must like vegetables. If I am a fan of a particular President, it does not necessarily mean my partner has to share the sentiments as I do. Thus, it is important to strike a balance by not allowing the clash of interests to become the very concomitants of conflicts, which could easily escalate to the realities of gender-based violence.

Respecting your partner's choices does not mean that you like their choices. It is an acknowledgment of their uniqueness. It is an acknowledgment of individualism.

This is the main reason, I do not like the term 'acceptance' when it comes to sexuality because it is disempowering. In a world where everybody has different likes and dislikes it would be irrational to force everybody to accept everybody. I prefer the term 'respect' when it comes to sexuality because it is empowering. Humanity must respect other human beings despite their differences.

I MAY NOT ACCEPT YOU, BUT I AM OBLIGED TO RESPECT YOU.

In an abusive relationship, one person may be willing to use their force for the other person to be uplifted, but the other person may not be willing to submit their will to this. The final picture is that one person is always using their force, so they remain down, and the other person is always uplifted and uses power and threats to keep the other person's force always uplifting them. It is very unbalanced and there is no pleasure in riding this seesaw board. A relationship where there is mistreatment means that one party is submissive and cannot be lifted. This is unbalanced. I was that one person that always gave my best in my Shipping career and for a long time, I never received any acknowledgments for the work I did. This was so unbalanced because I always uplifted the employer, but I could not be uplifted.

Only after acknowledging that I am in an unbalanced state of a relationship, I started self-evaluating and making changes to how I approach my career. It is this self-evaluation that enabled me to pursue so much of my calling in entrepreneurial writing – I then gathered the courage to compile a Shipping guide that was based on my working experience as a Shipping Administrator for big companies like Evergreen Shipping line, Euro steel, Power mite, Mganu group, and Grindrod.

The ultimate lesson to take from the 'seesaw' analogy is that a good relationship can be made possible if both parties are willing to be courageous enough to let go of their pride, humble themselves and see to it that their beloved is uplifted. Happiness in a relationship is made possible if there is mutual humility that is not self-seeking but selfless. The pleasure in riding the see-saw board calls for a team effort. In the same way, the pleasure of being in a relationship calls for the selfless effort of both parties.

I challenge the parenting family...

To take their child to a seesaw board and share this analogy with their children as they seesaw. It is a powerfully captivating, practical way of giving them the truth so profound...a truth that should govern any relationship that aspires to a balanced state of happiness.

50
REJECTION

The rejection that acts as an opposing force to the strong quest of achieving dreams can be discouraging and at best de-motivating. The agony of the pain of rejection is so real – it is only a matter of time that the rejected will become the rejecter.

Like any other challenge, the lesson is not so much in the rejection but in our response to the rejection that holds much power and impact in this world. After graduating in International Trade and Transport Logistics, I have had to come across a lot of rejections in my career path. Today I reflect and I see; if it was not for the appalling rejections I have had to encounter in my professional career, I would not have had the courage to give birth to my shipping company, Bright Shipping Services (Pty) Ltd. I could have given up on my career, but I chose to make lemonade out of all the lemons that life threw at me.

The response that one gives to the agony of rejection has the potential to build or destroy them. If taken to heart, rejection's pain has the potential to create so much hatred within, such that a person that has suffered rejection can only feel better after an endless series of rejecting others. Rejection has the power to change a good person to the devil herself. At best, rejection has the power to change the loving, humble, and caring man to a very dangerous thug the town has ever had - the kind of a thug that is even revered and feared by law authorities. Rejection's power changes motives, perceptions, and attitudes. It can be that toxic if it is taken personally and negatively. One will be surprised at the number of people that have become abusive due to the countless rejections they have come across. Rejection has the potential to build up anger, frustration, and feelings of inadequacy, if encountered by a character that is not intrinsically motivated and that does not have a strong foundation of self-worth.

The pangs of rejection are so real; they could be the very concomitants of self-doubt and self-hatred. Doubt is oftentimes birthed by the unfair analysis of one's performance and the unqualified opinions of other people. Discard the limitations of self-doubt from the realms of your child's mind by affirming them of their inert ability. Convincingly tell them:

"You are a champion"

Genuinely and persistently uttering these words to your children has enormous effects on their well-being, without a shadow of a doubt it eliminates self-doubt that may sprout up due to discouragements or failures.

As someone that has experienced rejection, it is vital to sass out the decisions that you make. Never make your decision about somebody based on your rejections. Do not allow your rejections to cloud your judgment and therefore propel you to reject deserving people.

The pain of rejection cannot be resolved by rejecting others.

It can only be resolved by giving others that which you were deprived of.

The rejected who becomes the rejecter is like a victim of abuse that becomes the perpetrator of human abuse and justifies their actions by their past pains.

Pains cannot eliminate pain – genuine love can.

Rejections are unfair; however healing humanity at large cannot be short-sighted to the repetition of the same mistake. The cycle of rejection needs to be broken and it starts with how you treat a young person that deserves a chance in life due to their potential despite their sexual identity.

After all, it is their work that speaks volumes and not their sexuality.

Untangling the psychological chains of human abuse calls for people that will have the courage to positively perceive the rejections that they face. It is not rocket science, it is just a matter of submitting to greater positive energy, to think constructively in the face of discouragements. It is a matter of igniting the eternal flame in the fire of your ambitions. It means safely guarding this flame so that no storm can turn it off. Rejection is encountered even at an early age of our life; thus, it is vital to prepare the young minds to be strong enough to withstand the breaking nature of rejection. Rejection should come and shift situations in our lives, but it must not be allowed to shift us from positioning ourselves in positivity, ambition, and determination.

To all the big dreamers that have had to make it amid all the rejections, let me make a toast...

Cheers to the lemonade that is the product of all the lemons that life has thrown at us.

PART THREE

51
PATTERNS

The essay would not have ended for me if a neatly, catchy, and boldly written pattern is not screaming at the bottom of my writing. I always loved patterns from my schooling days. I wrote my patterns with this in mind; the design must be consistent. It is the consistency of the design that qualifies it to be called a neat pattern.

My love of patterns must be the main reason why:

The one quality that I have always valued in life is the power of consistency. A good thing done once is better. Good things done persistently are the best. It is the consistency in my writing passion that has made this self-help guide a possibility.

I am convinced:
"Nothing is impossible if you consistently put your mind to it, the word itself says I'm possible" *(exclude the use of this quote in abusive situations)*

Of course, the interpretation of the above quote does not necessarily mean that one must endure the pains of human abuse because 'nothing is impossible'. It does not mean that one who is abused must have the unwavering hope that the perpetrator of human abuse may change, so they must just stay in an abusive relationship and not make any plans to walk away.

The 'nothing' contextualizes the achievement of dreams, visions, overcoming a bad habit, healing from traumatizing experiences, and restoration of health.

The emphasis of the above quote is the power of consistency which simply implies that persistent practice is the best.

It is the consistency of the good qualities in a relationship that will see to it that the parties in a relationship are satisfied and there is profound meaning in the relationship. It is in human nature to change behavior and attitudes based on the surroundings and the situations encountered. Maintaining good qualities in a relationship calls for a greater will and commitment. It is a great responsibility that needs the effort of both parties in a relationship.

Remember - It seizes to be a neat pattern unless there is consistency in the design. Oftentimes the problems faced by humanity stem from inconsistency in behavior and attitude. If virtues such as love, care, humility, and passion are kept consistent then the chains of human abuse will be untangled easily.

Reflecting on the value of forgiveness, consistency is one of the effective tools to protect the value of forgiveness. It is worth it to forgive someone consistent in doing the right thing. It is not worth it to forgive someone inconsistent in doing the noble thing.

The value of forgiveness can be protected by forgiving those that are consistent in doing the right thing.

Consistency is a sure way that leads to growth. Remember growth is not in the big steps taken, but it is the small leaps of faith that are taken in courage and hope. One can be taken to the best relationship coaches the world has ever had but unless consistency is applied to the advice that they receive, it is impossible to grow and improve. One can be taken to the best rehabilitation centers that the world has ever had, with the best practitioners to help them. It is only a greater human will in the consistent application of advice received that will produce growth and activate effortless changes. Consistency is the key to adopting the behavior that liberates humanity from the chains of human abuse. I have said it - I will say it again that practice is good, however, practice-practice-practice is best. It strengthens one's efforts and activates the phenomenal transformation

The value of consistency is evident even in the early stages of a young child. It is the small steps that are consistently taken by a crawling child that will strengthen their muscle to walk with greater firmness and graduate to the phase of running. If the child does not consistently use their legs to walk, it could lead to drastic effects in their walking rhythm and they could be disabled due to neglecting the consistent practice of walking. Remember, falling forms a part and parcel of this exercise. It is the falling and pulling themselves up to walk again that will strengthen their muscle and build an attitude of resilience. I by no means intend to equate falling with being abused. I would rather equate it with failing. Failing is normal, but one must consistently keep their focus.

Falling is part of the game, but like Johnnie Walker...one has got to keep walking.

Consistently...!

52
BROKEN VESSELS

The more my mother expressed her dislike for my fashion style. The more I was deeply attached to my high heels. The more she affirmed me I must dress in a way that she deems as 'normal'. The more I saw the other side as strongly normal for me. This parent-to-child tension that was triggered by my sense of style has more than anything else facilitated in me the truth that one's normalcy is not necessarily another person's normalcy. Everybody is unique. If you like the taste of apples, it does not necessarily mean that everybody must like them.

Convinced:
'NO-ONE IS ME; THIS IS MY POWER'.

I have come to have my revelation of the truth that, one can take a horse to the river, but one cannot force it to drink the water. The horse must have the will to put the effort of titling its head to reach out for the water.

This to me still speaks to human will and effort that one has to put in to see a change. Forcing somebody has never been exciting - it takes a whole lot of strength and power to force somebody into something, even if in your perspective that something gives them life. If it is important and valuable, then one should not be forced to see this value. A solution applied forcefully does not have any long-lasting effect in the mind of the one who makes use of it. An abuser can only make long-lasting changes to their abusive behavior - in opening their eyes to the value of the healing mechanism that is introduced to them.

Broken vessels are not separate pieces that are useless or to be thrown away instantaneously. One who gathers broken vessels can still put mud on the pores of the vessels so that they can contain and therefore function as per what they were purposed to be. One who picks up these pieces can still glue these pieces together so that they become whole and functional again. One who is given these vessels can still polish them and clean them up so that they look new, fresh, and attractive again.

Do not instantly despise these vessels by destroying them or throwing them in the litter bin.

I still believe there is 'hope' to heal the abuser only if a greater will to change is at work. The mind will automatically conform to this will and healing will be simultaneously activated - In the same way that the horse must see the value in drinking the water and be willing to put in the effort to tilt its neck to allow the process of swallowing. As much as the abuser's action can never be justified, it will be ignorance at bliss to turn a blind eye to the background of the abuser. For the mere reason that it is this background that opens more knowledge about human abuse. It is this background that is used to help come up with a healing mechanism not just for the current abuser but for the future generation. It is this background that makes it possible for the fighters of human abuse to reflect and revise the best solution that best nullifies the impact of human abuse. In other words, the background of the abuser allows humanity to detect the root of his or her or their abusive tendencies and therefore come up with the best healing mechanism.

Some of the most influential people today, were once perpetrators of human abuse. They are beaming with gratitude toward those that did not dispose of them, but that still saw their value. Behind the human abuser, is a social worker, a pastor, and a lawyer to be born – thus, it is wise to help perpetrators to overcome the violent nature in them so that ultimately their purpose can bear fruits. Brothers for life is a South African organization that keeps on working with these vessels, cleaning them up and mending them – so that they become positively functional in embracing their intricate purpose – and reaching their destiny.

We salute all loyal broken vessel keepers!

If I had not reflected on the background of the human abuser, I surely would not have suggested that the most effective pill to this psychological illness is in restoring the love in young minds…it is in replacing the scarcity of love that is felt at an early age with the abundance of love.

It is my objective to create a world that makes it easy for the abuser to drink in the fountain of hope and a greater will to change their minds. Open minds do not just limit the effects of human abuse and direct anger to the abuser. Open minds think for the future generation. Open-minds see the abuser as a broken vessel that still has the potential to be mended to whom they are truly supposed to be – an abuse-free human being.

They may be broken, but they are not useless:

Open minds believe it is still possible to mend these broken vessels…

53
NOBODY IS DISABLED!

The world would have been the ugliest place of all places if all of humanity was the same. Same color, same features, same body structures, and appearance. It is indisputable that our differences complement each other, and the beauty of the world can only be attributed to these differences. It just gives the eye the zeal to want to stare on the right, left, front, and back. If all humanity was the same, then the eye would not have the appetite to look around. I mean, just look at the rainbow, the beauty of a rainbow can only be attributed to the different colors that complement one another…isn't it stunningly beautiful?

This is the reason why South Africa is one of the most beautiful countries in the world, it is a rainbow nation.

Some prefer to call it a disability, I prefer to call it uniqueness for the mere fact that one can never be disabled, they can only be unique. The word disability is an insult to the creator who created us and instilled ability in everyone from birth. Of course, we all have limitations. One person can be gifted with the ability to do things that others cannot do. This does not mean that they are disabled; it simply means they are limited in that regard, but they still can carry out certain things as well. Therefore, the word disability is largely used out of context. I don't know about you, but I struggle to find peace in saying that another human being is disabled. It doesn't sound right. I appeal to all of humanity to chuck away this word from their vocabulary.

Refreshing the context in which the word disability is used will be very instrumental in supporting everybody despite the nature of their uniqueness (broken leg, broken arm, blind or short-sighted) to achieve their dreams.

Behind these unfitting names, there are authors, doctors, builders, cleaners, lawyers, and Presidents. The emphasis of the continuous usage of unfitting names (*dis-abled*) has a psychological effect that cripples the expression of potential. It acts as a demotivating agent. There is power in the affirmation of ability.

Endorphins of ability are produced in the mind of a human being that is constantly receptive of the words:

'You are able'

Imagine the positive psychological impact created by changing the name 'Disability center' to 'Center of uniqueness'.

On one hand:
'Dis-ability center' is a negative name; it is not encouraging at all. It keeps the mind in the bondage of being unable to do what is possible to be done – it entangles the mind with the psychological chains of human abuse because those who dwell in this place are bound to suffer from low self-esteem and issues of insecurity.

On the other hand:
'Center of uniqueness' is a positive name, it speaks to individualism and uniqueness, which is a quality that all human beings have in common – it is a name that untangles the mind from the psychological chains of human abuse because those who dwell in this place feel like every other human being, they do not feel separate from all of humanity which eliminates esteem and insecurity issues.

This is my proposal to the world:
Based on the above differences:

How about we start changing 'Disability centers' to 'Centers of uniqueness'

It is upsetting, the connotations and views that humanity has built around the word disability. These connotations suggest that some people are able and other people are not able, which is a big lie to be ever told in the history of lies. The impact of continuously using this word slowly but surely seeks to bring about division among humanity which makes it impossible to untangle the psychological chains of human abuse. So many people have had to be subjected to the realities of human abuse because they have been deemed as disabled. The word itself is a form of abuse to the ear that is inclined to listen to it. It is intolerable and destroys the motivation and drive within humanity.

It is only when humanity awakens to the negative impact of this word that the healing process in the mind can be activated. Young minds should be channeled to believe that it is an insult to call a human being disabled. It is an insult and a very limiting word whose roots should be cut off from the human family.

I emphasize:
NOBODY IS DISABLED…
EVERYBODY IS ABLE, EVERYBODY IS UNIQUE AND EVERYBODY IS LIMITED!

54
OCEANS

The ocean is fascinating - I love the waves, the currents, and the tides of the ocean. The co-ordination with which these waves move is amazing. The bigger the wave, the intense the current and the longer the tide created by the wave. The smaller the wave, the lesser the intensity of the current and the shorter the tide created by the wave. The bigger the wave the greater the force and the impact created. One does not just swim in the ocean, time needs to be taken to observe the waves, read the current and measure the tides. Failure to do so may lead to one's drowning and suffocation. It is misleading to just step into the ocean and begin to swim against the waves.

It is vital to critically evaluate any relationship before giving all of yourself in it. Develop an attitude of being able to be aware of the surrounding energy and learn to fit in well with this energy. In my three-year relationship with a handsome man, I met while in my tertiary studies. He knew me well enough to describe me as a person whose personality is larger than life. He would always advise me to learn to be aware of the energy that surrounds me before I bring in the gigantic energy for life that I have. He would always say, "Your energy should gel in with the surrounding energy – it should not be separate – attractive energy fits in well with the surrounding energy. Ignorantly using your magnanimous energy for life without reading the surrounding energy may lead to an imbalance and suffocation of other people's personalities".

I must admit my love for this advice – it keeps me anchored.

Stepping in on a new working environment can be very terrifying. It can be stressful and at best seek to shake the foundation that holds a firm character. I have seen them all, those that step into the working environment and fix their eyes only on the boss or manager and nobody else. Such an individual has a lot to lose than gain. The main objective for them is to please the boss. They will go to the ends of the earth to see to it that the boss feels their presence and is pleased by their performance. I have watched, with great intent, these innocent souls suffering human abuse at the hands of the boss due to their unrelenting desire to please the boss.

One needs to bear in mind the different characters and personalities before forming a strong bond with any of the employees, including the boss. This means observing the personalities, reading the behaviors, and measuring actions and reactions before forming strong bonds with any person in a working environment.

Fixing eyes on the boss only will trigger hatred from other employees. The moment one opens their eyes to focus on other employees, it could be too late. It is so vital not to be entangled in the psychological chains of abuse by not succumbing to being the boss's puppet but a dignified worker that knows their right and respects not only the boss but all the employees.

My experience of the working environment is one that encompasses an array of personalities; I have met and worked with employees of all portfolios. The endless list is made up of the feisty, the humorous, the fighters, the blame gamers, the fragile, the good, and the bad. It is for this reason that I still see it best for one to take time in finding a way to relate to all these personalities in a good way.

It makes working life easy if one can first acknowledge and honor the uniqueness in everybody, then find a way to fit in nicely and bond with the different personalities. One who cannot have the capacity to fit in with different characters will always find it challenging to fit in with other employees.

Do not just dive in and swim...

OBSERVE THE WAVES; READ THE CURRENT AND MEASURE THE TIDES!

55
I AM THE LIGHT

After a handful series of denials and disapprovals, I finally gathered the courage to boldly utter in their midst, motivational words that were immersed and saturated with a strong desire to empower the one who has been denied, by life's fate, of what they rightfully deserve.

Accompanied by an unrelenting inner conviction that screamed through my facial expression; "I have experienced countless denials, but my focus is not swerved by discouragements!"

I said...

"If it has the potential to burn the bed to ashes in their attempt to hide it, it is genuine light..."
"If it can burn them in their attempt to blow it off, it is genuine light..."
"If it can ignite even brighter flames, in their attempt to cover it with a wet woolen blanket, damn that light is genuine!

In my final year of schooling, apart from the pressure that stemmed from meeting result expectations set by myself, teachers, and family. I frequently went to a prophetic church – where those that had the gift of prophecy could foresee the past, present, and future. I remember it vividly well – on this day I was with my mother and young sister when the prophetess by the name of Percia Ndlovu ordered me to stand up. Prophetess Percia spoke a word of prophecy in my life, a word whose roots have never been shaken from my life. As I stood amid the whole congregation – The prophetess spoke,

"You are the light of your family"

...I believed it.

I love the concept behind the light. Ever heard of the saying; "As you let your light shine brighter, you unconsciously give others permission to do the same". The world would have been so void if the light was absent. The light is just attractive and appealing in its nature.

Everybody wants to move to a place where there is light. It's like the epitome of life itself. Everybody has the potential to shine their light in their area of work. It can be a career, gift, sport, or success. It is undeniable that other people's light just seems to shine brighter than other people. This could be attributed to commitment, patience, resilience, attitude, or character. People whose light seems to shine brighter have one thing in common. They are the best version of themselves, they do not live their lives for approvals, they make the most out of that which they have, and it is their boldness to stay true to their identity that makes their light shine even brighter. The point of reference I use to pin-point bright-lighted people is the immense contribution that they bring, not only to their lives but to the greater good of humanity. They have a selfless spirit running in the fiber of their genes.

As a bright light with an attractive character,
It cannot be denied that not everybody who is attracted to my character has good intentions or will be of benefit. Oftentimes some seek to turn off my light, some seek to use it to enlighten their shadows and some seek to use it for their esteem-elevation.

Out of all the intentions, the one that almost chokes my breath is esteem-elevation. The person who creates a close intimate relationship with another person for the sake of their self-esteem elevation is most likely to be an abusive person. I know of so many great people who have passed away in the hands of their abusive partners.

As much as I respect everybody, not everybody has the right to speak into my life. Trust can never be thrust upon an individual; it is certainly a virtue that is earned.

The brighter the light the more the people that it attracts, the sustainability of the light lies in the firmness of character. It is the firmness of character that prolongs the lifespan of the light. It is this firmness that empowers others and unconsciously permits them to turn on their light.

Perhaps, as a reader who has been told you will never mount-up to anything. You have had your fair share of light neglected and attacked. Do you feel like you are bound by the psychological chains of human abuse? This is my heartfelt piece of motivation:

"People's unqualified opinions of you should end where the tip of your nose begins. Do not allow people's negative judgments to taint your self-reflection. Rather, give room for your attitude to define your altitude"

To all the bright lights, I say:

Keep on shining brighter!

May your soul so rest in eternal peace Prophetess Percia Ndlovu.

56
THE OVER-SIZE SHOE

Shoes are fascinating, if they could sing, I think the genre that would best suit some of our shoes is the 'Blues' simply because it will allow them to deeply express an element of sadness, abuse, and frustration that is imposed by some human legs.

Let's face it:

Some legs just find it difficult to find the fitting shoe-size.

The discomfort that comes with putting on an oversize shoe or a small size shoe is evident in the steps that are taken by the walking legs that are putting them on. Believe me when I say, by merely observing the steps taken and the facial expression, the size of the shoe seizes to be a secret, it is revealed to all. That's the power that is brought about by this discomfort.

I applaud the courage to take on the responsibility without complaining. It is good to tackle responsibility without shifting it. It speaks to one's maturity and sense of accountability. It is a very attractive quality. However, there is just enough measure of responsibility for everyone to tackle. The measure of the amount of responsibility tackled by an individual can be determined by physical strength, mental strength, emotional strength, and at times spiritual strength. A state of equilibrium must be achieved between these determinants and the amount of responsibility that is tackled. Tackling maximum responsibility can have drastic effects. Maximum responsibility has the potential to have drastic effects on one's physical, emotional, mental, and spiritual state of being. I call it maximum responsibility, but it is only fitting to call it human abuse.

The drive to achieve goals contributes to determining the amount of responsibility that we are willing to tackle. One who is living in a toxic abusive environment will be willing to overload themselves with maximum work so that they see themselves out of this environment. Their goal is to get to a safe place and this goal is driven so much by the harmful nature of their environment. It is this discomfort that ignites even a greater desire to tackle maximum responsibility so that ultimately, they can get to that safe place.

I choose to equate an oversize shoe to maximum responsibility, because of the discomfort that it causes. Maximum responsibility will harm a person's state of being thus curbing the progression in their lives. The pressure that is brought about by maximum responsibility can be a lot for any being to take in. This pressure could lead to alcoholism and depression which are the strong fasteners of the psychological chains of human abuse. Untangling these chains calls for a people that will see to it that responsibility is tackled but adequately and objectively.

Highly driven people and ambitious people are bound to push their work to extremes. Ambition is captivating and attractive; however, it must be treated with great care. I have witnessed the health of many brilliant people succumbing and suffering due to neglect that stems from the need to attain excellence. It is important to maintain a balance between attaining excellence and living a healthy lifestyle. Hard work should never rob you of enough sleep. Ambition should never rob you of a balanced diet. Neglect is in and of itself a form of self-mistreatment.

Do not allow hard work to bind you with the psychological chains of human abuse.

Take care of the one precious life that you have.

On the other hand, I choose to equate a small size shoe to meager responsibility. This shoe has just the same effect as an oversize shoe; it brings about discomfort on the legs and has the potential to affect the rhythm of walking. Meager responsibility is attributed to one who is lazy and reluctant to tackle their tasks. The result is they procrastinate, or they do not get to finish off their tasks. These are less productive people that abuse the employer because they get paid but struggle to carry out their tasks within the allocated time. This is a form of human abuse to the employer and should not be tolerated.

Laziness is such an unattractive quality; it is the thin line that lies between freedom and the continual perpetual tangling of the mind by the psychological chains of human abuse. The lazy one is most likely to go for the small shoes. He/She/They fail to attain total independence from a hard worker. The lazy one remains dependent on the breadwinner. It is easy for them to be manipulated, brainwashed, violated, and abused.

Teach the young minds to tackle just enough responsibility,

To keep walking forward...one needs to put on the fitting shoe size...no exceptions!

57
JUDGEMENT

It will be reasonable for someone to argue that; "If 'judgment' is wrong, then why do we have judges in the court of law?"

First and foremost, bear in mind the educational background of the judges in the court of law. These are not people that just wake up and choose to judge. They have been trained to professionally weigh the pros and cons of cases and to find the best verdict that will best suit different cases. Having judges in the court of law does not necessarily mean that justice has been served. For example, briberies are still used as tokens of silencing some judges. Again, there are courts of law that still see it fit and just to imprison people from the LGBTQI+ community.

In the eyes and minds of these people, they think justice is served if they imprison people for their sexuality. However, in the eyes of genuine love – they are wrong and ignorant. In a world where sexuality has evolved to such an extent that there are people that are born with two genitals (*hermaphrodites*) it will be 'ignorance' at best not to redeem such courts of law from continuously fastening humanity with the psychological chains of human abuse.

The kind of judgment I am referring to below is directed to one's sexual status in a religious context. I am not referring to the kind of judgment that is directed to criminals, drug traffickers, or human traffickers by the court of law.

The impact that religion has on humanity can never be argued. It forms the basis of decision-making for most people. So great is the impact of religion, it influences one's identity, self-worth, image, confidence, attitude, and perception of life. If religion has so much of an impact on humanity, then it can only make sense for religion to be anchored in the roots of abundant love. Love that never judges but Love that unifies.

The debate around the word judgment is one battle that I am not prepared to tackle in my guide, for the mere fact that people relate to this word differently. Over and above, I am certain that judgment within the religious corridors has brought about division and not unity. My issue with judgment lies so much in the intention that it radiates. Nevertheless, someone can judge with good intention, but the receiver of the judgment can still be offended regardless of the intention. Thus, offense that is brought about by judgment can ultimately result in division. It is not until the religious corridors are deeply anchored in abundant love that unity can be the foundation of religion.

My message is simple, yet fundamental; love should overshadow 'judgment'.

If the 'judgment' overtakes the love, then one can be certain that religion is heading on to a disastrous journey that is offensive and divisive. For a greater noble course, the religious leaders must preach the message of love to the masses.

Impartial love – love that knows no judgment – love that knows no discrimination.

To truly know and love God is to love the condemned, the under-estimated, the weak, and those that have been told they will mount up to nothing. It is this that will birth a refreshed and better perception of religion. The face of religion has been tainted by those that continue to condemn others unfairly. It has been dragged in the mud by those that see themselves as better and deserving of a place in heaven than other people.
Genuine love must refresh and rekindle unity and peace back into the religious corridors.

Humanity must not turn a blind eye to the human abuses that have been suffered due to the misconduct of religion. The suicides and depression cases that are attributed to the misconduct of religion are heart-breaking. The objective of religion should be to make people feel loved and welcomed. Failure to achieve this objective is failing humanity at large. Honestly, I am angered by the suicides that are attributed to the misconduct of religion. It is completely unacceptable. I will not rest until these are curbed and brought to a halt. Sadly, judgment in the name of Christianity has been the root cause of so many suicidal cases. It is not surprising that many openly gay people find it toxic to be in Church, simply because of the endless insults and judgments from the very same people that have been entrusted by God to spread a message of love to all people, indiscriminately so.

If God valued judgment more than love, he never would have said; "Out of the three things that will remain which are faith, hope and love, the greatest of these is love". (*1 Corinthians 13 verse 13*)

Isn't it the best irony that we have suicides within the corridors of a church? A place that is meant to preach love cannot be subjected to blood. It is unacceptable and inappropriate. I am calling out all facets of religion to stop becoming vehicles of human abuse. Young minds should not be exposed to such. It is intolerable. Human abuse that is experienced within the confines of the church is a definite killer of the human spirit.

The solution is:
LET LOVE LEAD!

58
THE UNATTAINABLE

Perfection is nothing but a fallacy that human beings aspire to. Human nature in and of itself is not designed to be flexible enough to work hard to attain perfection. It is but a fallacy that human beings wish to attain but they will never, they can be close to it but will never reach it.

In the light that perfection is unattainable, I hate it when abusers use the statement; 'Nobody is perfect' as a scapegoat to continuously perpetuate abusive behavior. It is completely irrational to inflict pain on a human being and still hide behind the veil of human beings not being perfect.

Abuse has got nothing to do with imperfection, but everything to do with selfishness. The act of willingly and intentionally mistreating other human beings is intolerable misconduct that is inhuman. One who has inhuman behavioral tendencies cannot be deemed as imperfect, this is a monster that breeds danger for humanity. What do you do to a monster? Do you allow a monster to just continue preying on humanity because of the inability to be perfect? No.

A monster is kept in a cage and ostracized from contact with humanity. A monster is not fit to be part of the human family. A monster is isolated from humanity. A monster remains a monster even after using make-up. Not until the monster decides to submit their will to be courageous enough to see their weakness and be willing to change their attitude towards others – that they can be fit to be part of humanity. The monster needs to have a greater will to change so that their mind can be transformed. Mind-transformation is what will qualify the monster to be a part of the human family. Until then, the ideology of perfection cannot be used to justify the atrocious actions of monsters.

The ideology of perfection is fit for human beings, not monsters that continuously and intentionally perpetrate abusive behavior.

Imperfection is an ideology that is fit in cases such as:

- Failure on a particular activity
- Mispronunciation of words
- Late coming
- Being forgetful

I still accentuate that humanity should refrain from using statements such as 'Nobody is perfect' to justify the atrocious acts of hurting others.

You are imperfect for the mispronunciation of words. However, you are a monster for abusing another human being.

The distinction is:

Imperfect beings are tolerable,

Monsters are intolerable.

59
THE POWER OF ENTHUSIASM

To a young immature mind, it can be one of the scariest experiences to have hair on the most unexpected part of the body. It can be a blow to one's confidence to wake up to a face that is sprouting up of pimples. I am convinced...puberty can be one of the most terrifying experiences if there is a lack of knowledge about it.

Unfortunately, this experience can never be avoided. It is part of human nature that is necessary for growth and maturity. Without puberty, there will be no growth. There are no shortcuts to growth and maturity. If the adolescent stage has the potential to lower one's confidence - Then human abuse can be a by-product of failing to cope with this growth stage.

Irrespective of the changes stimulated by puberty, a young person must have a reason to wear a smile as they - peacefully and with understanding embrace all these bodily changes. Pimples can undress a young person's face of their smile if the young person is not strong enough to cope with the changes. The impact that puberty has on a young mind is enormous, it even affects the thinking patterns and sound decision-making process of the young mind.

Mood swings are a critical element in this teenage growth stage; these refer to the sudden change of emotions. At this stage, emotions become unpredictable, at the blink of an eye, the happiest soul becomes the angriest human being. In a short space of time, the most talkative soul becomes the most silent.

These unpredictable emotions are still vented out by a human being that has a will. Therefore, as much as the body chemicals produced by this stage have a role to play. It will be ignorance to shift the blame on body chemicals when behavior accountability should be at the forefront of blame.

These mood swings if taken to extremes will result in the propping up of the victims and perpetrators of human abuse. Teenagers should be responsible enough to be able to harness an attitude of self-control when it comes to their emotions. Self-discipline will see them through. Self-discipline is not a once-off achievement; it is a process – one that calls for commitment, listening skill, and patience.

Failure to be in control of these mood swings will result in adults that are either very angry or short-tempered people or adults that have low self-esteem and a poor self-image.

These are the very concomitants that result in great exposure to abuse and mistreatment. Using genuine love as a solution to curb gender-based violence must be infused with some sense of practicality. It considers the impact of the growth phase that is an unavoidable path for the young person. The solution rather remains in finding answers to the question; What is the best way to navigate the social shoals of the stage of puberty so that ultimately it is not an obstruction or triggering of abusive tendencies, but in such a manner that it is embraced with care and understanding?

It is an undefiled truth - people perish because of a lack of know-how. Education about poverty can still be revised and improved. How about linking the education on puberty with the realities of human abuse? Linking the education that schools provide on puberty with the agony of abuse holds much more substance for a young mind, it is ideal for the cultivation of an abuse-free generation. I strongly believe; education has value, only if it can produce independent minds that can tackle complex problems. It is for this noble reason that those that are actively involved with educating young minds should do so with enthusiasm, passion, and zeal, knowing that they are actively at work freeing the chained minds of the young so that they become free and independent and have the capacity to make sound decisions.

Conjoining the education on puberty with the knowledge on the psychological chains of human abuse means linking the negative effects that puberty can have on the mind and the bad concomitants birthed by these effects such as loss of self-worth which triggers mistreatment of oneself and others.

This is a sure way of grooming adults that will understand that puberty is just an affirmation that one is becoming a fully grown-up human being. Puberty should not lead to loss of one's confidence and should therefore be fully embraced and cherished with understanding. It should not expose one to the realities of human abuse - it should just be allowed to take its course naturally as it was designed to be.

Instill enthusiasm when educating these young minds.

Remember...

Knowledge is power, but enthusiasm pulls the switch!

60
RUN-AWAY

The principle of diffusion suggests that particles can only move from a high concentrated area to a low concentrated area. Taking in this truth - means that concerning an object, the heat particles produced by a fire can only move from a high concentrated area to a low concentrated area. That is, the closer one moves towards the fire, the more intense the heat. The further one moves away from the fire, the less intense the heat.

In the same way, the closer that one gets to the abuser, the more pain one feels. The further that one moves away from the abuser the lesser the pain. It takes will and effort to decide to draw closer to the fire. Nobody can force one to take this step. If it is the love that keeps this fire burning that attracts one to draw closer to the fire, then one is taking the risk of burning in their quest to draw close to it. If it is the cold and the strong wind experienced, that causes one to draw closer to the fire, then one can be lured by the heat that the fire produces, but ultimately burning is a high possibility that comes with the continuous drawing closer to the fire. For example, there are a lot of circumstances that cause the victim of abuse to be continuously attached to the perpetrator. It could be circumstantial love and the insecurities such as inability to be independent and fear of letting go. However, the conviction that there is a lot of pain that is caused by attachment to the perpetrator will see the victim through.

Nobody likes pain. It takes away one's peace and happiness. Isn't it mind-boggling that; abuse encapsulates all the characteristics of pain, but some choose to stay in it against all odds? Perhaps, one of the main reasons could be that it comes in the form of pretense and superficial love. Perhaps, it could be the materialism that comes with it or it could just be the fickle hope that things will change. Either way, these reasons are not enough to justify the reasons to stick with a relationship of such a nature. One must be very careful not to run the risk of being addicted to the pain. The pain experienced in an abusive relationship may in a subtle way suggest to the victim that they are important in the life of the perpetrator or the perpetrator cannot live without them.

The pain that comes with burning because of drawing closer to the fire is much greater than the comfort that lures the victim to it. The pain is much greater than the cold weather and the strong winds encountered. It could ultimately lead to death. Therefore, nothing is enough to justify the gesture of drawing too close to the fire. It is a dangerous mission that can only lead to drastically painful effects. Love can be very attractive, and winds can be a pain to take, but these should not be convincing enough for one to decide to draw too close to the fire. After feeling the heat of the fire, one must be convinced that drawing closer can only lead to a deadly end.

Make the right decision and move away from the comfort of the fire. Your life is worth more than the comfort of the fire.

One, who has experienced the intensity of heat, does not behave like a toddler who just ignorantly goes to touch the fire. One who knows how hot the fire is, stands in a better position to raise awareness and educate others by warning them not to stay too close to the fire for fear that they will burn. One who knows how hot the fire is - is not lured by anything to draw close to the fire. Even if they are in the cold, they would rather prefer the warmth of the blanket than the fire.

I know the intensity of the fire; therefore, I will not stand aside for others to burn while I watch them helplessly.

I choose to be the fire rescuer.

A firm decision to stay away from the fire means that one must endure the pains of the cold. It means that one must be prepared to face the discomfort that is brought about by the cold. Only a strong mind and perseverance in the cold will save one from burning. It is not easy, but possible, with practice and an awakened sense of awareness

An awakened sense of awareness means that a young mind is prepared not to succumb to the traps that promise heaven and earth at a cost of their happiness, identity, self-worth, and dignity. It means respecting oneself enough not to fall into the trap of being lured by a lack of material possessions. It means being bold enough to say NO!

Thank heavens it is warm but never forget that fire has the potential to burn you to ashes as well so...DO NOT JUST BE LURED TO IT...for ALL THAT GLITTERS IS NOT GOLD!

61
SORRY

The uttering of the word sorry can be very comforting. The first big fight I had as a young child was because after unintentionally hurting me with a ball, the person could not see the need to say sorry to me. The inferno within me began to blaze! As I felt that I have been wronged and rightfully deserved to have the word sorry uttered to my ears.

'Sorry' is an affirmation of care, concern, and empathy. It shows remorse for the other person's emotions. The world would be a very cold place if the word 'sorry' was non-existent. Two different people may say the word 'sorry'. The distinction between these two is the motive and meaning given to the word. One person may say the word 'sorry' with an impure or inauthentic motive. Another person may say the same word with a pure and authentic motive.

Beyond the saying of the word sorry, some actions are in alignment with corrective behavior so that the word is given meaning. Failure to couple this word with corrective behavior cripples the meaning of saying the word sorry. A meaningless sorry is better kept unsaid. It is deceptive and it does not tolerate or consider the emotions of the other party.

The comfort and peace that stems from the word sorry are amazing. It is just fitting for one who has been hurt to receive the word sorry. Most importantly humanity must understand that the value is not so much in saying the word sorry. The value is in the intention that is attached to the uttering of this word. It is the intention that remains long after the word has been uttered. It is the intention that will determine whether the same action will be repeated without a care of the other person's feelings or not. A meaningless sorry is better kept unsaid. If the intention is not genuine then there is no value in saying the word - sorry. What is the point of saying sorry if the abuser intentionally continues mistreating the victim?

Deep interrogation of the motive of one's sorry is necessary. Most importantly, it is vital to not just pay lip service but to mean every word of the phrase "I am sorry". It adds to one's self-worth and self-esteem. The psychological chains of human abuse can only start untangling if the call to attach meaning to the word 'sorry' is adhered to.

Failure to attach meaning to the word 'sorry' is very detrimental.

Sorry is like the glue that mends two broken pieces, however for this glue to be effective it must have the original qualities of a shoe mending glue. Otherwise, the two sides will remain separate and not unified. A pure motive is one of these qualities; Meaning is another of these qualities. Without the fitting qualities, the glue that is used to mend the shoes remains ineffective.

The fact remains:

Uttering the word 'sorry' is an effortless act in comparison to the agony that one must endure. Thus, it can only be an effective act if it is coupled with a genuine heart. The pains that Joyce Meyer had to endure in the hands of her father were insurmountable, from her book she iterates that she was raped multiple times; however, she, with time was able to gain the strength to genuinely forgive and forget.

So effective was this act of forgiveness, it was coupled with so much meaning because her father did not continuously repeat abusing his child.

He stopped after being genuinely forgiven

The countless number of 'sorry' that is received by the victims of human abuse daily is shocking. Human abusers are good at uttering this word to their partners. To them it's become like a Justin Bieber song, they can just sing it to the victim anytime without meaning it. In other words, the abuser knows the value in saying the word – sorry - but they struggle to give value to the word. This is displayed in the repetition of their actions. As they continue to abuse the victim regardless of having said the word sorry.

Perpetual cycles of human abuse followed by meaningless sorriest episodes and quests for forgiveness have become the daily realities of our lives.

Positively breaking this cycle calls for the mind-transformation of the abuser. If only the abuser can start saying the word sorry with genuine intention, then the cycle of abuse can be broken much faster. The intention that governs the word sorry needs to be authentic and meaningful. The effects of a meaningful apology far-much outweigh the effects of a million meaningless apologies.

"Sorry can only be the best-dressed word if it puts on the full armor of an authentic and meaningful intention".

- Brightwell Dube

62
AWARDS

One cannot help but long for the excitement and recognition that comes with achievements, accolades, and awards. The feeling that graces winning these is great. It is one feeling whose effects will always be resurrected even in the after-moment.

Awards are a great recognition of the unrelenting restless effort of a person. They are a great stimulator of energy and ambition. They propel a person into a forward motion. The only time that awards can become toxic is when they can become the tape measure that is used to measure our potential. A life that says it's either an award or you are not good, is pressurizing. As much as an award is a symbol of recognition. It is not wise to use it as a criterion in sassing out the potential that someone holds. Awards can be used as badges of mediocrity in the sense that they are symbols that are because of being judged by consensus of what is known, good and acceptable. They take away the element of uniqueness. They take away the individualism in people's work.

It can be heartbreaking for a multi-award-winning artist to drop the standard of winning awards. This could pose a threat to their career. It could potentially result in bad publicity. This can ultimately break the greatest artist of all time. Some suicides by artists can be attributed to this drop in the standard of scooping awards. It is that heartbreaking and painful. Depression can certainly be the result. Isolation can seemingly be the best solution. The question that faces the artist who after a series of winning awards is now failing to win awards is - "How do you make a comeback?" If treaded with much desperation the artist will soon find themselves having to endure the pains of human abuse to make this 'comeback' a possibility. Some give their bodies to the jury that is connected to the winning of awards for favors. This I must say is a reality in the entertainment industry.

Don't get me wrong…it is good to win awards, but the ideology behind winning these should not be warped. It certainly should not bind humanity to the psychological chains of human abuse.

Awards are satisfying; they come with a lot of satisfaction and gratification. However, one must be genuinely deserving of an award, they should not lose their dignity in-order to attain one.

Awards should be instrumental in the acknowledgment of those that are at the forefront of fighting the scourge of human abuse. I am talking of all the fraternities, from authors to activists, musicians, counselors, psychiatrists, and motivational speakers. These awards will encourage all artists from all facets of life to increase their involvement in the battle against human abuse.

Please note, by 'encouraging', I am not insinuating that artists will help fight the scourge of human abuse because of awards, I am saying they will be affirmed that they are doing the right and noble thing for humanity; as such they should continue.

Here is my proposal:
How about a night with fighters of gender-based violence, we can call it –
"Love with a noble course"
Stop Gender-Based Violence Movement!

A once-off in a year event of recognizing, highlighting, and raising awareness on gender-based violence issues - Infused with poets, contemporary dancers, musicians, motivational speakers, and authors –an event like this will positively contribute to curbing the escalating levels of human abuse. Think about the impact that will be created by an event of this caliber in encouraging the young generation to be active and vocal partakers in this battle with human abuse. With social media doing the rounds, an event of such a caliber cannot be paralleled.

Its impact will be historical and timeless.
It will certainly go down the history books.
An event like this will create dialogues and encourage social cohesion among young people. Young people must also be acknowledged for their resilience and those among their peers that are poets and motivational speakers should embrace this event with performances that will be significant for the night.

Not winning awards should never be equated to failure or a lack of potential. If winning awards is a symbol of being judged by consensus for what is good, acceptable, and enjoyable. Then not winning means the power of the uniqueness of what has not won should not be weighed down or degraded. For in its respect, it is still impactful, good, acceptable, and enjoyable.

I love this truth; I feel like saying it again –
"The power of the uniqueness of what has not won should never be under-estimated - For in its respect it is still impactful, good, acceptable and enjoyable".
- Brightwell Dube

63
INDEPENDENCE

As I took the firm decision to move out of my parents' house to stay in my own rental space, I felt a certain element of freedom. Freedom that knows no boundaries, Freedom to finally dance to my tune and play by my own rules – Independence creates room for growth and maturity.

Independence remains idealistic if the courage to think on one's feet is not pursued. The independent one must have the courage to stand alone and positively tackle complex problems.

The title of being a parent can be very empowering. It means that one has the power to control the activities, lives, behaviors, and attitudes of a child. However, be cautious: The heavy hand of control that a parent has on their child can be very detrimental to the child's well-being.

When taken to extreme measures, this sense of control can be very toxic to both, the parent, and the child. One cannot expect a parent that is raising a 10-year-old child to instill the same amount of control on a 24- year-old. It is not healthy for both the parent and the child. Room for growth and embracing oneself should not be shattered. A heavily controlling hand can only cripple the child's ability to think on their own. It builds an unhealthy dependency syndrome in the mind of the child. Reflecting – I promulgated - education has value only if it produces independent minds that can tackle complex problems. Thus, after educating them, it is more effective to sit back as a parent and trust in the value of the education that they have acquired and the principles you have instilled in them when they were young: Let them go.

Psychologically, some parents find it difficult to let go of their children even if they are at a stage when they are grown up enough to take care of themselves. It could be the fear of the unknown and it could be the fear of being alone. The pangs of detachment may be painful, but at some point, in time, it is necessary for the healthy upkeep of a relationship. To overcome all these fears, professional advice can be pursued from counselors and psychologists. One good friend of mine that helps you overcome these fears is the author of the self-help guide – Magic Mirror Mind –Juan de Beer Odendal.

The undefiled truth is:

The heavy hand of control of the parent can only cripple the child's search for their own identity and therefore the child's ability to make a sound decision becomes painful if not an impossible mission. Life is not crossing a football field. It is very tough and only when the child comprehends this truth, then, they will strive to stand on their own two feet. Think about it, the parent is not going to hold the hand of the child till eternity. If this is true, then it can only make sense for the parent to let go of the child's hand just at the right stage, especially if the child has acquired an education and sound values. It is this heavy hand of control that parents continue putting on the child even at the wrong stage that ensures that crippled adults are propped up. The result is adults that cannot think and that will continuously need the parent to think for them. It becomes like a parent- addiction-scheme, where one is solely dependent on the parent for life. Letting go of the hand of the child just at the right stage will teach them to be independent, to make sound decisions on their own. It is not easy for the psychological chains of human abuse to entangle the mind of a child whose hand is not firmly holding on to the parent because independence teaches the child:

Do not be afraid to be alone.

Prepare them to be truly independent by now and again giving them room to decide which works for them. Let them be involved in the decision-making that involves the making of decisions that are central to families, the nation, and the community. Action their suggestions and show them, their voice is valuable – they are an assertive mouthpiece of the decision-making process. It is this that will ensure that they are not just independent but responsible, self-disciplined, and accountable in their independence as well.

I am not ignorant of the fact that some children did not have access to formal education. Thus, I intentionally did not use any connotation to the type of education obtained. The reason being education is not only acquired in a classroom set-up. Parents can educate a child, the community can educate a child, Circumstances and experiences can educate as well. It is the priority of the child to gather the value in every form of education to see to it that it prepares them for an independent mind that can tackle complex problems.

The hand of comfort is good but a temporary one; it provides a short-sighted sense of relief.

The young minds must know that there comes a time when one must -Let go of the hand that pampers them.

Experience what it means to live life...BE INDEPENDENT!

64
THE CELL-PHONE BUCKET

Social media has become the mouthpiece of humanity. The purpose of the mouth is slowly getting replaced by the evident heavy influence that social media has on society. In the frame of my mind, I am picturing a family that is treated to a dinner table. What shocks me most at this dinner table is the loud silence that is caused by the heavy usage of their cellphones. The social aspect of humanity is getting neglected and abused every day. We are slowly progressing to becoming human-robot machines that are controlled by our technological gadgets.

Social media is good, but like anything else, a balance is vital. The superficiality in the lives of the people displayed by social media can be very deceptive. The idea that social media pushes is that life is about materialism. Rarely do people post-natural pictures of themselves while in pain or hurting. It is always smiley and happy faces. This builds up a warped view of life, especially to the young mind. It facilitates the impression that; they are important and acceptable only when they post materialistic pictures. It may give them some sense of worth and shortly elevate their self-esteem but ultimately deep down they will not be redeemed of their deep wounded scars. Superficiality is like an imaginary life, it is easy, fake, and a waste of time.

My advice: Post the pictures, but do not forget that realism is important. It is important to also maintain the human-social-facial interaction aspect of humanity.

If so, much social influence can be held by social media, then humanity has the potential to suffer human abuse as a result. If the young mind can only feel good and a sense of meaning after getting a hundred likes on their Facebook page, then the human family is surely heading up to a socially crippled generation. Social beings cannot neglect an aspect as vital as the social aspect of life. A parent can never rear a child and heavily use social media. That will mean that the child that is reared-up by this parent will grow up as a socially crippled child because the parent could not communicate with them. This is a form of abuse to the child. The parent needs to give the child a fair share of social food so that they build their social muscle and in introspect the child does the same to their child. The absence of socializing is crippling and killing the human family.

The cell-phone bucket should be one of the most important items that families should pack when going for dinner. It should be positioned right in the middle of the dinner table.

Everybody should conform to the rule...

Chuck away the gadgets in the cell-phone bucket...EAT... SOCIALIZE...BE HUMAN!

65
MAN-HOOD

What makes a real man?

Is it character, wealth, strength, cultural-initiation ceremonies, or power?

The unjust and unwise unpacking of this question has triggered so many abusive behaviors. Men are still widely perceived as a symbol of strength especially in the African continent. An African boy child is oftentimes channeled and pressurized into this short-sighted ideology of what consensus generally thinks a man should be.

This is the reason why:

Most African men are so hideous about their sexual identity. To them, it is a guilty trip to go against their mother's words. You will be surprised at the amount of control that an African woman will want to have on their boy-child. It is this that causes these men to continue falling into a pit of depression that is intricately designed by their mothers. I have seen African men choosing to love their mothers more than their partners. I have seen them tremble at the thought of opening about their sexuality because of what their mothers will think of them.

African women:

"Give your boy child room to breathe and to make their own life choices.

Stop putting your sons at crossroads of choosing between loving you or their partners".
Stop making the boys prove their manhood!
Stop suffocating the boys…
Let them embrace their identity
Let them choose what is best for them sexually.
Give them room to breathe,
Do not force them to be who they are not
Do not pressurize them into preferring that which they do not love.
Applaud their courage to be unique and still be counted.

The ideas that are attached to the concept of manhood can be very misleading. One begins to wonder if this concept should be subjected to provision, strength, or mentality. The worldly projection of a man is a strong figure, a provider and that is not sentimental or expressive of feelings of hurt and pain. It is a very misleading projection that only seeks to fasten the psychological chains of human abuse.

The truth is, every human being has the potential to cry, be sentimental and be vulnerable. It comes with the territory of being fully human. Even media still largely portrays a misleading concept of roles, sex, and gender. I speak of media because it is a tool whose influence on the human mind can never be paralleled to any tool. The influence that media has on the human mind is magnanimous. Thus, mass-mind-transformation can only be activated by instilling changes and improvements to this tool. This is a platform that humanity should take advantage of by portraying open-minded people that will convey an unorthodox message of roles, sex, and gender. This is the answer to curb even the brutal killings of people because of their sexuality. Human abuse has seen escalating levels of such incidents. It is intolerable and at most pathetic to have atrocious killings of humanity that are attributed to sexuality. Not today…Not tomorrow…Not in the 21st century or ever…STOP THE KILLING!

One cannot help but begin to wonder if the warped portrayal of manhood should not be attributed to a continuous lack of knowledge about sexuality. If humanity only has a limited approach to what a man should be and what is expected of a man, then it can only make sense for the minds to drift into a continuous lack of enlightenment and ignorance. Taking time to open our minds on this subject by gaining knowledge is vital. In the mind of the killer, it is the limited knowledge and their views that will cause them to do such. It is inhuman and foolish to kill others on the grounds of sexuality. Mass-mind-transformation should portray manhood in such a manner that it can never be attributed to such. Not in my world...

To gain knowledge on the subject of manhood, one should take time to tune in to radio stations such as 702 with open-minded African-men presenters like Aubrey Masango who largely explore the subject of manhood.

What goes through the young minds when every corner of the world is lamenting abuse because of sexual identity? Is this not going to result in more fear and suicides by young people? Young people who feel sexually different can only resort to suicide because they fear the treatment that they will be subjected to in their respective societies and families.

They may all have the same private part, but they are unique; some prefer apples, and some prefer bananas.

Stop generalizing and respect everybody's sexual identity!

66
THE AGONY OF A BLACK CHILD

No child can better-tell a story of being subjected to a lot of human abuse because of sexuality than a black African child. The extremes in which family, community, and society will take this child in the hope that they wake up a different person are completely uncalled for. I know it all...from the drinking of bitter medicine to getting cleansed in almost all the rivers. Only a strong mind will cause this child not to succumb to suicide; because believe me when I say, the pain is just too much to take in.

Opening-up about one's sexuality in the African context could be a matter of life or death. I still do not understand the reason behind treating sexuality as a separate entity from the individual, it's like something that we buy or impose. Just like a boy child can never choose to be sexually attracted to a girl child. It comes naturally; it is a natural sexual feeling. The same goes for a boy child that is sexually attracted to another boy child. It comes naturally; it is not a matter of choice, but nature taking its course.

Let it be known:

You do not buy or choose your sexuality, it comes naturally.

My bitter experience with sexuality has allowed me to discover the fact that:

"Human sexual attraction is a gift that exists naturally among all of humanity, indiscriminately so - between a boy and a girl, a boy and a boy, a girl and a girl. However, the desire to sexually explore with the other party is what defines a person's sexual identity".

Therefore, I concluded that:

Sexual identity is not defined by sexual attraction; rather it is determined by desire.

'Desire cannot be imposed'
One cannot be forced to have a desire for something; it must deeply resonate with a person's heart – otherwise, it will be forced-love.

Heavens know what goes through the mind of the child who is subjected to pains in the name of their sexuality – something they do not buy or choose. This is a sad state of mind for any child. The psychological chains of human abuse can strongly fasten their bind on such a young mind.

The courage to educate humanity and restoring the young mind that has drowned in these deep waters of abuse is a call not to be ignored. The relevant organizations should see to it that no stone is left unturned when it comes to holding the hand of a child that has been rejected, abandoned, and traumatized because of sexual identity.

Now, is the right time to rewrite the story of a black African child. Now is the time to restore that which an African child has always been deprived of – the freedom to express their sexuality without any obstructions or painful episodes.
It starts with you.

It is not my objective to override any religion's views on this subject. However, one thing I know for sure is that no religion will support the brutal killing and abuse of humanity on any grounds. It is completely uncalled for and should be curbed at all costs. Killing and abuse can never be the solution. It only strips away the dignity, integrity, and self-worth of humanity. The only time I detest being human is when I continuously come across such despicable actions. I for one cannot stand these abuses. I despise them.

The progression of time has taught us that, human beings are different. In the early stages of a young child, one can never deny that signs of being different are displayed by a young child. It is denial at best, to override this truth. It will be ignorance at bliss to say that there is something wrong with the child. Lack of knowledge will second that there is something wrong with such a child...but the truth is - the child is a fearfully and wonderfully crafted creation.

It is warped views and stereotypes that stand against the truth that everybody is wonderfully and fearfully created with a unique purpose.

The dilemma of a black child is in your hands, guard your words and actions for they can be the very concomitants that will keep a black child in chains.

Colonization, apartheid, and slavery were enough!
OUR LIVES MATTER!

67
THE POWER OF MENTAL STRENGTH

Mind-power is the bridge that allows one to cross to a different realm of life. It is the ticket that can take you to that place of happiness while in misery. It is the transporter that can give you a fulfilling experience of what it is to be at one of the world's wonders such as Mount Everest or the Eiffel Tower or Table Mountain while in the dusty roads of KwaMashu.

Mental strength is the key to healing most of the illnesses that are faced by humanity. It is not so much the illness that is a problem - it is the mentality around the sickness that activates the healing process. This explains the reason why by merely taking a pill with a package that is written painkillers, even if it is not a painkiller, one can get healed of the pain. It is the mentality around the word 'painkiller' that produces the healing enzymes in the body of the one that is ill. Examples of effective books that delve deeper into the techniques of using mind power for healing abuse trauma include – Magic Mirror Mind by Juan de Beer Odendal and Mind Power by John Kehoe.

John Kehoe suggests that the impact created by one who physically goes to the gym and uses the machines, instruments, and tools to exercise is as equally important as one who uses the power of imagination to go to the gym and exercise within the realm of their mind.

One might not physically go to the gym and exercise, however, by using the power of imagination to gym and exercise – the results will be the same.

That is the power of mental strength.

You will be surprised at the impact of mind power techniques if you effectively, wisely, persistently, and genuinely use them. My success in becoming an author is attributed to the use of some of these techniques. This is my story in brief:

During my tertiary studies, I stayed in Braamfontein for three and a half years with a man called Cecil Robert Jordaan. On my first day in his house, I was welcomed by a countless number of books. You would swear he had turned his house into a library. The books were not just plenty, but they were neatly arranged.

As I cleaned this house every day; I immersed myself in these books. Taking them in, like one who discovers a treasure of a well, would gallop their deep-seated thirst for water in a desert. I read, I read, and I read until I began imagining my name on the front of the book cover. This self-help guide is a product of the power of imagination and affirmation. As I imagined, I also affirmed the universe that whatever I desire and keep in my heart, I shall conceive it.

It works – the universe will conspire in your favor if you believe.

The atmosphere or the setting of our environment becomes central in igniting deep-seated desires that have always been there, but that we were unaware of – blinded by the unfamiliar settings we found ourselves in.

- A musical atmosphere ignites a desire of singing,
- An athletic atmosphere ignites a desire to be fit,
- An atmosphere of praise and worship ignites a desire to pray.
- A book-filled atmosphere ignites a desire to write.

The energy of the book-filled room encapsulated the deep-seated desire within me to delve into the wisdom of these books. As I consistently did, I was getting prepared for my writing adventure and here I am – enjoying the ups and downs of writing.

Mental strength calls for a greater will to think positively. The mental damage that is a result of being abused is a greater call for using techniques of mind power to heal. In my quest to heal the physical abuse I endured at the hands of a stranger who beat me up for no reason in an orphanage. In my quest to heal the emotional abuse I endured at the hands of those that could not accept my sexuality. In my quest to heal the spiritual abuse I endured in the church – I discovered that mind power techniques are effective. Most significantly I found out the truth that healing is a journey – a process that calls for greater commitment and resilience.

Abuse can cause a big dreamer to settle for less because it just deters the determination that drives the mind. It is the active use of mental strength that will ignite a refreshed courage and affirm the victory of the victim's battlefield with brutal experiences. No pill is taken for mental strength; it is activated by reflecting on positive thoughts and feeding the mind with powerful self-help guides such as '**Untangled' 'The Psychological Chains Of Human abuse**'. One's intrinsic motivation and drive to improve must be actively at work.

If mental strength can heal the sick and pro-long the old-aged, then it can be a useful tool to keeping one safe from the pangs of human abuse. It is not easy, it takes practice.

Unrelenting and persistent practice to strengthen the mental muscle starts by affirming positivity into life's situations.

Healing begins in the realm that governs the mind.

The mind will then dissipate the healing energy to every part of the body.

A HEALTHY MIND IS A HEALTHY BODY!

68
EXPECTATIONS

I have seen the anguishing pain that is a result of being disappointed because the expectations that a parent had for their children were not met. The only way to avoid these pains is to consciously guard the expectations that one has for the child. Expectations create an imaginary world – a world of false hope. A parent that holds their child at birth should not put a lot of expectations on this infant, because it is these expectations that will haunt them if that child grows to become a different person from what the parent had expected. Expectations should be open in the sense that, the parent should acknowledge the individualism and uniqueness of this infant at birth.

It is this conscious guard of expectations that will see to it that the parent will still love their child indiscriminately, despite the decisions that the child makes later in their life.

I have seen and observed the mother sing praises to their boy infant who has not even had an anchored identity. The mother heart-fully looks at their child and iterates that the boy must be married to an ambitious and hard-working woman, she continues singing praises of the expectations that she has for the child. The boy must be a lawyer and have a lot of children so that she can be a grandmother to someone.

The dangers behind such utterances and expectations are:

- After discovering that the boy is gay, it will be very painful for this mother to accept their child's sexuality.

- Upon discovering that the boy does not want children, it will be very agonizing for the mother to accept and respect their child's decision.

- If the boy resorts to being a cleaner as his life-time career, the mother will be heartbroken by her boy's career choice.

- In the case that the son gets married to a lazy woman, the mother will rather encourage their son to walk out of this marriage.

The above scenario suggests that the mother is tormented not so much by the boy's decision, but the mother is tormented by the failure of the boy's decisions to meet the expectations they had for him.

Lesson is:

Parents should not raise the bar of the expectations they have for their child too high. They must bear in mind that the child is unique, and their decisions thereof must be respected even if they do not agree with them or prefer them.

Expectations can be the driving force that causes one to tap into the best of their ability. It has the power to ignite passion, ambition, and determination. On the other hand, it has the power to create unnecessary pressure. It can be very depressing if taken to extremes.

Without a shadow of a doubt, the expectations that fans hold for those in the limelight are great and at most pressurizing. For those in the public eye - It is not about maintaining the standard that they see fit for them anymore, but it's about maintaining the standard that will be judged as good and reasonable by their fans. It's like their own life is not theirs anymore – their supporters are certainly a part and parcel of their lives. Impressing their fans becomes the heartbeat of efforts. It becomes the epitome of their hard work.

As motivating as it may seem, the effects of great expectations can be toxic. The human cruelty encountered today can be attributed to great expectations. It is the pressure to impress that is a by-product of these expectations that poses a huge problem. Life becomes an externally controlled adventure. If not self-controlled the effect of these expectations could cause one to succumb to depression and isolation. One cannot be blind to the alcohol and drug abuse that is created by the failure to live up to expectations. It boxes one into a life that is far from reality. Realism supports that expectations must be met, but at the same time leaves room for failures to take part without resistance.

Resistance to one's failure is a sure way to molding one over-confident and arrogant human being. A balanced state of confidence is possible, to a human being who is not blind to their weaknesses. Resistance to weakness and failure is an enemy to overcoming. It does not leave room for one to overcome. There is freedom in the acceptance of one's weaknesses. There is suffering in the resistance of one's weaknesses.

Arrogance is the best friend of resistance - it seeks its way and never leaves room for correction. Humility is the best friend of freedom - it is selfless and leaves room for correction
CHOOSE HUMILITY!

69
FORCED-LOVE

Love is a natural flow.
Love cannot be forced.

The idea of forced love implies that a human being is forced to love another human being. One's will to love is not respected. That is, one must love despite their will. Relationships of forced love continue to entangle the human mind with the psychological chains of human abuse. Forced love is a phenomenon that is still prevalent in certain cultures. Some even go to the length of joining the children at birth. The child grows up with a husband or wife that was already chosen for them at birth.

The result of forced love is an unhappy human being that is not genuinely involved in a marriage or a relationship with their chosen partner. This is a form of human abuse because it seizes to respect the other person's will.

Human relationships that have progressed to becoming obligatory are very toxic. Humanity should cultivate relationships that seek to instill respect and keep a clear line of individualism. Love another human being, but still have the courage to breathe and live normally even after that human being is not with you. I have seen it with parental love. It's like some parents want to live their lives through their children. It's like a parent that comes from a family of doctors who expects the child to follow the doctrine of being a doctor against the child's will. The child must have the passion to be a doctor. The child must willingly want to pursue the same doctrine. It is a call that should be answered by the child - the call should not be answered by the parent or the relatives on behalf of the child. It can only be human abuse if the child is forced to do what they do not have a passion for.

You cannot force a young adult that is in love with John to love Marble. The relationship of forced love does not bear any fruit for those involved in the relationship. It is one bitter hell of a ride.

The problem in learning to love someone is that you do not have any choice, it's either you love this person, you are indifferent, or you hate them. The hatred that stems from loving someone forcefully will escalate to numerous episodes of abuse. In a matter of time, one of the parties involved in a forced relationship will become a victim and or perpetrator of human abuse. The hatred of the other person and frustration of the relationship will bear fruits of mistreatment. The result is a nasty abusive experience that requires one of the parties to call it quits.

Passion can never be imposed upon an individual, it must emanate from within one's soul. For example, one who becomes a doctor, not because they had a passion for it but because they were forced into the medical fraternity – will always be miserable even on duty because the long hours of helping sick patients is not a calling that they resonate with. It is not something that gives them a reason to wake up in the morning because they were forced into it.

It will not be surprising that the standard of work produced by this doctor will not be good – patients will die at the care of this doctor because they are in a forced job position. It is not what they solely wanted for life.

Young people should follow their passion; they should not be forced into job positions or relationships. It is this that will shield them from the psychological chains of human abuse and bear fruits in their line of work or relationships.

For one to be truly fruitful in any line of work - passion should be instilled. If there is no passion, there can never be productivity. Productivity is a by-product of passion and a greater will to perform an activity. It is not ideal for humanity to be forced to love and have a passion for any activity. Passion comes from within; it is intrinsically driven. Parents cannot live their lives and find meaning in their lives through the life of their child - it is inappropriate. The parent's respect for the child's dreams implies that the parent honors the child's passion and vision for life. It will be very limiting for the child to succumb to the passion and vision that the parent has for them. The child may look at it as respecting and honoring the parent's wishes, I call it self-mistreatment.

A child should honor and respect their parent. However, this respect should not be sacrificial of their passion, talent, skills, future career, or vision. The decision that they make with regards to what they do in the future is a cornerstone of their happiness, not the parent's happiness. Therefore, it can only make sense for the parent to respect their child's decision in this regard.

Love is not sacrificial or forceful - it is patient, caring, and kind.

70
TRUST

The core reason why so many leadership fraternities are breaking down is that power is no longer earned but thrust upon the shoulders of those who cannot influence others. We have witnessed companies such as the VBS Bank in South Africa falling to its knees because of looting. Honestly, the trust that entities had for this bank was largely betrayed due to the despicable action of looting.

For argument's sake, if the bank had re-gained its position, the public would not have instilled the same amount of trust in this bank as they did before the looting incident took place.

Lesson worth noting:
Attitude and actions are the determinants that will see to it that trust is maintained. Therefore, one should guard their attitude and actions for these determine the magnitude of one's trust.

If there is one pivotal lesson the shipping industry has taught me, it is the value of building trust with the supplier. It is the trust that will ensure that payment and delivery of goods to their destination is a success. In the same way, a relationship must be anchored on the firm pillars of trust among the parties involved. Without trust, the result is an unproductive relationship that leans on the unstable foundation of mistrust. A small child cannot be scared if they are tied at the back of the parent simply because of trust. The child can only trust that the love the parent has for them is enough not to let them fall on the ground.

This is the unwavering trust that the child bestows on the parent. A relationship without trust curbs growth. It can never be beneficial. Such a relationship has no love in it. It might be infatuation but not love. I concur that trust must not be imposed upon an individual. It must be earned based on the evident actions that have been done or carried out. The actions of an individual can be a useful criterion that determines whether that individual can be trusted or not. Unfortunately, words can sound convincing, but action carries more weight. If there is trust, the chances of experiencing human abuse are drastically reduced.

On one hand,
The kind of trust that is bestowed on the perpetrator of human abuse by the victim of abuse is a wavering one. It fluctuates as per how they continue to be treated. It can easily move from a ten to a 1, because of the unpredictable violent nature of the human abuser. It is this uncertainty

that increases the degree of harm imposed by abusive relationships.

On the other hand,
The perpetrator of human abuse proves to have absolute trust in the victim, because of how they mistreat them. May believe that the heavier the hand of violence they impose on the victim, the more their trust for them is secured. May harp on the misleading belief that trust is secured by force or violence, which is far from the truth.

The psychological chains of human abuse continue to be strongly fastened by the warped belief of equating trust to violence.

Trust is earned; it is not secured by threats or abuse.

A lack of trust is a lack of peace. Where there is no trust there can never be peace. Peace is a product of trust. I would not trust an abusive person to drive me around and I certainly would not trust an abusive person to work for me.
Their abusive tendencies become an enemy to pro-found peace.

Trust is directly paralleled to love in the sense that, where there is no trust, there is no love and where there is trust there is love. Lack of trust is triggering of abusive tendencies. The lover who lacks trust in their partner seeks to know the notifications and the messages of their partner's phone. This kind of lover is likely to suffer from a deep sense of insecurity, so they can't help but constantly monitor and guard their partner. Where they go, whom they talk to, and what they engage in. The constant monitoring of one's partner is in and of itself is a form of human abuse because it quickly escalates to the invasion of the partner's privacy – which is abusive.

Love enough to respect your partner's privacy.

It starts with deep introspection and self-reflection –

Am I worth the trust of another person?

71
CALCULATED ACCURACY

The lyrics of the Gospel song 'Walking' by Mary Mary say:

"Some people say walking takes too long,
But I say with walking you can't go wrong,
Why should you rush your way through life?
You won't get very far, running all the time".

These lyrics are so cognizant of the truth that, so much of life's beauty is missed by someone who is always in a hurry. In the same way, healing from an abusive relationship may take time, but a slow and impactful effect is much better than a fast and impact-less effect.

"Surely, the slow movement of a tiger is not a mistake, but a calculated accuracy"

- PROPHET T.B JOSHUA

The most complex of all creations is not the universe and the stars. The most complex of all creations is humanity. The complexity of human nature means that the healing process that is directed to the human mind will take t-i-me to truly heal the human family. The healing process of abuse always takes time to effectively take root in the human mind.

It can be a very slow process, one that calls for unrelenting patience, commitment, and resilience to be upheld consistently.

Do not tire when it comes to working with your soul and digging up the unearthed treasures within yourself. The slow process of healing can be improved by someone patient enough not to allow the fruit of self-doubt to curb the healing process. In trying to work with yourself towards achieving a greater course, there will inevitably be resistance; the pull him or her down syndrome that we can all relate to in our quest to achieve our goals and dreams.

Amid resistance, one's conviction and trust in the power of the healing process must be greater than any doubt. In discouragements, one's trust in the effectiveness of the healing process must be greater than any negative or opposing forces that slow-down the healing process.

Time is all that humanity can work with to ensure that effective healing takes root in untangling humanity from the psychological chains of human abuse. Rome was not built on one night, but each day a brick was laid. That is, the manifestation of greater results is but a result of considering and rightfully channeling every necessary step that should be taken. The principle lies in putting an effort into taking the step. The principle lies not in giving up along the way. The principle is in committing oneself to the healing process and giving oneself fully to its ability to mold and form the final product.

Like a tiger - move slowly, but purposefully.

Move slowly but aim at the target and get healed. Neither running nor jumping can bring about total mind-transformation. Running will cause one to miss important aspects that should be considered. Running will cause one to miss the stones, trip, and fall again. Do not run to your victory lane…Walk to your victory lane. The game of life can only be carefully adventured by those who keep a steady pace on their toes.

Being calculative means that one is mature enough to trust in the value of the healing process - It means taking in information that brings about a balance – a balance that is vital for producing healing toxins. It may be going through self-help guides, books, or newspaper articles. Attend the counseling sessions but most importantly keep yourself informed.

Take a step towards your healing, the universe will follow to support and cheer you up.

The impact that is created by walking is very effective. It allows one to see the view that lies on their path. Healing the pains of human abuse and allowing time to take its course will allow one to clearly see their shortfalls and therefore adjust and make improvements. Rushing the healing process will make room for a lot of downfalls because one cannot see the view of where they might be lagging. It is a wrong miscalculated approach that is not ideal to becoming human abuse over-comers. Adopting a good approach to the healing of human abuse is ideal for the human soul. It creates a great impact and never retaliates.

What differentiates the healers of human abuse is the value that is captured in the healing. If there is no value in the healing, then it is not useful but a short-sighted illusion that will see one resorting back to the realities of human abuse.

THE VALUE OF EFFECTIVE HEALING IS IN THE LONG-TERM LASTING EFFECTS.

72
OPPORTUNITY COST

Opportunity cost is an economic term that refers to the value that is lost in choosing one thing over another thing. For example, the opportunity cost of using a bicycle instead of a car is much lower. And the opportunity cost of using super glue on a shoe instead of paper glue is much higher.
In the same way, it is reasonable to say:
The opportunity cost of holding on to an abusive relationship instead of walking-away is much higher.

The green traffic light says that one should go. One should maximize the time that is created by the green light for going. Delaying will only change the green light to a red light and one will have to stop and wait again for the green light to start reflecting. This is the idea behind a traffic robotic light. The lesson is in maximizing the opportunity that allows one to go before the time for that opportunity elapses.

Victims of human abuse must maximize at all costs the opportunity that allows them to exit a relationship before the time for that opportunity elapses. Time is a factor that one needs to consider when faced with a decision to exit.

Indecisiveness can cause the exit time to lapse. We have all been faced with indecisiveness. It is one of the worst positions to find oneself in. That is especially if the two given scenarios are seemingly balanced. The principle of opportunity cost from economics suggests that there is a value in choosing one option over another option. The opportunity cost of letting go of an abusive relationship for another relationship or being single is much lower than the opportunity cost of not letting go. That is, the value of staying in an abusive relationship is much higher than the value of letting go.

Where is the gain in getting hurt in the name of love? There is no gain. The only benefit lies in letting go of such a relationship. The young mind can be indecisive in choosing the right pair of shoes, choosing fruits over sweets, staying home, or going to school, choosing friends over family, choosing faithfulness, or cheating, and choosing friends' advice or the parent's advice. There is an array of decisions that a young mind must make before making a hasty, wrong, and miscalculated decision.

Teach them the principle of opportunity cost, it allows their minds to be flexible enough to look at both sides of a coin, the negative and the positive. By so doing they will have a clear view of the value of choosing one decision over another decision. The idea is that if a decision's value is outweighed by the alternative then they must discard that decision.

The most effective pill to the illness of indecisiveness is in making use of...

THE PRINCIPLE OF OPPORTUNITY COST

73
A 'COMMON-PRINCIPLED VILLAGE'

I have heard them say and sing the praise, 'It takes a village to raise a child'. This sounds good - the village should be involved in the raising of the child. My only concern with this statement is that it does not lay down clear parameters - it is too generic for such a huge responsibility that goes into the raising of a child. The meaning will be much enhanced if the praise is changed to - 'It takes a common-principled village to raise a child'. This lays down a clear parameter because let's face it - there are a lot of villages with varying principles. A common-principled village has the same vision, mission, purpose, and principles. It can never confuse or mislead a child. It is good for the proper growth and grooming of the child.

The notion of a 'common-principled village' considers, the activities of the child. It is made possible by dwellers that will have the capacity to care for all the children in the community. It does not segregate a child by blood, and it does not segregate a child by genes. Every parent becomes a role model and a guardian to every child. Without discriminating and separating their blood children from the other children – Common-principled parents take hands and take it upon themselves to love all children genuinely and infectiously like their own.

In a common-principled village, it becomes the priority of every parent to see to it that the children are always safe and protected from harm. Taking them away from bad influences such as alcohol intake, drug abuse, and risky sexual behaviors becomes the role of the dwellers of a common-principled village. Educating and motivating young people to achieve their dreams becomes the priority and the role of the dwellers of a 'common-principled village'. It is a place that radiates a different kind of love – an infectious love.

My ideal 'common-principled village' is one in which no child sleeps on a hungry stomach. The necessities of every child such as food, water, education, and good health are met, not just by their parents but with the help of the community. More especially if the parents are not working – the community must not fold their hands while the neighboring child is sleeping on an empty stomach. Everybody in the community needs to contribute to the upkeep of this child.

A 'common-principled village' is anchored into the belief that a child remains a child despite whose blood child it is. A child needs care.

Now the above is a true definition of a 'common-principled village'

Untangling the psychological chains of human abuse calls for a 'common-principled village to stand in solidarity against the scourge of abuse. Let us continue building within communities and societies 'common-principled villages' that we can all be proud of.
Homes that will cultivate an abuse-free generation –
Let us sort out our differences and stand for a greater and noble course:
Genuine love should be the pillar of a 'Common-principled Village'

The village of humanity should work in unison in cultivating the same vision, mission, purpose, and principles in grooming the young mind to be better prepared when facing the reality of mistreatment. It is working from a place of common ground that will not confuse or mislead the young mind. A common ground will facilitate and strengthen the force of the message conveyed. Ultimately - the more people who are speaking the same language - the louder and stronger the voice and the greater the impact created. Powerful and impactful is a human voice that supports the notion of eradicating human brutality.

Humanity should strive to speak a common universal language of love to every young mind. A village that is grounded and anchored in love is ideal in the raising of an abuse-free generation. A village whose main goal is to replace the scarcity of love with abundant love is ideal in raising a child that knows no pain from human abuse. A common universal language of love should be humanity's medicine to heal the psychological illness of human abuse. How powerful and loud it is for humanity to shout love in one unified voice, even a soul that is sinking deep in the hole of human abuse can hear this voice and find comfort and healing. How powerful it is for humanity to hold each other and march against human abuse, it is convincingly powerful...This is a 'common-principled village' that humanity should strive to build.

It takes a 'common-principled village' to raise a child. A 'common-principled village' with the same vision, purpose, and principles is a necessity for the raising of a child whose principles are aligned to a world that is free from the strong grip of human abuse.

74
THE MIRROR

One of the best lessons from my role model David Tlale, which has taken root in me, is that one should never argue with the mirror. It can never lie to you. It gives a precise image of exactly what is being reflected. If the mirror says change, do not argue just do it. If the mirror says no, do not argue just put in the effort of change. The only exception is when the mirror is unclean or is badly shattered. Then the reflection might be tainted. This will mean that some effort must be channeled into the cleaning of the mirror. It can also mean that some money must be used in replacing the broken mirror. All these efforts are channeled to the attainment of a true and untainted reflection.

A famous artist once said,
"Trust is like a mirror; you can fix it when it's broken"

In the same way, the parent is a mirror that mirrors the reflection of the child. The parent should ensure that they are a clean and un-shattered mirror to the child. If the parent is an unclean or shattered mirror, the reflected image of the child will be tainted. Thus, an effort to replace the mirror or clean the mirror should be considered. So important is the effort that goes into cleaning the mirror, it will restore the image of the child to its true and untainted state. Thus, if the parent can understand this concept - they will put into effect every action that is necessary for the enlightenment of the child. Thus, if the parent can be a mirror that mirrors the reflection of love to the child, then the child will reflect an image of love. If the parent can be a mirror that mirrors the reflection of abuse, then the child will reflect an image of abuse. Not until the parent takes an effort to clear the mirror of abuse with the dishwasher of love can the image of the child be a clean and untainted one.

Take a moment to ponder upon the kind of a reflection that you have so-far been to those that you love – Is it a reflection of love, trust, confidence, boldness, contentment or a reflection of hate, pain, mistrust, and ingenuity? It is in the way that you behave and treat others that ultimately continues to craft the kind of a mirror or reflection that you are to others.

I choose to reflect love, trust, confidence, boldness, and contentment.

Isn't it interesting to know that everybody that we meet in life is a mirror? - A reflection of our qualities. Of course, not everybody is going to fit in the caliber of qualities that we have. However, the bottom line is, as you look at this person that has qualities that are very contradictory to your own in a negative way (they may lie, steal, and manipulate), **the act of not accepting** this person as a normal person that is fit to live in harmony with other people is an affirmation of the kind of a mirror that they are towards you. It is an affirmation of the reflection that you see when looking at them.

The person is still a mirror, one whose reflection will ignite in you the desire to despise them as part of being accepted by society.

Interesting right…?

Take care of your mirror, so that the reflection that you radiate to others may empower, build, inspire, comfort, cheer, restores, give hope, elevate, and promote others. Before looking at you as their mirror, may they be inspired to turn on their light and clean their mirror first so that the reflection is accurate.

Isn't it interesting to know that parents have a great responsibility when it comes to the reflection of the child? If I were a parent, I would be actively at work cleaning the mirror that I am and replacing the shattered parts of the mirror in me. Sourcing out cleaning material from external parties by seeking out advice and implementing it can be an effective solution to improve a shattered mirror. External parties can motivate, encourage, and impart truths that we need to face for the mirror to be completely clean. It takes effort and humility to put into consideration the advice that external parties give. A clean spotless mirror is one that every parent should strive to attain. It is one that the universe should extend a helping hand for the parent to become. It is fulfilling and meaningful to attain a clean and spotless mirror. It gives a true and untainted reflection of the child.

I am strongly supporting the idea of continuously seeking a loving and wise approach to raising a child.

Remember,

A MIRROR CANNOT LIE...

UNLESS IF IT'S SHATTERED OR UNCLEAN...

I call upon all parents to become reflections of love to their children.

75
POINT OF CORRECTION

As an average Mathematics scholar, I knew of mistakes when it came to Mathematics. I loved the subject, but for some reason, it did not love me back with the same affection, I was just an average Mathematics scholar. It is only now that I have grown up, that I know of human mistakes. My intestines have had to grumble at the sound of a parent who uttered these words to their child, "You are a mistake that should have never been made". This is the only time I have come to know of human mistakes. Mistakes can never be good - they are the very contributing factor to one's failure. I do not want to be a mistake. Humanity can never be a mistake. Calling humanity or perceiving humanity as a mistake is a mistake that should be corrected.

It goes back to the phenomenon of the search for meaning that is at the disposal of all humanity. A human family that is in a perpetual hunt for answers of their existence constantly enquires:

Who am I?
Where do I come from?

How did I come here?
Where am I going?

A search for meaning and answers to the above questions will be confused by the referring to humanity as - 'mistakes. One who enquires while being called a 'mistake' will be misled into believing the responses that suggest that:

'You are a mistake'
'You came from an unplanned pregnancy'
'You came by mistake'
'You are going to hell'

These responses will bind the human mind with the psychological chains of human abuse. The one who is told they are a mistake goes through life with a limited sense of confidence in oneself. They have a lot of self-doubt about their potential and ability. It is not cool to refer to another human being as a mistake.

One who is told they are a mistake is likely to suffer from low self-esteem and a poor self-image. They might believe they do not deserve to love and to be loved because they were not made in love.

The ultimate result is a human being that struggles with self-love and loving others as well. The final product is a generation of young people that are entangled by the psychological chains of human abuse due to low self-esteem and a poor self-image.

Think about the thoughts that are ignited by this statement in the mind of the child that is receptive to these words... "I am a mistake; my existence is a burden to my parent, and I should never have existed". In and of itself, it is human abuse to say such utterances to a child. It is emotionally damaging to the human soul. Upon hearing these words, the child grows up with a warped sense of meaning for life. Without proper guidance and motivation, this child's life will be meaningless and filled with a deep sense of thirst to know what life is about. There can never be mistakes in the human family. A child might have been the product of unplanned pregnancy and negligence, but they can never bear the burden of the events that took place in their making. This is a human being that did not ask to be created. One must just holistically and fully embrace the child with an abundance of love. An unplanned pregnancy may be a call for the parent to be extra careful with their sexual behavior, but it certainly does not mean the child is a mistake.

I strongly believe one can correct mistakes, learn from mistakes, and despise mistakes. One can never love mistakes, it's humanly impossible. This statement gives an overview of the parent's perception of the child. A parent who perceives their child as a mistake will struggle to love the child - the parent's treatment of the child is always clouded by the misconception that the child is a mistake. There is a very thin line between loving this child and abusing this child. The human abuse that is directed to children today can be attributed to such utterances. They are poisonous to the human soul. They stand as an obstruction in the parent's approach to raising the child. They bury the child's self-worth, confidence, self-esteem, and dignity. Restoration calls for the parent to transform the perception they have of the child. It calls for a humanity that is willing to fully embrace and cherish its seed against all odds.

Assurance that the child is an abundantly loved soul, the world has been longing for is a sure step to build a foundation that is anchored deep in the roots of abundant love.

NEVER MAKE THE MISTAKE OF CALLING HUMANITY A MISTAKE...CORRECT IT!

PART FOUR

76
INTERPRETATION OF ART

The power of art lies in its massive influence to change mindsets, perceptions, behaviors, and attitudes. Art is one aspect that will stand the test of time. Its roots cannot be uprooted from the human family; it is that deep, running from the past to the present and the future generation. Art is an assertive asset that was, is, and will always be the heartbeat of the human soul. Life would be boring without art - I would not listen to any music, watch any movies, read any book, buy any portrait, and dance to any beat. I cannot even imagine such a miserable life. Out of all the beauty that art radiates to the human soul, I am captivated by its ability to hold various interpretations. Different people can have different interpretations of the same work of art. It is this open-minded approach that art holds that stands out for me...I love it.

A work of art is just that, a work of art – it leaves the end open in the sense that what someone may see or take from an artwork may be different from the view and interpretation of the other person. The power and relevance of uniqueness imply that we see the same things differently. It will be outrageous to want to force people to have a common way of interpreting a work of art.

In the light that art is open to different interpretations, humanity should be aware that there are certain artworks whose interpretations may trigger human abuse. Artwork such as poetry and motivational speaking must refrain from 'ambiguity' because these could be interpreted in such a manner that will strongly fasten the psychological chains of human abuse.

For example, a poet may sing praises of a poem that is titled "Hold on and be strong". It will be vital for the poet to explain that holding on and being strong cannot be used in an abusive relationship context, it can be used in achieving goals and dreams during calamities such as financial problems, however, it cannot be used in giving hope to the victim of abuse.

I earnestly appeal to all facets of art not to present abuse-triggering works of art.

In a world that is beaming with the reality and struggle of gender-based violence:

It would be vital to be upfront and transparent when it comes to the proper contextualization of words of encouragement.

It is our uniqueness as a people that causes different people to interpret the same situation differently. Human abuse can be interpreted differently by different people who experience it. Some of these interpretations can be misleading if the mind is not enlightened enough about human abuse. These form part of some of the misleading interpretations or stereotypes of abuse that should not be entertained:

- Abuse is a part of human nature.
- Abuse is an assurance that one is loved.
- Abuse is a normal part of a relationship.
- Abuse must be endured for one to prove the love they have for another.

These interpretations are rooted deep in the minds of the victims of abuse that do not know this subject. They are also deeply rooted in the psyche of those that have grown up in abusive homes. These homes have in introspect tainted the view that these individuals have on abuse. They view it as acceptable, tolerable, tough-love, and endurable. It is not until some light is shone on these minds that their interpretation of human abuse can be revised and changed for the better course of humanity.

These interpretations are the main reason that can be attributed to the sense of endurance that is attributed to abusive relationships. You will be greatly amazed at how some individuals can defend these relationships. They have birthed within their souls a deep sense of conviction that cannot be easily shaken or uprooted. It is a blinding and short-sighted sense of conviction that sees nothing wrong about an abusive relationship. Such issues are heavy to deal with, even as a human abuse activist. Helping a willing mind is better than helping an arrogant mind. It takes a whole lot of strength to help a human being rooted in misguided conviction.

There is hope, I still believe. The interpretation that young minds have for human abuse must be wise and based on knowledge…they must not fall victim to misinterpretations or stereotypes.

Human abuse can never be a work of art:

The human mind can only have:

ONE LOVE…ONE PEACE…ONE INTERPRETATION

77
THE POWER OF SOLITUDE

I love the company of friends and relatives - it is just awesome especially on a weekend-special vibe. The social aspect of it keeps me on my toes. I just love telling stories and listening to stories...all forms of stories. Gossip just adds that flavor to the dish of life. The problem is when a company of friends becomes the lifeblood of life. It's like one cannot stand their own company. Their happiness revolves and is anchored around the company of friends. As much as the company of friends is great, it must not be taken to extremes. One should be at peace with one's own company. It is powerful and refreshing. It is the only time that one gets the opportunity to tap into their power without sharing it or competing for it. Enjoy the company of friends, but never forget that solitude can be one of the most powerful tools to help fight the human dependency syndrome.

Solitude affirms one's peace and power. The gold (*treasures of wisdom*) that is mined in a time of solitude is great. One who is happy and peaceful in solitude will not fail to be happy and peaceful while in other people's company. It is very empowering and eye-opening to spend some time with oneself. It is important at this moment to guard one's thoughts. It would be positive and beneficial to keep thoughts that nourish and enrich the soul. Thoughts that are a great stimulator of genuine love are ideal for cultivating a human being that is untangled from the psychological chains of human abuse.

It is this time that opens realms and avenues of one's soul. A secret ingredient worth telling to aspiring writers; a writer cannot always be surrounded by people. It is this that allows them to tap into the unearthed treasures of their soul so that they can tap into the wells of unexplored wisdom. A writer on gender-based violence is a critical component to help fight the scourge of human abuse and as such, they need a time of reflection and introspection both within and without.

Solitude allows one to listen to one soul without competing for it; it creates an atmosphere that allows a richness of the soul and sharpening of one's sense of awareness which are vital elements in untangling the psychological chains of human abuse. In a world where radio and television sets are so vocal with gender-based violence issues, one cannot help but show some sense of care. I for one, at one point in time, could not switch on my radio or television set, because of the large magnitude of violent cases – I knew deep down within my soul that something had to be done –

I had to search for the missing antidote – I am confident that I found it now; it is nothing but genuine love.

Some people miss their mark on earth, not because they do not know, but because of failure to spend time in solitude. Teach children to be content and flexible enough to spend time in solitude. It produces alignment that is powerful enough to attract positive energy that will untangle them from the psychological chains of human abuse.

Solitude allows one to self-analyze their happiness and peace. Spending time with one-self allows one to note if there are any deviations along the way so that a restoration solution can be implemented.

Tune into your soul and listen to the voices within yourself. Discard all the negativities and only entertain the positives. This is not easy to master; it takes consistent and persistent practice. Balance your life, enjoy some time with a company of friends and take time in solitude as well. I call the solitude time 'the-me-time'...it is a necessary time to connect with one's soul. A human being that cannot stand their own company can be prone to the realities of human abuse because this implies that they have a dependency syndrome of being with another human being. They cannot stand their own company. This speaks to the voices within them in times of solitude. They cannot stand these voices;

these can only be negative, horrific voices. A sense of dependency on the company of other people means that one cannot stand a time of solitude. Isn't this the nature of an abuser? They abuse the victim but at the same time cannot live without the victim. Be powerful and content enough to enjoy, laugh and converse in your solitude time. It is powerful and reassuring of one's bold and confident existence.

I have met friends who would rather endure the hand of abuse than endure solitude. They would rather have pain inflicted on them than for them to have their own company. The pain endured from the person that gives them the company is worth much more to them than the pain of having their own company. Their own company must be a terrific one if the opportunity cost of it is much more than being in an abusive relationship. They find so much gain in being in an abusive relationship than the gain of being in their own company. The solution is cultivating a culture of balancing company and solitude. These are both significant in the life of a human being that aspires to happiness and contentment. Discontentment is not enough, it always thirsts, it is always hungry, and it can never be satisfied. Be content in both company and solitude.

The ability to balance company and solitude must be mastered at a young age by clearly setting boundaries and making time for these two vital aspects of life.

78
THE POWER OF SERVING

I have always said it and I will say it again that, a child is a child regardless of whose blood and gene it is. That child needs, love, care, education, and guidance. Adoption is a good decision for me if one is in a good position to do it. The staunch absurd belief in a parent to care less about a child that is not their blood moves humanity further away from the plan of untangling the psychological chains of human abuse. If humanity is serious about seeing this plan to its fruition, then the attitude that every parent has on any child regardless of genes and blood should be revised. Every parent must have the capacity to make any child feel the abundant love that surrounds them.

Serving is so powerful and significant, even leaders are born from serving. True and genuine leaders are those that find pleasure in serving. The course of time has had to mistake being a servant from being a slave – confusing these two and ignorantly binding humanity with the psychological chains of human abuse. To untangle these starts by knowing the difference between these two:

Serving is within the confines of respect for the servant. The meaning and sense of satisfaction derived from serving by the servant and those that are served qualifies the act of serving as one that is none-abusive.

Slavery is outside the confines of respect for the slave. The sense of dissatisfaction that is derived from being a slave qualifies the act of slavery as one that is abusive.

Humanity should rather choose to serve rather than be a slave because serving will ensure that they are not entangled by the psychological chains of human abuse.

The power of serving is indescribable; serving is what a 'common-principled village' is all about. It runs the inner workings of society. The only element that should not be buried by those that serve is the ability to serve from the heart. Serving from the heart means being considerate enough to use genuine love while serving – a kind of love that is infectious - Love that touches the very core of the beings that you serve.

It is genuine love that births a serving spirit that is timeless and meaningful so that those that are served remain with a kind of love that can be spread to others.

Serving should be done in authenticity and genuineness so that ultimately those that are oppressed can become freed from the psychological chains of human abuse.

I prefer the serving of orphans as an instrumental tool in curbing the scourge of human abuse because it is impactful for a child that grows up without parents not just to receive the act of being served - But to receive genuine love while getting served.

A love so significant such that they will be untangled from the psychological chains of human abuse – a kind of love that encourages a non-violent attitude:
Love and serve an orphan today!

I hope that I may find healing as I immerse myself in this chapter of serving orphans, because of my painful experiences with one of them. Upon self-reflecting on the boy that beat me up for no reason while I was serving at an orphanage – I must let go on the grounds of my discovery - They were deprived of love from birth. It will be outrageously cruel to deprive them of it now.

I am not blind to the parameters that can be set by parents when it comes to their child. I am not talking of immense involvement in a child that is not your own. I am awakening awareness in the parent to just have it in them to treat any child with abundant love. It's in the small things like sharing the little that one has with the child at the orphanage. It may seem like a small act, but the effect goes a long way. The upkeep of orphanages lies in the hand of every human being. One might not have material things to share with the orphans but so great is the quality of sharing, it is not just expressed in monetary value or materialism. One can share a gesture of love by just playing and getting involved in the activities of the orphans. One can share a word of motivation with the orphans. One can perform some chores at the orphanage. It does not take money to express these gestures of love. It only takes a willing and loving heart.

The human abuse that some of the orphans have been subjected to in the hands of those that are meant to take good care of them can be appalling. Taking time to listen to some of the orphans 'stories, I felt sick. I am appealing to humanity to extend a gesture of abundant love to all the orphans and give them eternal hope in the midst of all that they have faced. How can humanity forget - a child that has not had the pleasure of being told the three universal words affirming affection from a parent? It certainly does not hurt to say to the orphan, "I love you". It might be their first time to hear such words uttered to them. The effect is the orphan will grow up knowing they are loved.

Untangling the psychological chains of human abuse calls for a people that will extend genuine love to an orphan. Humanity must never forget the power of love. Embedded in these orphans might be a President, a Doctor, a Teacher, a human abuse Activist, and a Farmer. It is the responsibility of all of humanity to ignite the passion in them and to see to it that an orphan grows up to be what they aspire to become.

Remember,

The best way to find one is to lose oneself in the service of others...SERVE ORPHANS!

79
STATUS

It would not be surprising to get a buzz of laughter in a class, if, upon being asked by a teacher, "What do you want to be when you grow up?" John responds – "A cleaner".

The laughter speaks to the status that is attached to this career. The laughter is a sign that it is taboo for a scholar to aspire to be a cleaner. It is this status that is attached to different treatment that is rendered to different job descriptions that is a problem. Humanity at large must transform the mindset it has on job descriptions. This starts by transforming the mind of the young not to see it as taboo to become a cleaner. It should be well accepted and perceived as equally important as all the other job descriptions. A change of perception in this regard will reduce the amount of human abuse that humanity must endure due to the status that is attached to the job description.

The education system needs to revise the perception that it has long imprinted on the young minds when it comes to different jobs. These misleading pre-conceived ideas attached to job statuses can only fasten the psychological chains of human abuse. Schools need to start encouraging learners to become cleaners, plumbers, designers, shoe menders, farmers, poultry owners, cattle ranchers, miners, builders, painters, and childcare takers without seemingly promulgating the idea that one will not be respected if they go for these kinds of jobs.

In so doing, they in the long run will curb the low self-esteem, insecurity, and poor self-image that are attached to jobs of such a caliber. Schools must facilitate the noble truth that all jobs are equally important. It is this that will curb the violence and injustice suffered by humanity that has a passion for hands-on jobs. Elevating the status of all jobs will ensure that income is distributed, and most importantly one's dignity is respected.

Eradication of the warped idea that one job is more important than the other will ultimately untangle the human mind from the pangs of mistreatment. Elimination of the misleading fallacy that one human being is less of a human being loosens the agonizing violence suffered by people of all job sectors.

Everybody is important and so is their job.

The compartmentalizing and classifying of job descriptions according to status is a very toxic approach to the human mind. It gives a perception that certain jobs are more important and highly esteemed than other jobs. This causes the human mind to vary its level of respect on the grounds of the job that one holds. The fickle idea that a lawyer must be respected more than the tea lady or tea gentlemen is then built in the human mind. With such a mindset it will be more fitting for the cleaner to be more prone to the realities of human abuse than the lawyer. The truth that will bring humanity closer to healing human abuse is that no job description is more important than the other. All job descriptions must be equally perceived, and an equal amount of respect must be attributed to all of them. A job is a job, there are no exceptions...everybody is putting in the effort to see a greater course achieved. Nobody is more important in the job sector.

All people in the job sector are equally important. Without a cleaner, the courtroom will be a filthy place for the jury. Without the lawyer, the courtroom cannot proceed. Both entities are uniquely involved in the proper procedures of the courtroom. Thus, they are equally important.

The education system needs to open more opportunities and more schools for hands-on jobs such as cleaning, building, plumbing, and child-care taking and farming such that the levels of unemployment can be drastically reduced. Formalizing these sectors is a sure way to elevate the esteem attributed to them and addressing the depressing levels of unemployment that slowly but surely becoming more-like a pandemic of its kind.

The formalization of practically hands-on jobs will see to it that young people that are passionate about these industries are groomed and nurtured from a young age. It is this that will ultimately take young people out of the streets and away from activities that may expose them to the realities of human abuse. The level of crime will be reduced by such avenues.

Remember:
"An idle mind is the devil's playground" – Keep them busy.

It will not be surprising that the never-ending job-hopping dilemma that is evident today can be attributed to the status of jobs and the perceived respect that humanity has built around the job. Nobody wants to settle for a job that is perceived as a low standard. Humanity has built these standards and needs to break them for the greater good for all.

The classification of jobs according to status will only result in abusive behavior that is attributed to the status of the job. It is high time that humanity restores the respect and dignity of every worker who is involved in a common goal.

If a palace needs a builder, then the significance of the builder cannot go unnoticed.
YOUR JOB IS AS EQUALLY IMPORTANT AS ALL THE OTHER JOBS...NO EXCEPTIONS!

80
THE CHILD-BIRTH CRISIS

There is one thing that has always astounded me in population studies. The idea that developing countries such as Burundi and Kenya have a birth rate that is much higher than that of developed countries such as Canada and the United States of America. Don't get me wrong, a child is a blessing - one can have a lot of children, if they will be able to support the child. I am astounded by the mind-blogging question:

If the proper raising of a child calls for a lot of money, why would developing countries have an increased birth rate?

Any child needs to be provided with the proper care that considers all their necessities. However, the pressure only mounts up very high especially for the poor. If this is so, then what is the reason that developing countries have a birth rate that is much higher than that of developed countries? Can it be attributed to a lack of knowledge; can it be attributed to frustration or is it merely because the poor just love the company of a lot of children? – Food for thought...

One of my dearest teachers used to humorously tell us that the dilemma of increased birth-rate in developing countries should be largely attributed to the resorting of sexual pleasure as a way of making up for the frustration that stems from doing nothing. He used to say, making babies becomes a hobby to those that do nothing. It gives them some sense of relief and satisfaction.

Growing up I finally made sense out of what he used to teach us – sex has the power to ease the pressure, however, I had to deduce that the reason has to be beyond just resorting to sexual pleasure as a way of releasing pressure and frustration. There is something more and bigger to it.

The dilemma of developing countries comes with a lot of lack of knowledge and resources that facilitate birth preventative measures. Some of the cultures in these countries do not recognize and encourage the usage of birth control measures such as the use of condoms during sexual intercourse, the use of birth control pills, and birth preventative injections. A lack of resources such as condoms, birth control pills, and injections could also be the core reason behind the escalating levels of the birth rate in developing countries. This is a greater call for developed countries that can extend a helping hand to intervene in the increasing birth-rate crisis that developing countries are faced with.

I strongly concur with the above reasoning, and as such, I urge societies and communities to engage in dialogues that will improve their knowledge on birth rates and the preventative measures thereof.

My concern is - the human abuse that is encountered in these big families, because of a lack of resources is too much. Frustration aroused by hunger can be the sorriest excuse that justifies one's anger and negligence. There is no doubt that the level of frustration is much higher for the poor. One cannot create that which they cannot handle. Even hands were designed to hold a certain amount of content. If hands have a lot of content to handle, that which is handled starts falling.

It can be a challenge for the necessities of the child that comes from a poor background to be met. A child in most of these big families grows up without an education that allows them to be independent enough to fend for themselves. This exposes them to the realities of human abuse because they become vulnerable, weak, and dependent victims that will hold on to the abusive relationship for the mere sake of meeting the necessities they lack and not for the love. It is deep-seated poverty that will instill in this child tremendous fear – that ultimately holds them back from walking out of an abusive relationship. They would rather be a punching bag to a person that can see to it that their necessities are met. They would rather endure the pangs of abuse for the mere fact of the bread that is buttered in the relationship. This, I must say, is the sad reality that is faced by a lot of abuse victims in poor places. To this kind of victim - the decision of walking out of an abusive relationship is not so much a choice than it is an enemy to meeting one's needs.

The call is for humanity to transform its mindset concerning the idea of birth. It is completely irrational to continuously increase the number of births without the corresponding means to take care of these human lives.

The major African problem is that:

A hungry man continues to ignorantly make a bountiful number of children that he cannot feed, children that will grow up under the heavy hand of abuse due to a lack of necessities such as food and shelter.

What will it take for humanity to see...A HUNGRY MAN IS AN ANGRY MAN?

81
THE AUDIENCE APPLAUDS

It is a great feeling to have the audience applause, in honor of the noble work that one has presented. It is a moment whose glory can only be reflected upon long-after it has passed. However, the obsessive need of being affirmed by the audience applause is a problem. Confidence is bold enough to suggest that one's work is enough despite the applause that is received from the audience. Hunting for people's approval is not healthy. If one is not confident enough, it will not be surprising to fall into the pit of depression because of failure to hear the audience applaud. The sound is assuring of one's capabilities, but it is not the lifeblood of one's potential. True happiness lies not in the applause of the audience but within oneself. Thus, it is vital, even after getting the audience's applause one should still look at the mirror and genuinely strip naked the question:

"Am I truly happy with myself?" ...

So powerful is the effect of the audience's applause, the extremes that some go to satisfy the desire to hear the audience applauding can be appalling. Part of these is cheating, stealing, and pretense.

What if one who is hunting for approval starts being affected by their mischief – they start suffocating in the after-effects of their misdeeds such that they cannot even hear the audience applaud them. The negative effects of their misdeeds become so loud in their consciousness to such an extent that it becomes impossible for them to hear the appraisals of the audience.

It is important to have a clean and pure consciousness that will not block the sound of the audience's applause.

Take a moment to reflect on the appraisals that you have been showered with from birth up until now.

- 'You are smart'
- 'You are caring'
- 'You have a neat hand-writing'
- 'You are a Mathematics genius'
- 'You are such a good cook'
- 'You will make a successful builder'
- 'Your plumbing skills are of a high standard'
- 'Your cleaning is phenomenal'

The above compliments are so positive, and they have the potential to activate drive and ambition only if one's soul can deeply resonate with them. It's one thing for people to be happy for you and to shower you with compliments. The key to genuine happiness lies solely in how you feel about yourself. True happiness emanates within one's soul and not without.

'Pretense' is certainly a serious illness - I love those that hate me openly more than those that pretend to love me. 'Pretense' is such a toxic illusion that destroys humanity to the core. Pretense can never allow one to get to their power. 'Pretense' is the illusion that one puts on for approval. It hides one's true potential and ability. Living under the shadow of pretense covers one's identity. Deep down this shadow, it is most likely that there are hidden scars and unexpressed pain. One who pretends is like a child that is still in the womb, this child is still to be born.

Taking off the illusion of pretense will mean that one must have the courage to be truly oneself. To courageously face themselves without denials - to take in all the criticism that comes with it. It is the courage to let go of the concomitants of pretense that strengthens one and causes one to self-reflect, introspect and be better. The illusion of pretense is blinding, it is like the darkness that can only lament for the dawn of some light.

In taking off this shadow of pretense the unappealing parts of one's body can be a blow to one's confidence. The courage to face these truthfully is the first step to activate the power of self-love. Remember, one cannot have the capacity to love others if one fails to love one-self.

Untangling the psychological chains of human abuse calls for people that will be bold and confident enough to genuinely look at their image, scars, blemishes, smile, beauty, and all and be deeply content with these before extending their hand or heart to another human being.

Like an oxygen mask,

First breathe and gather enough air to sustain your lungs before helping a suffocating person.

82
MY DEFINITION OF WEALTH

I have come to deduce a new definition of wealth - it is not the money that one possesses, it is not the car that one drives, it is not the mansion that one owns. I strongly believe wealth is best defined as a state of mind. This might not sound like realism, but it is the truth, hard truth but truth that needs to be explored. It is an undeniable truth that some states of minds are just poor, and some states of minds are just wealthy.

The worst kind of poverty is to live in a huge mansion but have a poor state of mind.

The acquisition of materialism is good; however, it should not be paralleled to pro-found virtues such as peace, contentment, and happiness. The existence of these virtues should not be conditioned by the acquisition of materialism. The inert ability to refrain from conditioned tranquility, satisfaction, and joy make up a wealthy stand of mind. A practical way of measuring one's state of mind is to guard and take note of their emotions if one has money and if one does not have money.

One who remains happy despite their monetary position has a wealthy state of mind and higher chances of even acquiring more of it.

One whose happiness is conditioned by their monetary position has a poor state of mind and at-most leads a miserable life.

A wealthy state of mind is taps into the consciousness of contentment, fullness, accountability, and happiness regardless of the material manifestation of things. This state of mind is very attractive, it is not easily swerved - it is content and prioritizes happiness more than material things. Acquisition of material things can only be truly enjoyed by a wealthy state of mind. On the other hand, a poor state of mind taps into the consciousness of lack, emptiness, unaccountability, and misery despite the attainment of materialism. This state of mind is very toxic - it is discontent and only sees misery out of the abundant materialism that surrounds it. Take away the material possessions one has, a wealthy state of mind remains sound and positive. Take away the material possessions, a poor state of mind is left shattered and becomes negative.

Humanity's identity is not anchored around a poor state of mind.

Materialism or not, please make sure you still have a face to wear a bright smile.

It is healthy and fulfilling for young people to cultivate a wealthy state of mind. A mind that is free from the bondage of human abuse that stems from discontentment, misery, and unhappiness because of a lack of materialism. In a world that values gold and silver, making these the epitome of life itself, it is inevitable for one to succumb to sadness and misery because of a lack of money. This could only mean one thing; a wealthy state of mind is not a once-off achievement – one cannot wake up with a wealthy state of mind. Rather, it is a life-time endeavor that takes a lot of practice and persistence.

The practice to acquire a wealthy state of mind starts in the small things such as how to handle the little food or money that one has, how to maximize the opportunities that one has, how to handle disappointments, how to handle rejections in your career path, how to handle financial loss and instability.

It is a discipline on its own – a vital kind of self-discipline.

The most effective solution to the above inquiries that will allow one to have a wealthy state of mind is Detachment.

First and foremost, one needs to be aware that they are a separate entity from materialism. It is this inner conviction about detachment that will not see one controlled, manipulated, and succumbing to the social shoals of life. Do not attach oneself to materialism – rather acknowledge that you are not your money, flashy cars, and a golden watch. You are a separate entity that is deserving of peace, health, and success in abundance despite your material position.

Truly successful people are those that are disciplined enough to acknowledge they are not one with their possessions and therefore a healthy and balanced distance from these is significant.

The psychological chains of human abuse can only be strengthened by a poor state of mind. Humanity must have the courage to tap into a wealthy state of mind to start untangling these chains. It takes consistent cultivation and practice; it is possible and attainable. It is a journey, one that begins by appreciating the small things one has such as life, bread, water, and support. If one can appreciate the bread they have and are truly happy with that. Then the same attitude can be carried on to the attainment of an expensive cake. The key is appreciating and being grateful for the small things. The key is in being content with the small things. The key is in wearing a smile on one's face even if they have little to get along with. Appreciating the little things is a sure way to cultivating a wealthy state of mind.

The young mind must be taught to appreciate the small things and actions of love so that they can wealthily cherish the bigger things…BE GRATEFUL FOR ALL!

83
ISOLATION

Isolation can be the scariest and sickening of all experiences. I have come to understand that it comes in two forms. It can either be intentional where one separates oneself from others or it can be unintentional where others avoid associating with a person. However, out of all forms of isolation - I must say - the worst form of isolation is when you are surrounded by people but still feel a deep sense of loneliness.

The company and presence of friends, relatives, and significant others produce toxins that propel us to want to keep going – especially if it is positively affirmative. The failure of such a company to reach the depth of our being is a report that something - somewhere is drastically neglected and wrong. In the fast-paced technological world that we live in – so many reasons can be attributed to this failure of deeply connecting with other human beings. It could be a strong attachment to technological gadgets such as a cellphone, a television, or a laptop.

Humanity has for a long time now worn the belt of self-abandonment that is because of the strong attachment they have with these technological gadgets that ultimately cripples their socialization skill.

Think about it,
Other people still feel lonely in the presence of best friends, relatives, and significant others if the reality of load-shedding curbs them from charging their technological gadgets so that while communicating with their friends, the veil of loneliness can be removed by peering into their social media accounts.

Strong attachment to technological gadgets has become so strong to such an extent that human beings have built barriers and demarcations of isolation around themselves. These gadgets have boxed human beings into anti-social-self-isolated human beings that would rather value the company of technological gadgets than human beings.

Self-isolation has dire effects on the human mind. A human being is not meant to live on their island. A human being is meant to be in the company of friends. Keeping in mind the pandemic of coronavirus whose humbling impact was largely felt by all of humanity – the doctor that takes care of the positively tested corona-virus patient is advised to communicate and engage positively with the patient. This will speed up the recovery rate of the patient.

A huge part of being a human being is the ability to connect with other human beings on a deeper social level.

As social beings, the value of being with a company and socialize with others can never be compromised. It affirms one's human existence. Believe me when I say it comes with the territory of being human. A mind that has experienced unintentional isolation can never be in a healthy state unless the effects of isolation are unleashed out of it. It is what goes through the isolated mind that is at most toxic. It is not surprising - there will always be a sense of thirst and hunger in such a mind to know what life is about and to be affirmed of one's human existence.

The illness of antisocialism is birthed by isolation. A social being can only sharpen social skills by associating and socializing with other social beings. Failure to attain this can only lead to a dead social zone. If one is a stranger to company and true love, then it only makes perfect sense for that being to develop a strong sense of attachment – attachment on to that which promises to love and keep them company. A sense of attachment that knows the depressing feeling of isolation will not want to go back to the same feeling. One who has experienced isolation will find it difficult to walk out of an abusive relationship because their experience with isolation has birthed within them the fear of being alone. Long-struggle with Isolation only breeds a strong sense of attachment. The call is for humanity not to allow isolation to get in the way of one's decision-making as it is a very poor and blinding point of reference for sound decision-making.

Sound decision-making can be tainted by isolation. While deciding to walk out of an abusive relationship, isolation whispers:
"There is some bit of love and company in this relationship, stay in it because you do want to feel isolated again".

The task is for parents to unleash feelings of isolation that may be embedded in the young mind. I call it a task because it takes a whole lot of effort to create an atmosphere that allows young people to be vulnerable enough to open about the isolation experiences, they have had. It is one of those innate experiences that are always best kept inside. Only an unrelenting, caring and abundantly loving parent can untangle chains of isolation from the young mind.

Parents or guardians should be aware...

VULNERABILITY IS A BY-PRODUCT OF GENUINE LOVE AND IMMENSE CARE!

84
THE GOLDEN VOICES

"You can have it all, but not my voice – it is the weapon that will take it all back".

- Brightwell Dube

It is the sound of a crying baby at birth that affirms the life of the newly born baby. It is the silence that affirms the death of the newly born baby. It is for this reason that births within me a deep sense of conviction that out of all the precious things that life holds for humanity. One's voice takes the golden cup. It is the epitome of human existence. It is the determinant of life and death. Humanity must be propelled to choose to let their voice out, as this can only signify the presence of life. To me, killing is not just stabbing, gunning, or poisoning. I strongly believe the worst form of murder is in silencing the human voice.

If it wasn't for the desperate shout and screams from victims of armed robbery – heavens know what could have transpired. If it wasn't for the provocative songs such as '*One love*' that were sung by musical icons such as Lucky

Dube, the world would not have had a drop of unconditional love in its desperate times. If it wasn't for the timeless and meaningful speeches by phenomenal icons such as Abraham Lincoln, Nelson Mandela, and Martin Luther King, the world would have been left in so much conflict.

The one instrument that remains a powerful tool to fight the scourge of gender-based violence is the power of the human voice. Therefore, we ought to be objective with our voices. I recognize and applaud the vocal significance of the human beings that drive the transformation of toxic or abusive environments. Icons such as Steve Harvey, Tyler Perry, Oprah Winfrey, and Ellen DeGeneres have been very vocal in raising awareness and educating humanity at large about Gender-Based Violence.

It is the power of their consistency and persistence that breeds power and impact on their work.

Objective voices become the pillar that anchors young people when they are at the crossroads of love and hate.

Statistically – young people that immerse themselves in shows, works, and words of these icons have a greater chance of transforming their minds and untangling their minds from the psychological chains of human abuse. This confirms that media is not out-rightly a bad tool – if positively and objectively used with balance it can be pivotal in fighting the scourge of human violence.

An icon: was once young at some point in time and these icons have always been very objectively vocal from their early stages of life. Parents must be conscious of the fact that they are raising icons and role models. As such, they must treat their children like one.

I know from my own experience that - the streets of Johannesburg close to the taxi rank are a no-go zone at 08:00 of midnight. I was walking alone in this area on this day on my way from Braamfontein as I was rushing for a taxi in the middle of the night. When a countless number of street beggars surrounded me – the worst could have happened – I could have been killed, beaten up, raped, and robbed of my possessions. I screamed out loud as they extended their hands to take my purse from me. In the blink of an eye – I saw them laughing right back at my screaming and backing off from me. I was free and unharmed.

The above experience birthed a profound conviction within me – the conviction that there is power in a human voice.

There is so much embedded in this voice than what meets the eye. Humanity's voice when used positively, it has the power to comfort, motivate, inspire, transform mindsets, encourage, strengthen, revolutionize, and instill hope. The world would not have been the same without the voiced words, "I have a dream" …uttered by the legendary Martin Luther King. Think about it, the immense influence that these words have had on humanity at large. They resurrected even the souls that were close to giving up on a noble course.

The power of the human voice is undeniable, thus human abuse that is in the form of silencing the voices of humanity must be one of the worst forms of human brutality. The treasures that one holds are revealed in the venting out of their voice. It is the influence of these treasures that terrifies the perpetrator of human mistreatment.

Think about the voices of Nelson Mandela, Mother Teresa, and Steve Biko. These are voices that went down the history books because of the magnitude of influence that they carried. The great impact of these voices on humanity is evident today.

Long live the loud echoes of these voices!

If it was not for the strong voice that was inherent within these legendary individuals, humanity would have continued to be subjected to so much torture. The human abuse that these legends were subjected to was because of the strong, bold, influential voices radiated by their souls.

Think about the effects on humanity when their voices were forcibly silenced. The tower of hope and victory that had begun to stand tall in people began to crumble. The change that was beginning to manifest began to fade away.

I speak of power - a power that is inherent within humanity, a power that if positively used has the potential to bring about a complete human revolution. This is the power of the human voice.

The influence of the voices of these legends did not start in their adulthood stage of life. These legends reflected this influence in their young early stages of life.

Do not curb young voices from practicing their freedom of speech if it is within the confines of respect for oneself and others. Let them voice their views on public platforms such as debate and speech. Young and bold voices are the Mandela (s) of tomorrow...this I strongly believe.

85
KINDNESS

Kindness is an attractive quality. Every positive-minded soul loves the energy of a kind person. Like any quality there are levels to kindness, some people are just extremely kind. This is very attractive - however, the response that is received from this level of kindness can be discouraging. Instead of receiving appreciation as a gesture of kindness, extremely kind-hearted people are prone to be used by others.

I have heard them say; "Your kindness will kill you".
Isn't it interesting that a noble quality such as kindness has the potential to kill?

I know of a lot of kind-hearted people that have been changed by the response they received to the act of kindness they offered. My own experience of forgiving those that have hurt me has taught me to be very careful with continuous acts of kindness. I have been in a cycle of forgiving and getting hurt. Often-times people have had to abuse me emotionally and spiritually because of my kindness. It's like they continuously did it intentionally because they knew my kindness will not allow me not to forgive them. Sometimes being quick to forgive can cause people not to stop their bad actions on the victim. I had to learn that forgiveness is a principle that should be anchored in acknowledging that someone is wrong, and they should stop. My approach to forgiveness has now changed to - I can only forgive on the condition that one stops their evil deeds on me.

It is very sad, that gratitude can be a very scarce quality in humanity when it should be a priority. Kindness can expose one to the realities of human abuse, because of kindness - one is bound to tolerate the pain that stems from human abuse. It is the kindness that consistently forgives and forgets in the hope that the abuser will seize to abuse with time. It is this kindness that kills the victim of abuse. No amount of kindness should be applied in deciding to walk out of an abusive relationship. It is just a firm decision that calls for courage. The courage that sees a dead end and that is not willing to settle for less than walking out.

The act of kindness should be carefully given by humanity at large. Be kind, but with a sense of awakened awareness. Being king does not necessarily mean one has to sheepishly follow the painful or wrong guide. Being kind does not imply that one must be taken advantage of or abused or used. It simply means an equilibrium measure of generosity is rendered by one person onto another person. I call it equilibrium or balanced because if it is not balanced then it seizes to have an impact on the giver, rather, it seeks to act as a source of pain and strife. Everybody should strive to reach a balanced state of kindness. Balanced in the sense that it does not drain or discourage or manipulate, but it creates room for the desire to even do more. Kindness should not be used as a tool to manipulate or abuse. It should be one of the weapons that resonate with abundant love because love is kind.

Teach young minds to be kind but give them clear parameters that govern their act of kindness. Failure to do this will cause them to be abused because of their unlimited and unconditional act of kindness.

THE MAIN GOAL IS TO ATTAIN A BALANCED STATE OF KINDNESS - A Kindness that is appreciated, not abused.

86
EDUCATION INTO ACTION

Without proper application - education remains, a bunch of books that are read and studied for the sake of passing exams.

Take a moment to reflect and ponder upon the rich graveyards that are found in a cemetery yard. By rich graveyards, I am referring to the unexplored insurmountable knowledge that was buried with the corpse. These are treasures of knowledge that cannot be unearthed - Knowledge that was not turned into practical application. The value of such knowledge is useless.

Knowledge not shared is indeed valueless.

It is crucial to share knowledge and seeing to it that humanity that remains even after the source of this knowledge has passed away continues to pass this legacy on to the generation beyond the present generation. It is this that gives timeless value and meaning to knowledge – it must be practically passed on from one generation to the other.

My grave will certainly be one of the poorest graves that one can find because I love sharing my knowledge and wisdom with other people.

Every human being should work towards the attainment of a poor graveyard.
Be selfless with your knowledge – do not withhold it for your grave.

Some graves are rich in unshared experiences, experiences that could have helped shape the story of mankind. An abusive relationship is an experience that can help humanity at large to be aware of the psychological chains of human abuse and therefore loosen them before they strongly fasten the human mind. It could be a love story; it could be an incident with a teacher or a friend – share it.

Positively shared and interpreted experiences are impactful.
Remember you are the main character of your own life.
Tell us your story,
We are listening...
Do not die without sharing your own experience.

Don't get me wrong, it is good to be book smart. Knowing and interpreting the book from the start to the end can't be a bad thing. However, book smarts can be very arrogant;

they cannot deviate from their way of doing things. Therefore, a real world with real people calls for people who are more than book smarts to survive; Survival in the real-world means that humanity must balance out being book smart and street smart. Street smart people are more likely to survive the pangs of life than book smart people. Street smart means one can read people, fit in with people and apply the kind of communication that will be well-received by all people.

The most successful people in the face of the earth are those that have a balance of being book smart and street smart.

Humanity needs to start working on being a resemblance of what they study. If this attitude is applied to all scholars, then the value of education has no choice but to be upheld and highly esteemed because it will be a pill that will practically transform mindsets and attitudes. Education needs to be infused with some sense of practicality. By so doing a generation that has a balance of being book smart and street smart is cultivated. It is not surprising that people who are only book smart are more prone to the realities of human abuse. It is their failure to fit in and read people that make this a high possibility. I cannot emphasize enough the importance of being able to read people and to fit-in, in a highly social world. It acts as a shield even before committing to an abusive relationship.

One challenge that humanity encounters is the ability to put into practical use the education that is obtained. This could justify the reason for the escalating levels of unemployment and poor work ethic. I am of a strong idea that practically giving a marketing-job-seeking individual a pen to selling as a task to getting employment is much better than giving them an exam to write. An abuse-free generation is can read people, fit in, and apply communication that will be well received by other people without offending them. Failure to read people can be a blinding attitude that will cause one to fall into toxic relationships without reading the lines.

The best lesson in education is the value of what it does not teach you, to be able to read people, fit in, communicate effectively with all...AND SEAL THE BUSINESS DEAL.

87
IRREPLACEABLE

Gone are the days when writers wrote for the sake of writing, our content must shake to its core the human family so that it changes behaviors that govern the mindset. Our content must conjure beauty from rascals. Our content must create dialogues. Our content must challenge injustice. Our content must bring hope and healing where it seemingly does not exist. Writing can be a powerful tool used to express the voice within the human family. It is this power and influence that transforms mindsets. No amount of technological advancement can replace the timeless value of a pen and paper. Writing is just that, irreplaceable.

Awakening to this truth calls for a committed writer that will not only captivate the eyesight but challenge the character, attitude, and behavior of the reader. It is at the core of my purpose to challenge the reader to change and transform their mindset, attitude, and behavior. The truth is - if a message is held in mind for a long time, it is only a matter of time that the purpose of that message will be perceived. By writing this self-help guide - the message I want to be digested and held in mind is one of abundant love to the young child. My message is that - by giving abundant love to the young one - an abuse-free generation is possible. It is a message that appeals to people of all portfolios. I will be highly honored if the intricate purpose of this message is perceived within the mindset that governs humanity at large.

Growth, experience, and maturity as a writer come with the humility to acknowledge other writers and not to stop learning from them. One never gets to a point of knowing it all. It is impossible to know it all – there is always a better way of doing something and there is always someone to uphold us when we feel vulnerable, drained, pressurized, and weak. Humility to learn is what separates the different portfolios of writers.

The day that I will stop learning is the day that I die.

If I do not know, I am not afraid to say, "show me".

I am only a curious human being having a spiritual human experience with other human beings in an uncertain world.

The drive to want to know more keeps me anchored.
In a world where the upholding of reputations and egos has become the epicenter of life itself – it becomes a blow to one's ego for an experienced person to learn from a

newcomer. However, this attitude is blinding and limiting, in the sense that it closes the opportunity for growth and wisdom.

One could be in an abusive relationship, but because of pride and ego, they might continue to suffer because their ego holds them back from reading a self-help guide like '**Untangled**' '**The Psychological Chains Of Human Abuse**' that aims to break the agonizing cycle of human violence.

Do not suffer in silence.
Do not succumb to the unfruitful ploy of your pride and ego.
Do not journey the abusive relationship with blinkers.
Pick up the self-help guide and untangle your mind from the psychological chains of human abuse.

The subject of human abuse has been tackled by many writers. The power of this self-help guide lies in the value of what has not been written or spoken about in the topic that concerns human abuse. The self-help guide strives to highlight the intertwined relationship that exists between parents' way of raising a child and curbing human abuse. It aims to untangle the psychological chains that bind the human mind from a young age. It highlights the realities of human abuse in our everyday lives. It spots the nifty-gritty behaviors that may be looked down upon, but that have a great impact in strongly fastening the psychological chains of human abuse. It wisely and sensitively uses humor to enlighten the human soul on the serious subject of human abuse. It is a must-read for all human beings who share the vision of a human abuse-free generation.

The words that run through this writing are a breath of hope to the entire human family. These words are anchored deep in the roots of the daily experiences of humanity, from social media, family, school, parenting, growing up, human virtues, accolades, and role-models. Human abuse is highlighted in all these subjects.

I am confident that -
'Untangled' 'The Psychological Chains Of Human Abuse' is a beacon of hope to the human abuser and an unearthed treasure to the victim of human abuse. It is an enlightening self-help guide to the wise parent and a mentor to the young mind.

In a nutshell, it is an indispensable asset to the entire human family.
'Untangled' 'The Psychological Chains Of Human Abuse' is both an irreplaceable and timeless self-help guide.

88
EXTRAVAGANZA

I have come to understand that the uniqueness of humanity implies that they also come in different shapes and sizes. It is so sad, that human abuse is attributed to the different shapes and sizes of people. The dilemma of gaining weight, losing weight, and maintaining a figure will take humanity onto one hell of a ride. It all goes back to the desire of attaining an image that is deemed as good and acceptable. The effort that goes into building this image is enormous. Some starve themselves, some resort to body surgeries; some take weight-loss medicine, and some darken their skin color. This justifies the reason why some contestants just fail to cope with losing in beauty pageants.

Modeling and beauty pageants have evolved with time. These are now becoming more objective, coercive, positive, unifying, empowering, and encouraging to everybody, not just the contestants. They have certainly opened the arena – everybody can fit in modeling now - short, big, small, tall, and slim. I will not be surprised if this is news to somebody because the preconceived idea of modeling has been overtly tainted by the attaining of a typical image. (Skinny, tall, and long hair)

It is the failure to correct this pre-conceived idea that poses challenges and that consequently lays out a wrong impression of what modeling is about. The impression of what modeling is about can be corrected by increasing modeling contests and beauty pageants for those that have been shunned as not good enough to fit in the category of being a model.

How about a very short Ms. Universe for a change?
How about a chubby Ms. Universe for a change?
How about a paraplegic Ms. Universe for a change?

These changes will eliminate the warped impression that humanity has, for such a long time intricately weaved about what modeling is about, who qualifies and what are the traits that are required for one to become a champion in these contests.

In so doing the psychological chains that have entangled those that go to extremes of mistreatment to attain a 'typical, so-called, perfect' modeling image will start loosening.

Such a refreshing outlook of modeling will empower even the child that was told they will never mount up to anything because of their body weight. It will act positively in healing those that have suffered emotional abuse because of all the negative compliments that are directed to their body features.

Judging in beauty pageants such as the outspoken Mr. and Mrs. Extravaganza held in Heidelberg in a beautiful location called Ratanda has more than anything else ignited in me the desire to delve deeper into the mindset that governs these pageant Kings and Queens. Losing is certainly not part of their vocabulary. They all have the bold and confident mindset of winners. However, a contest being a contest, there must be losers and winners. Losing in these contests leads to a long struggle with depression, anxiety, and frustration. A depressed and frustrated mind can only be easily exposed to the realities of mistreatment.

The discipline instilled by these pageants is that lots of effort in building the ideal pageant image can be invested but ultimately there can only be one winner. Thus, one needs to be prepared for both winning and losing. Isn't this the same principle with life? Does one win all the time? Or the rule of the game is at times one loses and at times one wins. It comes with the territory of life. Life has victories and failures. It is the actions that one takes after failing that determine one's success. Failure should not discourage or cause one to succumb to self-pity, depression, or frustration. Failure should be embraced and used as a guide of the steps that must be taken to become victorious. Failure is an integral part of the human experience. It molds humanity into that which they are destined to become. It is a building muscle that brings about the strength that allows one to tap into greatness. Failure to embrace failure as a positive stimulant toward success can result in drastic measures taken to cope with it.

Failure that is not embraced can turn into anger - anger that is not expressed can be a danger to the human family. A balanced view of life is that there is 'failure' and winning. The young mind should be nurtured in how they handle their failures. Affirm the young mind that failure is normal. Some victories would have never come to pass if 'failure' was not first encountered. It is because of failure that some victories were granted a breath of life. Thus, humanity should not envy failure - humanity should positively deal with failure.

FAILURE'S MOTIVE IS NOT TO KILL - IT IS TO INCREASE THE PATIENCE, PREPARATION AND THE ZEAL THAT ONE HAS FOR LIFE.

89
PUZZLES

Broken pieces of a picture frame are just that, pieces that are very difficult to read and comprehend. Undone pieces of a puzzle are unattractive and very difficult to read and comprehend. Until an effort is channeled into the joining up of the broken pieces, what remains is a broken picture frame that is not appealing. Until some effort is instilled in joining the pieces of the puzzle. Then only an appealing clear picture that is easily comprehended is formed.

The human soul can carry a lot of unleashed brokenness. Brokenness comes from a lot of calamities and agonizing experiences. It could be the loss of a loved one, it could be un-forgiveness of self, it could be the disappearance of a close relative and it could be an experience with armed robbery and hijacking. If not vented out through the appropriate channel such as a counselor, social worker, or psychologist - This brokenness can only bear toxic gifts of impatience, anger, low self-esteem, and insecurity. These are the very concomitants that breed unbridled anger which then escalates to the tolerance of abuse and or the perpetration of human abuse.

Such personality tainting traits can only strongly fasten the psychological chains of human abuse.

Healing from brokenness is in essence a reduction factor of the chances of becoming either the victim or the perpetrator of human abuse.

Life's situations are bound to break the human soul. It is inevitable the brokenness that comes with situations encountered in life. There is a lot that can break the human soul, from the death of a loved one to the abuse that one may be subjected to. Situations are bound to break the human soul. It comes with the territory of living life. The response that one who is faced with brokenness activates will determine whether the cycle of human abuse is broken or not. Oftentimes brokenness that is kept inside, not shared or expressed can be very deadly to the human soul. Later, it manifests as maltreatment to humanity and oneself. It is like heaping a pile of burning coals within the heart. The heart can only feel a sense of relief after depositing some of these hot coals in the form of human abuse that is projected onto another human being. Human abuse that stems from brokenness is a dead zone to humanity. So many deaths are a result of brokenness.

The key is in expressing the brokenness at an early stage before it escalates to a heap of burning coals.

It takes a whole lot of courage to heal and nurse the wound of brokenness. It is a process, one that begins by first accepting, acknowledging, and a sense of awareness of one's brokenness. In other words, you first need to deeply accept that you are broken and therefore you need to overcome. The act of acceptance will activate the healing enzymes that will align body, mind, and soul to the healing course. One can be taken to the best rehabilitation center; however, if they are in denial of their problem it becomes a problem to restore their mind.

Restoration is activated in the realm that governs human will, acceptance, and courage.

My desk-top research has shown that the first most critical questions to be asked for a first-time counseling session are:

- Do you recognize that you have a problem? -
    If you do, explain the problem.

- Do you want to be healed or to overcome or to be restored? -
    If you do, what are the changes that you want to see manifest?

Failure to express brokenness is a sure way to heaping a pile of burning coals within the fragile human heart. The human heart is too fragile a part of the human body to keep the intensity of these coals without projecting this pain onto other human beings. The key is the courage to speak to a listening heart. The process of healing, comfort, and letting go is one that is activated by the courage to speak up. Failure to speak up is certainly one way leading to the distraction of the mind. The pain must be released at an early stage before it builds up into an agonizing part of the heart that is just too hot to be kept inside. It is a process, one that takes a willing and courageous heart to be carried out effectively. Healing needs the victim and the perpetrator to become harmlessly vulnerable with their emotions. To all the broken hearts, I say, it is never too late to heal and find comfort. It's only a matter of willingness and time. All hope is not lost...I strongly believe.

The young generation should be given room to be vulnerable in all the brokenness that they face. It is this attitude that will cultivate the courage that only sees it fit to open-up about their painful abusive experiences, even in adulthood.

I do hope that the publication success of this self-help guide is an answer to the question asked by my psychologist.

What will be effective enough to heal you?

90
THE POWER OF INFLUENCE

Influence is great - it allows one to have a book that will sell like peanuts. Sometimes the reader buys so much the influence of the author and not the content that is portrayed by the book. Influence can either be positive or negative. Positive influence creates a good impact on all of humanity. It positively changes attitudes and mindsets for a greater course. On the other hand, the negative influence is not ideal for the human soul and mind. This form of influence manipulates, abuses, and even kills. The danger of this influence is so much in the pretense and the false hope that it portrays if dug underneath - it bears nothing good but a lot of danger to the human soul. It may glitter on the outside but attachment to it can only mean a drastically dead end. I still maintain that the power of influence, if not safeguarded, can be misused for the destruction of humanity.

Influence is so sweet, if influential people are revered on the grounds of their influence in-spite of their shortcomings, then it will only make sense for everybody to have a strong desire to accumulate influence. The fragility of the human mind means that it can take to heart that which is uttered by an influential person without truthfully discerning it. It is for this reason that many victims of human abuse continue clutching on to the hand of the abuser based on the magnitude of the influence and not really on positive substance and growth. It is the sweetness that comes with the power of influence that builds a stronger desire for humanity to attain more of it with unswerving passion. The extremes taken to attain this influence can be shocking - some kill, some lie, some manipulate, some brainwash, some pretend and abuse others to strengthen the level of influence that they have.

The hunger and thirst for influence are portrayed by corrupt politicians today. This is an age where humanity is no longer driven by soundness and integrity but by influence. How can a blind person lead another blind person? It is impossible; they will both fall into a pit.

The lesson is to be careful whom you allow to exerting influence unto your life. Not everybody should speak into my life. Humanity should strip away the façade of influence and truthfully discern before they are led into a pit. One who is led into a pit might not find their way out of a pit. It is a dead-end that should be avoided at all costs. The outer cover should not be used to determine what is inside for - all that glitters is not gold.

The young mind should be wise enough to discern that which is spoken even by the people that they look up to. The person may be highly influential but what is uttered by them deserves a fair share of discernment before it takes root in their minds.

91
THE POWER OF MUSIC

The influence that music has on the human mind is undeniable. Music has the potential to comfort, unite, motivate, entertain, calm, and most significantly transform human behavior and attitude. The atmosphere and energy that is created by music is undeniable. If music can turn a sour person into the sweetest human being, then a need to revise the message behind the music is equally critical and significant. I don't know about you but if there is no message in it, my ear just struggles to be inclined to it. There is so much into music; it is the beat and the sound as well as the message that has the potential to create energy and different moods.

Life would be mundane without music. The sound of the birds in the morning is the sweetest music one can tune their ears to. If music is so vital, then the message behind the music can be a powerful instrument that is used to curb the pandemic of human abuse. It is for this reason that I had to infuse the message of this book with my poem that is inspired by one of South Africa's best jazz sounds.

I call upon all music artists to try their level best to convey an abuse-free message to all humanity. The impact that this sound has on the human soul is great. Music can be the best form of counseling for humanity. Some abusers and victims of human abuse just need to hear a love-inspired song to bring about transformation in the attitude that governs their mindsets. That is the power embedded in the melody and message behind the music.

Some of the best songs that I still find comfort in, that highlight the realities of human abuse are 'Akukho Lula' by Sjava, 'More than you' by Monea, 'Faraway' by Marsha Ambrosius, and 'Same Love' by Macklemore. I love the message behind these songs. The influence that these songs have had on humanity cannot be denied. Both the abuser and the abused can find healing by inclining their ears to these songs.

Music artists in all facets of the earth should take advantage of the influence of their music by pushing the 'Stop Gender-Based Violence' message to all of humanity. It has been written, it has been spoken, and it is high time that some melody can be infused into the message. As an activist, I would be highly honored if I am joined by willing and courageous music artists that are willing to untangle the psychological chains of human abuse. A team is better than one. Unity is better than disunity. Many voices are better heard than one voice...so,

Let us all sing in one united voice...STOP GENDER-BASED VIOLENCE

92
THE TRIP

It is a trip whose influence just seizes to be uprooted from my mind. Schooling days were given substance by these types of trips. The impact of the trip to the prisoners' cell is one that brightly flashes its message in my mind; "Behave and become a responsible citizen so that you do not see yourself in the prisoner's cell". I must say the idea behind prison is one of isolated rehabilitation. The impact that the prison cell has on the prisoners is massive. As much as some prisoners turn out to be the worst people coming out of prison. To a large extent prisoners' minds are positively transformed by the prison cell.

A prison cell is the worst place to find one in. However, I must say that some people need this space to be able and to have the time to truthfully reflect on their life. Interestingly this is the only time that some prisoners can get to reflect, tap into their brokenness, and heal the wounds within their hearts.

As much as the trip to the prison cell was awesome, it will be unwise to turn a blind eye to the episodes of tears that were part and parcel of these trips. These were not tears of joy - these were tears that were because of the human abuse that some prisoners were subjected to within the confines of their cell. A place that is meant to be a rehabilitation center is slowly but surely progressing into a den of abusive tendencies such as gang-rape and killings. If this is the case, then the authority that governs the prison cell should be at work to ensure that the main purpose of a prison is not tainted or altered. This is a call for this authority to implement harsher laws to those that partake in human abuse while in a prison. Revision of the prison purpose is a must.

If the purpose behind the idea of a prison cell is not revised, one can only be certain that - the perpetrator of abuse can only come out of prison like a vicious dog that is ready to hunt down those that reported them to the authorities.

A young person that is treated to this kind of trip should not have a warped view of the prison. The young mind should be affirmed that the prison is in essence a place of rehabilitation - this will instill in them the desire to find careers in a prison center. This will propel them to want to be partakers in curbing human abuse by working with prisoners. More abuse stories encountered within the confines of prison can most certainly pose questions among the young minds like, 'What is the point of going to a prison if one comes out the worst human being?' and 'Where is the meaning in working with prisoners if they have the potential to abuse you?' These are the relevant questions that govern the young mind that is treated on to a trip to the prison.

THE KEY IS REVISING AND STRATEGIZING THE PRISON TO BE THE IDEAL REHABILITATION CENTER THAT IT IS PURPOSED TO BE.

93
HUMAN CHARACTER FOR HUMAN COLOR

It is not so much the color of one's pigment - it is the character that is radiated by the human soul that carries substance. This I am convinced is the answer to the classifications and divisions that have brought nothing but abuse, discrimination, and hatred among the beloved human race.

I am appalled by the amount of hatred and discrimination that I see because of the classifications of human color. I have said it and I will always say that a human being is a human being to me regardless of the color of their skin. The world will be a much better place if only humanity was classified according to character, not color.

Instilling a non-color classification-attitude cannot start with adults. It is a message that should be preached to the young mind so that they have a different approach to life. Isn't it sad that today, humanity's vision has been blurred to see so much of the color and not the character of another human being?

Preferences and favors are gained because of the color of one's skin when they should be earned based on one's character. 'Character' holds substance in this world. Human abuses that have been endured on the grounds of human color are pathetic. My objective is to spread the message of love to all humanity regardless of color. If the secretion of humanity is the same, why should color divide humanity?

It is very disturbing that even within the same color of people there are divisions. Now humanity finds pleasure in using words such as 'yellow bone'. I appeal to humanity in all facets of the earth to nullify the effects of colorizing humanity. Propping up such words will only strengthen the grip that the effect of color has on humanity. The young mind should be taught about human beings and not the color classifications of humanity.

It is high time that classification of humanity is defined so much by character and not the color of one's pigment... this is a step towards a progressive world – most significantly a world that is untangled from the psychological chains of human abuse.

Note:
*My second baby '**Human 1st** will shed some fair share of light on burning issues such as racism. Coming soon...*

94
CHEERS TO THE PILLARS

I am not just a staunchly proud African soul. I am an enlightened child of the universe. My message appeals to the human family, without the limitation of race, culture, nationality, background, or sexuality. It is for this reason that drives me to delve even deeper into the depths of my character and being so that I can shed some light about human abuse from a humanly, worldly, and universal point of view. Bear in mind, I am not ignorant to the varying levels by which the magnitude of human abuse is experienced in different places all over the world.

The question that always astounds me is: "What is the reason for the reduced levels of human abuse in developed nations such as Canada, China, and The United Kingdom?"; "Can we attribute it to the law enforcement, economic development, level of education, religion or the morals?". Higher levels of education are equated to reduced levels of human abuse. In contrast, lower levels of education correlate to the rising levels of human abuse. This is a call for all nations to ensure that they work towards elevating their level of education in the high hope that this will also be a sure solution to wiping out human abuse.

Let us not take for granted, the effort that has been instilled by concerned individuals to bring about a change to the rising levels of human abuse. I speak to writers, activists, counselors, psychologists, and doctors all over the world. You are highly honored for your work in this regard. I appeal to the States of all nations to extend an unwavering hand into ensuring that organizations that are fighting human abuse are fully supported. Organizations such as Sisonke, Out, Moshe, Brothers for life, Child-line South Africa, Powa, and Zazi should be at the fore-front of receiving government assistance. These organizations should be supported by humanity at large for they stand for a greater and meaningful purpose.

I have brought to the light a deep conviction that human abuse is a worldly pandemic that starts at an early age but grows within an individual. An unwavering extension of assistance to ensure that young people are well informed should also be at work. Actively involve them in these troubling issues, let them be an active mouthpiece within the confines of their societies. Their voices hold lots of molecules of water...listen to them and action their suggestions.

To the entire human abuse activists, writers, counselors, psychologists, and doctors:

Thank you so much for being pillars of strength.

You are dearly loved!

RESOURCES

HELP-LINE FOR LGBTQI+ COMMUNITY

SONKE GENDER JUSTICE

Sonke Gender Justice is a South African-based non-profit organization working throughout Africa that believes women and men, girls and boys can work together to resist patriarchy, advocate for gender justice, and achieve gender transformation.

CONTACT

Email: info@genderjustice.org.za
Cape Town: +27 (0)21 423 7088
Johannesburg: +27 (0)11 339 3589
Bushbuckridge Satellite Office: +27 (0)13 795 5076
Gugulethu Satellite Office: +27 (0)21 633 3140

Servicing the Lesbian, Gay, Bisexual and Transgender community

PHYSICAL ADDRESS

CONTACT NUMBERS

1081 Pretorius Street
Hatfield
Pretoria, South Africa

Telephone
0124303272

HELPLINE FOR MEN

MOSHATE: The Voice of Men

The main purpose of this ESE or NPO is to fight and address the imbalance of gender and ill-treatment of men and boys by authorities in South Africa that include bias and ridicule by police, court officials, public health worker, and any other public officials rendering service, because of victimization and abuse by female counterparts.

Contact details

Tel: +27 11 050 0943   Email: info@sangonet.org.za

BROTHERS FOR LIFE

Brothers for Life are a social and well-being movement aimed at mobilizing men to take responsibility for their health. We hope to achieve this by promoting positive male norms and encourage men to test for HIV and undergo Medical Male Circumcision (MMC), actively take a stand against Gender-Based Violence (GBV) in their communities.

Contact details

Tel: +27123669300
Cell: 082 808 6152

97
HELPLINE FOR CHIDREN

CHILDLINE SOUTH AFRICA

Child-line is an effective non-profit organization that works collectively to protect children from all forms of violence and to create a culture of children's rights in South Africa.

Contact details

Child-line National Office

Tel: (+27) -(0)31-201 2059
Fax: (+27) -(0)86 511 0032
Postal Address: P O Box 51418, Musgrave, 4062
Physical Address: 24 Stephen Dlamini Road, Musgrave, Durban, 4000
Email: admin@childlinesa.org.za (General Enquiries)
Email: olcadmin@childlinesa.org.za (Counseling/Case Enquiries)

Regional Offices

Child-line Eastern Cape

Tel: (+27) -(0)43 722 1382
P. O. Box 11127, Southernwood, 5213
Email: admin@childlineec.org.za

Child-line Gauteng

Tel: (+27) -(0)11-6452000
PO Box 32453, Braamfontein
Email: admingauteng@childline.org.za
Web: www.childlinegauteng.co.za

98
HELPLINE FOR WOMEN

Powa's vision is to create a safe and equal society intolerant of all forms of violence against women and girls in all their diversity, where they are treated with respect and dignity and their rights are promoted.

CONTACT DETAILS

Head Office: Berea Johannesburg
Postal address: PO BOX 93416, Yeoville, 2143 Johannesburg
Tel: 011 642 4345/6
Fax: 011 484 3195
Email: info@powa.co.za

Life-Line Southern Africa

Zazi provides a 24-hour crisis intervention service, "Emotional First Aid station", Free confidential telephone counseling, rape counseling, trauma counseling, Aids counseling, and a range of other services.

Contact details

National counseling line: 0861-322-322

Website: www.lifeline.org.za

99
CONCLUSION

I rest my case by emphasizing:

The genuine and persistent affirmation we are infinitely loved beings at an early stage produces enzymes that consequently equip the human psyche to be empowered, secure, and bold enough to walk away from any abusive situations.

100
THE COURAGE TO LOVE
"A Beacon of Hope for the Human Abuser"

I speak to the heart that has been denied of its rightful right to be loved,
In its quest for an affectionate embrace,
In its longing for some heavenly comfort,
In its unquenched thirst for the three universal words affirming affection,
The loud echoes of the opposite just seize to be silenced...

These are the echoes that give birth to syndromes of entitlement and dependency,
These are the roots that perpetuate more harm, unbridled anger, and greed,
Not only the conviction but the application of the words written in red will save a generation:
"Guard your heart above all else for it determines the course of life", proverbially says the King.

Strip away the façade,
Dare not pretend!
Shade away the masquerade,

You cannot take your beloved to a place where you have never been,
Just acknowledge…just accept…just embrace
"You need a drop of unconditional love to ignite the courage to love, my heart…"

Denial's power will never take you to a place where you have never been,
Believe me when I say – "The power of acceptance will lead you to that place…."
Like Zama Jobe you will be singing Ndawo Yami…my place of genuine love. 🎵

ABOUT THE AUTHOR

Passion, ambition, determination, and resilience are some of the adjectives to describe this phenomenal human being who grew up in Olievenhoutbosch in South Africa.

Brightwell Dube is the world's first Human 1st author. Human 1st being a principle that this remarkable author had the sole pleasure of weaving, which states that "I am human 1st before my race, gender, status, religion, sexuality, and background"

Brightwell is a Godly inspired writer, motivational speaker, poet, singer, dancer, entrepreneur, and LGBTQI+ activist. Like one who dares to dance in the path of greatness, Brightwell highly esteems originality and authenticity.

Professionally, Brightwell has 5 years of shipping experience as an International Trade and Transport Logistics graduate with the UK ICM Institute. Brightwell's working experience involves reputational shipping companies such as Evergreen Shipping Line in Bedford view.

Brightwell may be confident, but not arrogant. Through the words of this author, there is a humble spirit that calls upon everyone not to be afraid to say:

"Inform me"

The Leadership roles that Brightwell was catapulted into from schooling days were not a mistake but a prophecy of destiny.

Brightwell's best advice to both young and grown-up people is:

"*Be the best version of yourself*"

www.ingramcontent.com/pod-product-compliance
Lightning Source LLC
Chambersburg PA
CBHW060103170426
43198CB00010B/747